16/12

SOCIAL STUDIES IN THE NEW EDUCATION POLICY ERA

Social Studies in the New Education Policy Era is a series of compelling open-ended education policy dialogues among various social studies scholars and stakeholders. By facilitating conversations about the relationships among policy, practice, and research in social studies education, this collection illuminates various positions— some similar, some divergent—on contested issues in the field, from the effects of standardized curriculum and assessment mandates on K–12 teaching to the appropriate roles of social studies educators as public policy advocates. Chapter authors bring diverse professional experiences to the questions at hand, offering readers multiple perspectives from which to delve into well-informed discussions about social studies education in past, present, and future policy contexts.

Collectively, their commentaries aim to inspire, challenge, and ultimately strengthen readers' beliefs about the place of social studies in present and future education policy environments.

Paul G. Fitchett, University of North Carolina at Charlotte, USA

Kevin W. Meuwissen, University of Rochester, USA

SOCIAL STUDIES IN THE NEW EDUCATION POLICY ERA

Conversations on Purposes, Perspectives, and Practices

Edited by Paul G. Fitchett and Kevin W. Meuwissen

Routledge
Taylor & Francis Group

NEW YORK AND LONDON

First published 2018
by Routledge
711 Third Avenue, New York, NY 10017

and by Routledge
2 Park Square, Milton Park, Abingdon, Oxon, OX14 4RN

Routledge is an imprint of the Taylor & Francis Group, an informa business

Library of Congress Cataloging-in-Publication Data
A catalog record for this book has been requested

ISBN: 978-1-138-28395-4 (hbk)
ISBN: 978-1-138-28396-1 (pbk)
ISBN: 978-1-315-26928-3 (ebk)

Typeset in Bembo
by Apex CoVantage, LLC

Paul: I would like to dedicate this book to my wife, Amy. Thanks for reading everything I have ever written and giving me insightful and "street-level" feedback. I also want to thank all of the social studies teachers and stakeholders with whom I have collaborated. I hope the conversations that arise from this book will help push our collective work forward.

Kevin: I wish to dedicate this book to Jamie, Sophie, and Paige, who motivate me to be a better listener, thinker, teacher, spouse, and father; to influential mentors and colleagues whose perspectives are represented herein and beyond this book; and to the social studies educators, and their students, who stand to benefit most from wise, ethical policy and practice.

CONTENTS

CONTRIBUTORS

Sarah Witham Bednarz, Texas A & M University

Steven Camicia, Utah State University

Margaret Smith Crocco, Michigan State University

Todd Dinkelman, University of Georgia

Paul G. Fitchett, University of North Carolina at Charlotte

Brad Fogo, San Francisco State University

David Gerwin, Queens College/CUNY

S.G. Grant, Binghamton University

Tina L. Heafner, University of North Carolina at Charlotte

Michelle M. Herczog, Past President, National Council for the Social Studies

John K. Lee, North Carolina State University

Bruce Lesh, Maryland State Department of Education

Peter Levine, Tufts University

Kevin W. Meuwissen, University of Rochester

Judith L. Pace, University of San Francisco

Jeff Passe, California State Polytechnic University Pomona

Gabriel A. Reich, Virginia Commonwealth University

Beth Rubin, Rutgers University

Alan Sears, University of New Brunswick

Tim Slekar, Edgewood College

Kathy Swan, University of Kentucky

Stephen J. Thornton, University of South Florida

Phillip J. VanFossen, Purdue University

Stephanie van Hover, University of Virginia

Bruce VanSledright, University of North Carolina at Charlotte

INTRODUCTION

Social Studies in the New Education Policy Era: Introducing Conversations on Purposes, Perspectives, and Practices

Kevin W. Meuwissen and Paul G. Fitchett

In the field of social studies education, scholars and practitioners often talk about and engage directly with policy, but they rarely write about it. The most overt discussions of policy in two recent handbooks on social studies research attend to the uses of curricula and assessments as regulatory instruments, but those are relatively brief discussions, compared to others about learning, teaching, and theories and principles related to citizenship and social justice (Levstik & Tyson, 2008; Manfra & Bolick, 2017). By contrast, Sykes and colleagues' (2009) comprehensive handbook of research in education policy presents numerous issues of direct relevance to social studies education, from scholarly and political rationales for the ways curricula and assessments are constructed, schools are organized, and collegial and pedagogical relationships are built and fostered to arguments about the impacts of policy on school segregation and privatization, teacher collectivization, technology uses in classrooms, definitions of achievement, and access to educational resources. Simply put, we think that the field of social studies education ought to pay more attention to policy, and we intend for this book to be an avenue for doing so.

What Is Policy?

We should begin with a clear definition of the central focus of this book. When talking about policy, we and the other authors use metaphors like instruments, mechanisms, and tools correspondingly to represent components of policy that are created and implemented by people with power to generate some kind of social change. Policy is a purposeful response to public demand that a social problem be addressed, arguably to improve circumstances for some people whose lives are affected by that problem. That response can take the form of laws, executive rules and regulations, funding decisions, standards of activity, programs comprised of material resources and governance practices, and so forth.

Problems on which education policies typically focus include conflicts over scarce resources (with decisions focused on costs, benefits, and modes of allocation) and conflicts over human activity (with decisions focused on the provision and protection of individual or collective rights or opportunities). Policy is necessary in circumstances where collective action is needed—where private solutions to problems that affect only certain populations of individuals will not suffice. Achievement of policy goals means both taking and avoiding particular actions, changing and maintaining some sets of conditions, via patterns or protocols of activity. Policy works under the authority of agents who create, enact, and enforce it, enabled by a social contract that such authority is legitimate.

How Does This Book Attend to Policy?

The aim of this volume is to enrich our understanding of, and facilitate conversations about, the situation of social studies education in policy landscapes. The scholars, leaders, and practitioners whose positions are represented herein attended to that aim in three general regards: (1) by illuminating and contextualizing the evolution of social studies education over time, relative to policy developments; (2) by offering contemporary perspectives on the intersections of policy with social studies learning, assessment, curriculum, teaching, and teacher education; and (3) by exploring possibilities for and modes of policy advocacy among social studies educators and researchers, with eyes toward the present and future. Structurally, this book is not a review of research on social studies education policy; rather, it is a series of conversations that coalesce around several overarching themes as they relate to policy, including the purposes of social studies education, the forms and functions of curriculum, teaching, learning, and assessment in specific disciplines, and political activity in K–12 and higher education contexts.

For each chapter, we invited different authors to respond to a common question. We purposefully chose scholars, leaders, and practitioners who represent a diversity of perspectives on social studies education, relative to policy. After writing an initial commentary, each author read her or his counterpart's position on the same question and crafted a follow-up response, or rejoinder. The purpose of this approach is to generate an authentic dialogue that offers readers multiple points of view from which to engage further conversation about social studies education in past, present, and future policy contexts.

How Might Readers Interpret the Commentaries in This Book?

Certainly, we do not intend to prescribe how this book should be used by readers, yet we do offer some direction and framing. The chapters could be considered discursive models, in terms of how people develop and warrant positions on social studies and education policy, define points of consensus and contention, and critically respond to each other, with an eye toward what ought to be done, how, and why. It is important to note that commentaries and corresponding rejoinders do not represent definitive positions or "last words" on policy-related issues in the social studies, and we acknowledge that there are numerous educational policy issues that the book's authors do not address, individually or collectively. We hope that the conversations herein will serve as an invitation for further discussions about, scholarship on, and activity around social studies education policy, related to various problems explored more or less extensively.

We imagine that social studies scholars, leaders, and activists, K–12 educators and administrators, educational policymakers and analysts, and those learning to take on such roles might enter these conversations via the following questions: If you were responding to the same question(s), what would your responses entail? Are these positions on policy credible, are their underlying warrants clear and compelling, and are recommended approaches worthwhile? What does the chapter accomplish, what does it evince in terms of work to be done, and what are its conceivable consequences? Additionally, we hope that social studies researchers might use this book as a springboard to future inquiry, considering what kinds of policy deserve scholarly attention and evaluation, what knowledge the field needs, and what modes of inquiry and analysis could meet those needs.

Readers will notice several regular themes across the book, including (1) the roles of various actors in the construction and implementation of policy, from federal to local levels; (2) the nature, importance, and impact of teacher agency as political activity; (3) the relationship of policy design and implementation to the contexts in and resources with which it is made and enacted; and (4) the ways in which people take active, neutral, and averse positions on influencing and responding to policy, and the consequences of those positions. There are different ways to look at these themes. One is by using a policy-evaluative framework. This approach, prevalent in the policy research literature, emphasizes the efficaciousness of policy using production-function models, whereby the complex characteristics of stakeholders, settings, and policy artifacts are represented as discrete variables (or inputs) that are theoretically assumed to generate particular outcomes (or outputs) (Hanushek, 2008; Monk, 1989). The strengths of this framework lie in the credibility and efficiency of research designs, the clear delineation of findings, and the potential to "scale up" policy initiatives.

And yet, policy-evaluative studies often fail to consider the complex, organic nature of education systems. By atomizing variables as they do, these studies risk perpetuating attribution error (Kennedy, 2010), whereby input and output definitions mischaracterize singular traits as representing more complex processes. Weimer (2009), by contrast, suggests that education policy studies be situated within a more policy-analytic framework. Rather than assuming linear input-to-output relationships, such a framework emphasizes understanding how multifaceted problems, contexts, actors, and practices converge to constitute and affect policy and its implications. Rather than focusing on generalizability and scalability, this descriptive and largely qualitative kind of inquiry tends to elucidate elements of policy development and engagement that go undefined or unaddressed in evaluative studies (e.g., Cohen & Moffitt, 2009).

While the chapters in this book suggest a propensity toward policy-analytical rather than policy-evaluative framing among social studies scholars, to our knowledge, neither is especially prevalent in the field. Outside a handful of studies that explicitly target policy (e.g., Evans, 2006; Fitchett, Heafner, & Lambert, 2014; Grant, 2001; Meuwissen, 2017; Parker et al., 2013; Reisman, 2012; VanSledright, 2010), little attention is paid to both the efficacy of policy mechanisms and the relational aspects of policy activity in the social studies. We contend that a healthy mix of policy-evaluative and policy-analytic scholarship might strengthen what we know about an important but understudied aspect of social studies education and elevate the position of social studies aims, practices, and research in policy discussions. And we hope that the following conversations illuminate pathways toward that work.

References

Cohen, D. K., & Moffitt, S. L. (2009). *The ordeal of equality: Did federal regulation fix the schools?* Cambridge, MA: Harvard University Press.

Evans, R. (2006). The social studies wars: Now and then. *Social Education, 70*(5), 317–321.

Fitchett, P. G., Heafner, T. L., & Lambert, R. G. (2014). Assessment, autonomy, and elementary social studies time. *Teachers College Record, 116*(10), 1–34.

Grant, S. G. (2001). An uncertain lever: Exploring the influence of state-level testing in New York state on teaching social studies. *Teachers College Record, 103*(3), 1–32.

Hanushek, E. A. (2008). Educational production functions. In S. N. Durlaf & B. L. E. (Eds.), *The new Palgrave dictionary of economics* (2nd ed., pp. 1–6). New York: Palgrave MacMillan.

Kennedy, M. M. (2010). Attribution error and the quest for teacher quality. *Educational Researcher, 39*(8), 591–598. doi:10.3102/0013189X10390804

Levstik, L. S., & Tyson, C. A. (Eds.). (2008). *Handbook of research in social studies education.* New York: Routledge.

Manfra, M. M., & Bolick, C. M. (Eds.). (2017). *The Wiley handbook of social studies research.* Malden, MA: Wiley Blackwell.

Meuwissen, K. W. (2017). "Happy professional development at an unhappy time": Learning to teach for historical thinking in a high-pressure accountability context. *Theory & Research in Social Education, 45*(2), 248–285.

Monk, D. H. (1989). The educational production function: Its evolving role in policy analysis. *Educational Evaluation and Policy Analysis, 11*(1), 31–45.

Parker, W. C., Lo, J., Yeo, A. J., Valencia, S. W., Nguyen, D., Abbott, R. D., . . . Vye, N. J. (2013). Beyond breadth-speed-test. *American Educational Research Journal, 50*(6), 1424–1459. doi:10.3102/0002831213504237

Reisman, A. (2012). Reading like a historian: A document-based history curriculum intervention in urban high schools. *Cognition and Instruction, 30*(1), 86–112. doi:10.1080/07370008.2011.634081

Sykes, G., Schneider, B., & Plank, D. N. (Eds.). (2009). *Handbook of education policy research.* New York: Routledge.

VanSledright, B. A. (2010). *The challenge of rethinking history education: On practices, theories, and policy.* New York: Routledge.

Weimer, D. L. (2009). Making education research more policy-analytic. In G. Sykes, B. Schneider, & D. N. Plank (Eds.), *Handbook of education policy research* (pp. 93–100). New York: Routledge.

SECTION I

Purposes

The Uncomfortable Gap Between What Social Studies Purports to Do and How It Is Positioned in K–12 Education

1

"WHY ARE THERE DISPARITIES AMONG THE GENERAL PUBLIC, POLICYMAKERS, AND SOCIAL STUDIES EDUCATORS RELATIVE TO THE AIMS OF THE SOCIAL STUDIES CURRICULUM, AND WHAT SHOULD BE DONE ABOUT THEM?"

Defining Social Studies: The Key to Bridging Gaps

Commentary by Jeff Passe, California State Polytechnic University, Pomona

Acknowledging the Gap

Disparities among the general public, policymakers, and social studies educators can be traced to the very birth of our field. Social studies as an integrated study was proposed by the 1916 NEA Committee on Social Studies, a cross-section of scholars, high school teachers, district administrators, and federal education officials. The proposal was offered as an antidote to isolated disciplines, but also as an opportunity to move away from having students regurgitate facts to having students engage in community study. These aims, influenced indirectly by Dewey (Fallace, 2009), are best exemplified by the Committee's recommendation for two inquiry-based, interdisciplinary courses, *Community Civics*, and a capstone senior course called *Problems of Democracy*.

That 1916 vision was never fully implemented. Some scholars argue that proponents of traditional American history resisted change, as did adherents to the "grammar of schooling" who rejected alterations to the structure of high schools (Evans, 2004). The Problems of Democracy course did grow in popularity for a decade or so, but social studies still appears to be much like it was a century ago. Thus, the general public (including many policymakers who, after all, are members of the general public) has never experienced interdisciplinary, inquiry-based social studies. The public's conceptions of social studies are based on the definitions they constructed through their own schooling, definitions that viewed social studies as old-fashioned history with a fancy name, much like language arts replaced English as a subject title.

In their schooling, most members of the public have been subjected to the dreadful chronology-based recitation of names, dates, and places that was anathema to the founders of our field. They experienced mind-numbing lectures that served to promote American nationalism, appreciation for various historic figures or events, and a presumed mental facility to organize and recall lists of information without context. Thus, for far too many, social studies has maintained its earlier designation as a time to memorize the presidents and the state capitals, as well as rivers, mountains, and political entities.

At this point, it is important to recognize that governmental policymakers and social studies educators fall into at least two overlapping camps. Some policymakers and social studies educators have embraced the notion of social studies as an integrated field focused on community study. These progressive policymakers, who fill the ranks of the National Council for the Social Studies (NCSS) supervisors and chief state social studies supervisor organizations, tend to be former social studies educators who have studied and applied the modern concept of social studies. They evolved from their teaching positions to become principals, central office staff, superintendents, and sometimes political leaders. Unfortunately, even though most were or are in a position to advocate for progressive social studies, they were marginalized as their states and districts embraced, willingly or not, the "back to basics" and "standards" movements that promoted tested subjects like literacy and mathematics at the expense of other subjects. Professional development budgets and opportunities for curricular change were minimal. While a handful of political leaders, such as former Representative Lee Hamilton and former Supreme Court Justice Sandra Day O'Connor, have argued forcefully for a progressive approach to civic education, most policymakers fall into the second and more familiar camp—operating under the old-fashioned depictions of social studies as drudgery.

This distinction matters because policymakers with traditional views of the field can constrain or block attempts by progressive policymakers and social studies educators to implement their competing visions. This is not to say that there is open philosophic warfare, though that does occur from time to time. Instead, it is a matter of either competing priorities that relegate social studies to the back burner or an alternative vision within the social studies field, wherein a state institutes a high-stakes facts-based social studies exam that influences curricular decisions in the direction opposite that of integrated, community-based studies. In both situations, the definition of social studies is key. If educational leaders think of social studies as a collection of irrelevant facts, they can successfully argue that it is less important than the crucial foundational skills that need to be emphasized and tested. If the public considers social studies important enough to be tested but operates under the assumption that the field is merely a collection of basic facts, high-stakes social studies exams would only measure the basic facts. What we have is a classic conundrum: Policymakers with narrow views of the field limit student experiences to a less-desirable curriculum, thus promoting a narrow view of the field for future policymakers.

Progressive social studies educators are placed in the unfortunate situation of having to place social studies on the back burner and/or teach toward a test of basic facts, even though doing so violates their own conceptions of social studies. Some educators have the freedom to ignore policymaker mandates and others courageously violate them with the expectation that integrated community study will yield the same or better test scores. These educators may have earned this freedom on the virtue of their successful teaching performance over their careers; others have been given autonomy by progressive supervisors and other administrators. Whatever the cause, these progressive educators may be deemed exceptions because they operate stealthily or have never organized into a recognized force for change.

Traditionalist policymakers are winning because they have the power to punish teachers or schools that veer from established guidelines. This power has increased in recent generations as state and then federal politicians have gotten more involved in educational policy, with special attention to testing. The impact of high-stakes testing in social studies was revealed in a 2010 national survey of more than 100,000 social studies teachers which reported that K–12 educators in states that have a social studies test perceive significantly less control over content topics and skills than do counterparts in non-testing states (Patterson, Horner, Chandler, & Dahlgren, 2013). Over time, with the continued assaults on teacher curricular autonomy, the original conception of social studies has become less and less familiar to the general public, policymakers, and even educators as they succumb to the party line.

Minding the Gap

A negative cycle can only be broken by altering one or more of its components; we can influence teachers, policymakers and/or the general public to embrace the original conception of social studies. Assuming that methods professors have been teaching progressive social studies over the years and that the traditional definition still stands, it appears that teacher education, by itself, will only yield only minimal success. While many educators may be models of best practice in social studies, they have a limited reach. As mentioned, in states with high-stakes fact-driven exams, teachers cannot be expected to defy administrative edicts, especially in high-poverty communities where the consequences of poor student performance can cause a school to close. Furthermore, elementary-level teachers, who are overwhelmingly generalists, are not likely to have a strong background in the social sciences. They may not even have had a methods course taught by a scholar in social studies education. After all, non-tenure-track instructors, for whom scholarship is seldom required, now account for over 70 percent of all instructional staff appointments in American higher education (AAUP, 2017). Limitations to the better teacher education solution notwithstanding, there is evidence that pre-service teachers adopt the progressive conceptions of social studies when it is taught to them (Doppen, 2007). Those efforts should be maintained while seeking more robust solutions.

The general public solution offers a different yet achievable challenge, with the added benefit of harnessing civic activism—the very tools of democratic citizenship that reside at the heart of the field. To wit, if the public demands it, policymakers or their political patrons will enact necessary reforms if they wish to stay in office. This approach, involving strategies of marketing and public education has been heretofore unavailable to social studies leaders because, basically, the public did not care. Until now.

The presidential election campaign of 2016, following years of dysfunctional congressional activity, makes the time ripe for a "return to social studies" movement. Regardless of party or favored candidate, polls (e.g., Pew Research Center, 2016a) indicate that the public is fed up with flawed candidates and unpleasant campaign tactics. Voters express a preference for attention to the issues, avoidance of ad hominem attacks, and greater cooperation between political actors. Unfortunately, those criticisms are unlikely to alter campaign tactics because, like it or not, they tend to be effective in influencing voter behavior. Now that the 2016 campaigns have concluded, the public is more receptive to addressing underlying causes of ugly politics. Criticism of political parties, the press, social media, and even the voters themselves coincided with the campaigns' roller coaster events and revelations. People are interested in raising the level of political discourse (Pew Research Center, 2016b), and social studies is one part of the answer. A public relations campaign, similar to those that successfully promoted science, technology, engineering, and mathematics (STEM) (National Governors Association, 2008), could present a persuasive case for social studies that would be well-received by citizens seeking to avoid the negativity of the 2016 campaign (Pew Research Center, 2016b). A series of advertisements, op-ed articles, public forums, and multimedia discussions can highlight the role of civics, current events, historic study, and especially the rules for serious civic engagement— all are central elements of a quality social studies program. This crucial public relations can serve as an initial step to get people talking. Any public relations effort must focus attention on the structural constraints mentioned earlier that have hindered social studies in the past. Debates about high-stakes testing and an unbalanced curriculum that overemphasizes literacy and mathematics are integral to any possibility of reform. These issues are complex and often contentious; they must be carefully organized.

My many years of political action on behalf of social studies suggest that direct outreach to policymakers would yield disappointing results. Political partisanship at the national and state levels has resulted in rigid allegiance to the standards movement, back to basics, and favoring of history over social studies among Republican political leaders. It is reasonable, however, in 2016, to be optimistic about reform for several reasons. First, during the campaign, many leaders of the Republican Party expressed pointed criticism of its nominee's public comments, lack of depth, and failure to conform to standard expectations of political discourse. Despite its electoral success, some segments of the GOP may welcome efforts to elevate the civic process. A second encouraging development is that the public has demonstrated a growing resistance to high-stakes testing and federal intervention into what was once an exclusive state responsibility. The rejection of the Common Core and, to a lesser extent, Partnership for Assessment of Readiness for College and Careers (PARCC) testing has been most fervent in states led by Republicans. On the other side of the aisle, we see significant efforts to refuse high-stakes testing in blue states.

Thus, there may actually be a bipartisan concordance to step back from more unpopular elements of recent educational reform movements. This can open the door for a candid discussion of the school curriculum. Social studies could benefit by stepping into the breach, provided we do not try to go it alone. There is power in collective action. Fortunately, potential allies abound, ranging from good government groups such as Common Cause and the League of Women Voters to educational organizations like the parent teacher associations, teacher unions, honor societies, and subject-area counterparts to the National Council for the Social Studies, such as the National Council of Teachers of English. Public relations campaigns are expensive, so it is necessary for social studies advocates to search for foundations and philanthropists who are concerned about the decline in the quality of political discourse and worried about voter alienation. Here too, the time may be ripe, as philanthropists and foundations seek to move beyond merely studying the problems of civic engagement and supporting reform experiments.

Social studies scholars and political scientists can also play a major role in researching the effects of any reforms so that improvements are documented and publicized and mistakes are analyzed and corrected. The federal system that grants each state the power over its education policies allows for experimentation. Research designs can range from case studies of individual states to comparative analyses of multiple states that have tried or not tried different approaches. Social change takes years, not months, so public patience must be advised. We cannot know the success of any reforms until a few election cycles have been completed, though preliminary reports may accelerate the process.

In conclusion, the disparities between the general public, policymakers, and social studies educators can be reconciled if all parties can be convinced that the vision at the birth of social studies education can make our democratic system work better. Our field should strike while the iron is hot—right now!

References

AAUP. (2017). *Background facts on contingent faculty.* Retrieved from www.aaup.org/issues/contingency/background-facts

Doppen, F. (2007). The influence of a teacher preparation program on preservice social studies teachers' beliefs: A case study. *Journal of Social Studies Research, 31*(1), 54–64.

Evans, R. W. (2004). *The social studies wars: What should we teach the children?* New York, NY: Teachers College Press.

Fallace, T. (2009). John Dewey's influence on the origins of the social studies: An analysis of the historiography and new interpretation. *Review of Educational Research, 79*(2), 601–624.

National Governors Association. (2008). *Promoting STEM education: A communications toolkit.* Retrieved from www.nga.org/cms/home/nga-center-for-best-practices/center-publications/page-edu-publications/col2-content/main-content-list/promoting-stem-education-a-commu.html

Patterson, N., Horner, S., Chandler, P., & Dahlgren, R. (2013). Who is at the gate? An examination of secondary social studies teacher support and curricular control in testing and non-testing states. In J. Passe & P. Fitchett (Eds.), *The status of social studies: Views from the field* (pp. 289–300). Charlotte, NC: Information Age Press.

Pew Research Center. (2016a). *Already-low voter satisfaction with choice of candidates falls even further.* Retrieved from www.pewresearch.org/fact-tank/2016/09/12/already-low-voter-satisfaction-with-choice-of-candidates-falls-even-further/

Pew Research Center. (2016b). *Campaign engagement and interest.* Retrieved from www.people-press.org/2016/07/07/1-campaign-engagement-and-interest/

Disparate Aims for the Social Studies Curriculum

Commentary by Stephen J. Thornton, University of South Florida

In this brief commentary, I examine the purposes that stakeholder groups bring to social studies. Specifically, I ask how and why those purposes influence curriculum and instruction. I first look at policymakers and the general public, two groups often thought to be at odds over purposes, and suggest their divergences frequently arise as much from idiosyncratic situations of concern to one or more pressure groups as from broad-based disagreement about aims among the public at large. Episodes of conflict attract more attention that are possibly less vivid but nonetheless are significant norms of life in school social studies department offices and classrooms. Still, competing goals do sometimes come into conflict, even though the conscious or subconscious criteria that drive the actions of curricular-instructional decision-makers often tend to mute or sidestep controversy (Ochoa-Becker, 2007).

When conflicts about values do arise, however, they surface within the ecological context of schooling. Thus, value conflicts among stakeholders is not all there is to it. Organizational factors and the professional lives of teachers introduce competing values that interact with disputes over formal purposes. While value conflicts may be mitigated somewhat by improved communication among stakeholders, these conflicts cannot be resolved simply by research on which one "works" best.

Purposes of Social Studies

It is a staple in the literature that stakeholders in school social studies curricula do not always agree on what purposes those programs should serve. Sometimes, they disagree about the overall purposes of schooling to which social studies (or other school subject areas) can contribute—that is, aims. But in practice such disagreements are relatively rare in social studies, because aims tend to be pitched at such a level of abstraction that, in the absence of aims talk (Noddings, 2013), practically everybody can agree on them. Few Americans quibble, for example, with social studies contributing to the development of good citizens. At the same time, however, different Americans may hold disparate conceptions of what a "good" citizen is. Thus, disputes about social studies purposes more often occur at the level of goals, which are more specific than aims. For example, should the prime goal of United States history courses be to tie the content directly to civic life or should civic education be conceived as an indirect outcome of academic study?

A new educational era stressing efficiency and accountability reforms began unfolding in the 1980s. At the time, Fred Newmann (1985) took stock of the directions of the as-yet inchoate reform movement as it related to social studies. He identified a consensus that "endorses citizenship or civic understanding as a basic purpose [i.e., aim] of schooling" (p. 5). He added, however, that there were "differences in philosophy of social education" (p. 5), as well as "disagreements over priorities for social education" (p. 8). In other words, Newmann found consensus on aims but significant disagreement about what specific goals and objectives the aims implied.

Already in the 1980s, the ideas driving this situation drew on a long tradition in U.S. education. Now, after more than three decades of efficiency- and accountability-oriented school reform later, during which time the policy environment of education is said to have been transformed, that tradition remains largely intact. That is, however great the transformation, it does not appear to have resulted in equivalent shifts in social studies purposes among stakeholder groups.

Policymakers and the General Public

Policymaking entities include such disparate groups as curriculum commissions, federal and state departments of education, and school boards and curriculum directors at the local level. Such entities vary in how much weight their actions carry. And, the variation is context dependent. But policymakers are still ordinarily regarded as wielding authority, or at least considerable power, over the purposes of social studies programs. Nonetheless, complete fidelity to policymakers' wishes is rare. This is, at least in part, because policymakers typically operate at a distance from the curriculum in action (Lipsky, 1980).

The reality is that policymakers set broad parameters for the purposes and content of social studies programs, not script the curriculum itself. The objectives and subtopics for instruction, as well as the learning activities that embody them, are generally in the hands of decision-makers at the local level. Distal policymakers may mandate a study of the Civil War in the 11th grade, but local decision-makers are likely to determine the form taken by a lesson on Lincoln's intentions toward slavery as enunciated in the Emancipation Proclamation.

Those decision-makers are tending the curricular-instructional gate (Thornton, 1991, 2005). Gatekeepers include local writers of curriculum guides and instructional materials, district and school curriculum supervisors, and, most significantly, classroom teachers (of whom, more below). The dividing line between what policymakers and gatekeepers do blurs because the decisions they make overlap—and, sometimes, the same persons may occupy roles of policymaker and gatekeeper.

Other stakeholder groups, who as a rule do not occupy formal policymaker or gatekeeper roles, still may influence the purposes and content of the curriculum. For example, social studies education researchers through their publications and teacher education courses may provide curricular-instructional gatekeepers with alternative goals to what policymakers had in mind. Similarly, the general public may seek to influence the curriculum by communicating with policymakers and gatekeepers, directly as constituents or indirectly through mass or social media. Pressure groups, too, sometimes influence purposes. In sum, when various stakeholders exert influence on policy, it may be in different ways and by different means.

Nonetheless, there tends to be an assumed legitimacy afforded to the actions of those who occupy formal policymaking roles. This legitimacy can be consequential, because policymakers generally define social studies education as cultural transmission, which might include "rather low-level, fact-based, (even anti-intellectual) approaches to instruction" (Stanley, 2001, p. 2). Cultural transmission is a process by which the traditions and mores of the dominant culture are passed on, which is the culture with which policymakers themselves are likely to identify. Human agency in this approach takes the form of "personal[ly] responsible citizenship" (Westheimer, 2015). Even if not consciously intended, emphasis on cultural continuity and individualistic conceptions of citizenship usually have the effect of skewing the curriculum toward classroom methods of passive absorption of knowledge rather than active learning. Similar skewing occurs toward individual rather than communal and participatory conceptions of civic virtue. American policymakers have less often recommended active methods that combine "knowledge and actual civic participation" (Parker, 1991, p. vi). The net effect is policymakers tend to act as agents of the existing social order.

A cultural-transmission and individualistic orientation to civic education is echoed in the mass media. As a rule, these echoes serve to reinforce the already-conservative views of policymakers and thus amplify those views. For instance, as former National Council for the Social Studies president, Ted Levy (2005), learned from experience, what policymakers hear from the mass media is skewed to "conservative critics" over "academic and other observers" (p. 65).

There may also be a procedural reason why policymakers adopt relatively passive conceptions of civic education: control over curriculum enactment is enhanced by detailed instructions conveyed in prepackaged curricula versus delegating responsibility to practitioners who may sway the curriculum in more active and participatory directions (Ross, 2006). In this way, policymakers aspire to control the message.

Classroom Teachers

Whatever reservations policymakers may have about relinquishing control, their concern about curricular divergence from officially sanctioned goals may be unwarranted with the gatekeepers who matter most, classroom teachers. More often than not, social studies teachers aspire to fit in with peers, administrators, and the wider community. Generally, teachers' curriculum ideologies seem more or less compatible with community norms and expectations (see Farkas & Duffett, 2010). When coupled with a desire for practical instructional routines, this ends up in "coverage" of subject matter and classroom control as a likely unannounced but effective goal (Levstik, 2008).

But it seems a mistake to assume that teachers' behaviors represent scarcely more than conforming to (or already believing in) the goals and values of the communities where they teach. Rather, a combination of the constraints on and possibilities open to teachers—for example, available time and instructional materials, testing requirements, sense of community norms, perceived classroom autonomy—interact with their view of a social studies curriculum ideology. This interaction is apt to guide how teachers tend the curricular-instructional gate. It was once widely concluded that the predictable result of this interaction was a "contradiction," as the resultant gatekeeping by teachers contradicted the aims and goals announced for social studies programs (e.g., McNeil, 1986; Palonsky, 1986). But more recent scholarship suggests a less deterministic explanation.

Put simply, teachers do not weigh all constraints and possibilities equally. So while it is accurate to say that in their curriculum and instructional practices many secondary school teachers can, and often do, prioritize routines to make their classroom tasks manageable, what they define as "manageable" varies, perhaps considerably, from one teacher to the next. Nor must the setting in which they teach, though it sometimes appears to largely explain things, dictate a particular kind of gatekeeping (Barton & Levstik, 2004). "Workplace conditions and classroom realities," Milbrey McLaughlin (1989) once observed, "determine fundamentally or even whether teachers respond to policy mandates and objectives" (p. ix). But encompassed within this conclusion is the principle that teachers actively interpret policy mandates—acting as gatekeepers—and are not mere conduits for mandates (Flinders, 1996). The same mandate may result, therefore, in some teachers narrowing instruction to, say, what is tested, while other teachers reconcile testing demands with "ambitious" teaching of rich content (Grant, 2007).

Elementary school teaching of social studies is a special case. Its circumstances differ from secondary teaching in ways likely to undermine ambitious goals for social studies set by policymakers. Secondary teachers typically specialize in one or two subject fields, whereas elementary teachers ordinarily are responsible for a bevy of subjects. In addition, social studies is usually consigned to an enrichment rather than basic status in the elementary curriculum, and this marginality may be reinforced by elementary teachers seldom possessing deep acquaintance with social studies subject matter. Given these conditions, the purposes elementary teachers bring to social studies instructional programs may be intellectually unambitious (Levstik & Thornton, in press). Instead, priority may be afforded to "practical methods and materials that will help [teachers] to reach children and to survive in the classroom" (Muessig, 1987, p. 526).

And what of social studies teachers, elementary or secondary or both, who are purposeful and ambitious for significant portions of their professional activity? What singles them out from other teachers who are less purposeful and less ambitious? As important as answering these questions would appear to be in accounting for the goals enacted (or not enacted) in classrooms, we have only limited answers. Satisfying answers to such questions seems to demand thick description, so it is not surprising that most of the answers we do have come from case studies. But relatively few case studies concentrate to a significant degree on answering the two aforementioned questions (Grant, 2014). Thus, much of what we do know is obtained incidentally from studies designed to study other things—such as compliance with policies on content standards—rather than dedicated accounts specifically seeking to explain how and why teachers effectively tend the curricular-instructional gate and to what educational effects. Such accounts might help us answer, for example, what episodes in classroom life are actually instances of goal-conflict between teachers and policymakers and what is better accounted for by organizational factors.

Conclusion

I was asked to consider research-based policy explanations and solutions to the "dilemma" of disparate aims (which I have explained are more accurately in this case understood to be goals). As I have argued, however, the platform of beliefs uniting particular stakeholder groups, whether they recognize it or not, generally ends up in their favoring some values and policies over others. But the views held by stakeholders beyond the schoolhouse gate may be relatively monocular. Gatekeepers face more constraints imposed by the ecological system in which they practice their craft. In schools, practitioners must simultaneously confront value and policy questions and procedural and organizational questions. Thus, what might appear inconsistent to an outside observer, such as a policymaker, may in context make sense. For instance, a teacher may believe primary source analysis would be the preferred method for students to encounter the Emancipation Proclamation but at the same time doubt that getting through the subject matter is consistent with devoting significant time to such analysis.

It turns out research alone cannot resolve—or even fully account for—value conflicts that underlie disparate goals among stakeholders. Research will not resolve whether U.S. history should be taught primarily for its civic versus academic worth, because the two approaches are based, to some extent, on incommensurable values premises.

What researchers and teacher educators can offer is to serve as honest brokers who may be able to lead parties with conflicting values toward collaborating on areas of shared purposes. For instance, researchers can serve as mirrors that reveal to teachers what classroom life looks like from the other side of the teacher's desk. Similarly, they can help facilitate discussion that can, at least on occasion, show how stakeholders with seemingly disparate goals may be more alike than the parties themselves realize (e.g., see Stanley, 2001). There is considerable (albeit not universal) common ground on what should be taught and how it should be taught. Much depends on apprising and supporting teachers to move toward such approaches as ultimately good practice cannot be mandated.

References

Barton, K. C., & Levstik, L. S. (2004). *Teaching history for the common good*. Mahwah, NJ: Lawrence Erlbaum Associates.

Farkas, S., & Duffett, A. M. (2010, September 30). *High schools, civics, and citizenship: What social studies teachers think and do.* Washington, DC: American Enterprise Institute. Downloaded October 5, 2016, from www.aei.org/publication/high-schools-civics-and-citizenship

Flinders, D. J. (1996). Teaching for cultural literacy: A curriculum study. *Journal of Curriculum and Supervision, 11*, 351–366.

Grant, S. G. (2007). High-stakes testing: How are social studies teachers responding? *Social Education, 71*, 250–254.

Grant, S. G. (2014). Framing a scholarly life. In C. Woyshner (Ed.), *Leaders in social education: Intellectual self-portraits* (pp. 71–84). Rotterdam: Sense Publishers.

Levstik, L. S. (2008). *What happens in social studies classrooms? Research on K–12 social education* (pp. 50–62). New York: Routledge.

Levstik, L. S., & Thornton, S. J. (in press). Reconceptualizing history for early childhood through early adolescence. In S. A. Metzger & L. Harris (Eds.), *International handbook of history teaching and learning*. Malden, MA: Wiley-Blackwell.

Levy, T. (2005). Headlines and furrowed brows: NCSS engagement with social studies critics and the press. In M. S. Crocco (Ed.), *Social studies and the press: Keeping the beast at bay?* (pp. 55–66). Greenwich, CT: Information Age Publishing.

Lipsky, M. (1980). *Street-level bureaucracy: Dilemmas of the individual in public service.* New York: Russell Sage Foundation.

McLaughlin, M. (1989). Foreword. In D. J. Flinders (Ed.), *Voices from the classroom: Educational practice can inform policy* (pp. ix–x). Eugene, OR: ERIC Clearinghouse on Educational Management.

McNeil, L. M. (1986). *Contradictions of control: School structure and school knowledge.* New York: Routledge & Kegan Paul.

Muessig, R. H. (1987). An analysis of developments in geographic education. *The Elementary School Journal, 87*, 519–530.

Newmann, F. M. (1985). *Educational reform and social studies: Implications of six reports.* Boulder, CO: Social Science Education Consortium and ERIC Clearinghouse for Social Studies/Social Science Education.

Noddings, N. (2013). *Education and democracy*. New York: Teachers College Press.

Ochoa-Becker, A. S. (2007). *Democratic education for social studies: An issues-centered decision making curriculum*. Greenwich, CT: Information Age Publishing.

Palonsky, S. (1986). *900 Shows a year: A look at teaching from a teacher's side of the desk*. New York: Random House.

Parker, W. C. (1991). *Renewing the social studies curriculum*. Alexandria, VA: Association for Supervision and Curriculum Development.

Ross, E. W. (2006). The struggle for the social studies curriculum. In E. W. Ross (Ed.), *The social studies curriculum: Purposes, problems, and possibilities* (3rd. ed., pp. 17–36). Albany: State University of New York Press.

Stanley, W. B. (2001). Social studies: Problems and possibilities. In W. B. Stanley (Ed.), *Critical issues in social studies research for the 21st century* (pp. 1–13). Greenwich, CT: Information Age Publishing.

Thornton, S. J. (1991). Teacher as curricular-instructional gatekeeper in social studies. In J. P. Shaver (Ed.), *Handbook of research on social studies teaching and learning* (pp. 237–248). New York: Macmillan.

Thornton, S. J. (2005). *Teaching social studies that matters: Curriculum for active learning*. New York: Teachers College Press.

Westheimer, J. (2015). *What kind of a citizen: Educating our children for the common good*. New York: Teachers College Press.

Passe's Response to Thornton's Commentary

I agree with Steve Thornton about how teachers serve as curricular gatekeepers. I always tell my students to embrace that role, especially in states and school districts where the official curriculum does not effectively address the needs of students and the society. Unfortunately, that role is becoming less and less viable. Consider this anecdote from my early years of parenting: I learned to avoid arguments with my young children by presenting them with insignificant choices. On a breezy day, I would not ask, "Do you want to wear a jacket?" Instead, I offered a choice of the red jacket or the blue sweatshirt.

I fear that social studies teachers are falling into the same trap as my children. We take pride in our gatekeeping autonomy when we get to choose how to teach social studies minutiae, such as the various qualifications to hold office. But for deep, conceptual ideas that are most relevant to democratic citizenship, such as the tensions between the executive and legislative branches, we may not be given the choice of whether to emphasize that over other content. All gatekeeping is not the same; some gates are more important than others are.

It used to be, as Thornton states, citing Lipsky (1980), that "policymakers typically operate at a distance from the curriculum in action. . . . The reality is that policymakers set broad parameters for the purposes and content of social studies programs, not script the curriculum itself." That was true in 1980, but policymakers are savvier today. They have developed powerful strategies to compel teachers to stick to the script, sometimes using actual scripts!

Consider elementary schools, where the marginalization of social studies continues. Research conducted during the No Child Left Behind era discovered that the teachers themselves were making that gatekeeping decision to marginalize social studies, not because of some higher-level edict, but because they bought into the harsh system of accountability that NCLB authorized (Heafner & Passe, 2008). In other words, many elementary teachers stopped teaching social studies because they did not want their school to be closed due to low test scores in literacy and mathematics. Ask a secondary school teacher why there is not more interdisciplinary, inquiry-based social studies, and you will hear a litany of complaints about high-stakes tests and accountability systems that were *specifically designed to limit teacher flexibility*. The screws are getting tighter.

Thornton acknowledges that outside interest groups sometimes influence purposes, but I do not believe that goes far enough. These groups (e.g., foundations supported by the DeVos and Koch families) are not only influencing purposes; they're forcing conformity! These politically charged interests hold rigid views of what social studies content should be emphasized and have waged a sometimes stealth operation to secure powerful positions on policymaking bodies, such as school boards, state education departments, legislatures, and Congress. They have learned that practitioners largely ignore policy statements, so they are now in positions to enforce them. To carry the metaphor further, they are removing the gates.

Scholars have a greater role to play than merely serving as "mirrors that reveal to teachers what classroom life looks like from the other side of the teacher's desk." While we continue that important work, we must expand our audience beyond educators to educate the public (which includes policymakers) about the effects of the accountability and standards movements on civic life. We must also use our scholarly prowess to present a vision of what social studies classrooms can be like if educators are given appropriate support and autonomy.

Thornton avers, "There is considerable (albeit not universal) common ground on what should be taught and how it should be taught." Again, while that may have been true at one time, and may still be true for the mainstream of American thought, the individuals currently holding the reins of power appear to have very different views from those of social studies teachers. The Trump administration's recent broadsides against a free press, judicial review, limits to presidential power, and ethical government are just some of the stances that stand well outside the locus of what has always been taught in social studies classrooms. It's a new era, when even the nature of science is under attack. Social studies educators should not be complacent, maintaining business as usual. Gatekeeping functions may no longer provide a sense of security. We need to form alliances in academia, P–12 education, and the public to restore the autonomy of social studies educators for the interests of democratic citizenship.

References

Heafner, T., & Passe, J. (2008). Playing the high stakes accountability game: Social studies on the sideline. Paper presented to the annual meeting of the *National Council for the Social Studies*, Houston, TX.

Lipsky, M. (1980). *Street-level bureaucracy: Dilemmas of the individual in public service*. New York: Russell Sage Foundation.

Thornton's Response
to Passe's Commentary

Jeff Passe convincingly argues why we should feel uncomfortable (or worse) about the status quo in social studies. That is, social studies programs too often feature passive learning of forgettable information and skills from the academic disciplines rather than students drawing on the academic disciplines to support active inquiry into the demands of contemporary living. I have no hesitation in agreeing with him that we need more of the latter and less of the former. It is a position advanced by a long line of leaders in the field, including the select few who, like Professor Passe, have had the distinction of serving as president of NCSS. But, nonetheless, I do question his account of how we got where we are and what might be done about it.

The crux of his argument seems to be that the "1916 vision [i.e., *The Social Studies in Secondary Education* report issued by the National Education Association] was never fully implemented" (p. 1). He more or less equates this report with his vision of what social studies should be. If we stick to this vision and somehow overcome obstacles to implementing it, he continues, school social studies programs will become what they should be. He concedes that such a task is formidable but holds out hope there may be at present a political window of opportunity.

But however worthy the vision, Passe oversimplifies the situation in the field. Perhaps foremost, his account of why the plans in the 1916 report so often went awry in practice relies as much on academic folklore as it does on sound historical evidence. This may not appear to matter very much, but it does—perpetuation of this folklore is not merely a harmless tale, but rather hinders understanding why "full implementation" never took place.

Passe treats the report as the field's defining moment, a benchmark against which subsequent practice is measured. He is hardly alone in doing so; however, recent research undermines this notion of the report as the field's veritable sacred text. Rather it is better regarded as one point in the stream of events through which the idea of social studies took shape. The report is a sketchy document open to multiple interpretations as to its intended emphases. The process by which social studies took shape neither began nor ended in 1916 (Thornton, 2017).

The accuracy of his assumption that the report validated social studies as "integrated" or "interdisciplinary" in contrast to "isolated disciplines" is also questionable. One could just as well emphasize how the report, far from abandoning or relegating to isolation courses in academic disciplines such as American history, foresaw a vital role for them in social studies curricula. In sum, the report can be used to justify varying levels of integration between studies such as history, civics, and geography.

Even if we accept that an archetype for social studies was set in 1916, that model was built on earlier foundations. In addition, it often goes unappreciated that the report was not regarded at the time as the last word on the matter. The report was "taken seriously," historian of social studies Hazel Hertzberg (1981) observed 65 years later, but "It became a landmark only in retrospect" (p. 26). In the *next* two decades Harold Rugg and Paul Hanna, for instance, would construct social studies programs precisely because they were dissatisfied with extant curriculum models (Thornton, 2017).

Conclusion

Just as Rugg and Hanna, architects of two of the most widely disseminated curriculum models in the history of social studies, did not limit their ambitions to the report, we should not be too detained by it now. The problems of social studies will not be fixed by somehow getting everybody to agree that the report should be faithfully implemented. Of course, Passe is right that factors such as reduced time for social studies in recent decades have hurt, especially at the elementary level. But we should remember that even *before* the efficiency-driven cycle of school reform which took off some 30 or more years ago, one highly credible and widely read national study of schooling reached a devastating conclusion: "It appears we cannot assume the cultivation of the goals most appropriate to the social sciences even when social studies courses appear in the curriculum" (Goodlad, 1984, p. 213).

The issues undermining an effective social studies are longstanding and deep-seated: teachers themselves may not have experienced lively social studies courses; college and university courses in the subjects teachers will teach are seldom consciously designed to connect with what is in the K–12 curriculum; a teaching methods course or two is supposed to undo a lifetime of exposure by prospective teachers of social studies that violates the maxims Passe lays out; curriculum policymakers may be ignorant of or even opposed to an activist conception of social studies; and the culture of schools frequently values compliance more than critical thinking. Hopes for reform cannot rely on a change of heart among stakeholders about the aims and goals of social studies, which is unlikely to happen anyway, in my opinion. Rather we need to seek entry points in the ecology of school social studies where there may be some leverage. For example, altering teacher education programs to provide the kind of subject matter that would enable prospective teachers to teach social studies the way it could be taught (e.g., Noddings, 2015). We might also learn from successful social studies programs (e.g., Kirkwood, 2002): How were they constructed? Supported? Institutionalized?

Or else in another hundred years the same laments about social studies failing in its basic mission will still be heard.

References

Goodlad, J. I. (1984). *A place called school: Prospects for the future.* New York: McGraw-Hill.

Hertzberg, H. W. (1981). *Social studies reform, 1880–1980.* Boulder, CO: Social Science Education Consortium.

Kirkwood, T. F. (2002). Teaching about Japan: Global perspectives in teacher decision-making, context, and practice. *Theory and Research in Social Education, 30,* 88–115.

Noddings, N. (2015). *A richer, brighter vision for American high schools.* New York: Cambridge University Press.

Thornton, S. J. (2017). A concise historiography of the social studies. In M. M. Manfra & C. M. Bolick (Eds.), *The Wiley handbook of research on social studies research* (pp. 9–41). Boston, MA: Wiley-Blackwell.

2

"TO WHAT EXTENT ARE SOCIAL STUDIES STANDARDS USEFUL AND CONSEQUENTIAL AS POLICY TOOLS AT STATE, DISTRICT, AND CLASSROOM LEVELS?"

Policy as Metaphor

Commentary by S. G. Grant, Binghamton University

Although it sounds like a cop-out, the answer to this chapter's central question really is, "it depends." In some cases, it depends on who one asks, for teachers may offer a different view than their district superintendent. In other cases, it depends on what other reforms are jockeying for consideration. Because the stream of accountability-driven policy initiatives since *A Nation at Risk* in 1983 shows no sign of abating, educators can hardly be faulted for practicing selective attention. And in still other cases, the impact of standards depends on how one measures usefulness and consequence. Education is a notoriously difficult field to measure with any precision, so understanding the impact of a set of standards can prove challenging.

These factors, and more, lay behind my earlier characterization of social studies reforms in general and state testing policy in particular as an "uncertain lever" (Grant, 2001). Several years and several standards documents later, little has occurred to encourage me to rethink that metaphor. In this essay, however, I expand on the uncertain leverage of policy by examining three additional metaphors: policy as "steady work," policy as a "blunt instrument," and the "pocket veto" that teachers wield over most every policy initiative. Not surprisingly, I conclude that it is far easier to create new policies and new policy metaphors than it is to change the classroom lives of teachers and students.

Policy as Steady Work

Elmore and McLaughlin (1988) wrote, "the history of American education is, in large part, the history of reform, or rather of recurring cycles of reform" (p. 13). Although schools are among the most long-standing of social institutions in the

United States, they are also among the most susceptible to critique, evaluation, and reform efforts. I say reform "efforts" because reform and change are not always the same thing (Corbett & Wilson, 1991). Tyack and Cuban (1995) observe that schools do change, but such efforts typically reflect tinkering than rather than transformation.

I will have more to say about the impact of education policy initiatives below. In this section, I want to highlight the seeming unrelenting state of reform-minded efforts. Elmore and McLaughlin (1988) term this condition "steady work," which is characterized by "a limitless supply of new ideas for how schools should be changed and no shortage of political and social pressure to force those ideas onto the political agenda" (p. 15).

Since the *Nation at Risk* report in 1983, there has been a relentless stream of social studies reforms. Although some of the efforts aim at areas like testing (e.g., changes in Advanced Placement exams and the adoption of document-based questions on some state exams), most focus on curriculum. And there have been many groups interested in social studies curriculum standards. Professional organizations (e.g., National Council for the Social Studies, 1994), nonprofit organizations (e.g., Bradley Commission, 1989), national government-sponsored projects (e.g., Siegfried & Meszaros, 1997), and state governments have competed for teachers' attention and underscored the validity of the steady work metaphor.

One reason for the continued and varied interest in social studies standards is focus. Some entities present standards aimed at the entirety of the social studies field, while others focus on a single discipline. A second reason is that none of these groups has to pay attention to the others. With no single body in charge of curriculum, the standards terrain is wide open, and there is a long history of groups both inside and outside state government trying to influence teachers' practices. The decentralized nature of schooling ensures that each group's new policy proposal will gain some attention and that it need not worry about conflict with previous efforts.

The steady work of producing social studies standards expanded with the introduction of the Common Core State Standards. The détente that once existed among curriculum reformers—each group staying within the standard subject matter bounds—ended as social studies teachers now found themselves attending meetings with their English-language arts colleagues and hearing about *The Common Core State Standards for English Language Arts & Literacy in History / Social Studies, Science, and Technical Subjects.* In a single move, the authors of the Common Core appropriated content in science, technology education, and social studies. Social studies teachers, accustomed to curriculum documents written by experts in their field, now found themselves reading and reacting to standards from a very different source. The steady work of social studies standards gained another supply site.

Steady work around curriculum can be empowering if the results are viewed as productive by an array of stakeholders—e.g., students, teachers, parents, policymakers.

Viewed as just one more thing, it can be enervating. Social studies standards may be influencing teachers, but it may be inducing fatigue rather than fervor.

Policy as a Blunt Instrument

Standards fatigue may be rooted in the fact that so many reforms pass across teachers' desks. But a second source may lie in the fact that so many of those reforms seem so irrelevant. Sykes (1999) notes that policy is typically a blunt instrument when it comes to improving educational conditions: "Levers of top-down control are blunt instruments for change because they ignore [the idea that the] autonomy of local systems, not directives from the top, fosters the system's self-organization and ultimately its coordination and potential productivity" (p. 9). Elmore and Fuhrman (1995) are more direct: "Teaching and learning are the central aspects of schooling and the aspects most inaccessible to the blunt instruments of policy" (p. 3). When it comes to curriculum reforms, pervasiveness is not the same thing as persuasiveness.

The idea that policy is a crude influence on teaching and learning should surprise few observers. Reforms that target obvious and uncomplicated behaviors (e.g., following the speed limit, observing the drinking age) impact most but not all behavior. Despite clear aims, widespread publicity, and clear sanctions, slippage in compliance still defines the simplest policies. Little wonder, then, that teaching and learning, which are among the most complex behaviors in which humans engage, are ill responsive to broad-stroke policy enactment.

Looking closer, at least three conditions blunt the effect of curriculum standards on the nuanced work of teaching and learning. One is the *clarity of the aims*. Even though curriculum standards ought to offer useful content guidelines, they rarely do. Consider, for example, the list of people, places, actions, and ideas that make up the typical standards document. A cursory look suggests that each item is worth noting but, beyond that, what does such a list tell teachers to do in their classrooms? The foreword to such documents may talk about deep and engaged study of important constructs; the list, however, says march through this content at a lively pace. Teachers are right to wonder which aim is intended.

A second condition contributing to the dulling of curriculum standards is the potential for *incoherent consequences*. Many of the curriculum reforms offered in the last several years come with no consequences attached (e.g., the Bradley Commission and Council for Economic Education standards). Others, such as those issued by state education departments, can have high stakes associated with them. Although state-level tests reflecting some measure of new curriculum standards may influence classroom teaching and learning, slippage can occur (Grant, 2006). Finally, the emergence of associated consequences, as in the case of social studies teachers being held accountable for students' scores on the English-language portion of Common Core-based exams, underscores the incoherence of standards-related outcomes.

One last way in which the promise of curriculum standards can be dampened emerges through teachers' *selective attention*. Even if a set of social studies curriculum standards are clear and the consequences coherent, its impact may be muted by the fact that schools are complex places with lots of policies in motion, and teachers have only so much time and capacity to pay attention.

Classroom teachers well know how the complexities and vagaries of their work—a lesson that went brilliantly in one period that falls flat two hours later; variable sensitivities to students' ideas at different times; even the amount of sunshine pouring through the classroom windows—can factor into their pedagogical decisions and success. Curriculum standards are one of those factors; they are not the only one.

Teachers' Pocket Veto

Much has been made of the special policy challenges inherent in decentralized organizations like schools: multiple and largely autonomous actors, weak command and control structures, diffuse organizational goals, and capricious resource decisions. Yet well before the latest rounds of reforms, Kirst and Walker (1971) noted the central role that teachers play in policy enactment:

> Supposing that a policy decision survives emasculation by the administrative hierarchies of federal agencies and state and local officials, it still faces a pocket-veto by 2,000,000 classroom teachers. So long as teachers consider themselves professional agents with some autonomy in curriculum questions by virtue of their professional expertise, policy implementation will be a matter of persuasion rather than direction.
>
> *(p. 505)*

Kirst and Walker's point is as simple as it is disconcerting: curriculum policies matter, only if teachers decide that they do. Educational systems are too leaky and reforms are too amorphous for policy fidelity to be the rule. Teachers and their practices may be the direct object of reformers' actions, but that does not mean they are pawns to those actions.

The Value of Policy Metaphors

Lakoff and Johnson (1980) present a pretty compelling argument: metaphors structure our understandings and experiences such that they become "the metaphors we live by." Vincent (2008) agrees that metaphors are powerful, but he points to a key limitation:

> The problem lies in recognizing the limitations of using metaphors as a means to order our lives. In order to truly work, metaphors have to be every bit as complex, subtle and nuanced as the reality they are attempting to describe.

If Vincent (2008) is right, two points follow: although metaphors offer the value of shorthand descriptions of people and their experiences, that shorthand may obscure important nuances. In short, metaphors are no substitute for experience. And the experience of teaching and learning within the classroom environment defies simple metaphorical descriptions as much as it does simple policy prescriptions.

Of what value, then, are policies in general and policy metaphors in particular? The first is too big a question for this essay, so I will focus on the latter.

Metaphors can point to the problematic elements of policy enactment and, in doing so, offer keen insights. But are they equally valuable in identifying and suggesting solutions? If we consider each of the examples above, I think the answer is no.

The steady work metaphor suggests that teachers may not attend to policy because there are simply too many. So is the solution to limit the number of policy proposals offered? A moment's reflection on that suggestion undercuts its potential: the entities vying for teachers' attention are just too numerous and diverse to imagine a systemic effort to reduce or consolidate reform initiatives.

The blunt instrument metaphor identifies a more specific problem: the challenge policymakers face in directly influencing the complex and nuanced work of teachers and their students. So much of what passes for educational reform seems directed toward that interaction, yet the influence has been marginal at best. But what would it take for policy to be fully directive? Is the answer to mandate one or more acceptable approaches to teaching and assessing, for example, the French Revolution or economic scarcity? Sober reflection suggests that it is not. Not only does the idea of monitoring every teacher's every action seem overwhelming, but one can only imagine the volumes of regulations needed were every lesson to be scripted.

Turning finally to the metaphor of teachers' pocket veto over policy, we can immediately see the parameters of the issue: because teaching is complex and because teachers' actions cannot be monitored completely, teachers retain considerable power over policy intended to influence their pedagogical practices. Once again, however, we cannot find the solution in the inverse of the problem. Like parenting and each of the helping professions, teaching is more about understanding and reacting to the dynamics of a constantly changing context than it is about blindly applying a prescribed set of actions. Every good teacher knows the power of instructional planning *and* the power of revising that plan when circumstances demand. Educational policy in general and curriculum policy in particular are about general conditions; teaching is about the particular. A mandated policy approach that works with some but not all students should be pocket vetoed. Trusting teachers to make on-the-spot decisions, even if they run counter to a policy prescription, may simply be the price necessary for teachers to do their work.

We are left then with the circumstance that policy metaphors can never describe the full reality of teachers' classroom practice and, even when they describe a piece of that practice, they do not do so in ways that offer a clear and positive direction. But then policy is no better. Recall Vincent's (2008) caution about the value of metaphors cited above: "In order to truly work, metaphors have to be every bit as complex, subtle and nuanced as the reality they are attempting to describe." Substituting the word "policies" for "metaphors" brings us to the central conclusion of this essay: policies that miss the "complex, subtle, and nuanced" nature of schooling realities will fail.

I, for one, am not ready to give up on the possibilities of policy nor am I willing to abandon the use of metaphors to understand the relationship between policy and practice. What seems evident, however, is that the metaphor of policy as uncertain lever may be as apt now as it was 15 years ago and that teachers and their students deserve more from those who make and analyze policy.

References

Bradley Commission on History in Schools. (1989). Building a history curriculum: Guidelines for teaching. In P. Gagnon & The Bradley Commission on History in Schools (Eds.), *Historical literacy: The case for history in American education* (pp. 16–47). New York: MacMillan.

Corbett, H. D., & Wilson, B. (1991). *Testing, reform, and rebellion*. Norwood, NJ: Ablex.

Elmore, R., & Fuhrman, S. (1995). *Opportunity to learn and the state role in education*. Washington, DC: Consortium for Policy Research in Education, Office of Educational Research and Improvement, U.S. Department of Education.

Elmore, R., & McLaughlin, M. (1988). *Steady work: Policy, practice, and the reform of American education*. Santa Monica, CA: Rand.

Grant, S. G. (2001). An uncertain lever: The influence of state-level testing in New York state on teaching social studies. *Teachers College Record, 103*(3), 398–426.

Grant, S. G. (Ed.). (2006). *Measuring history: Cases of high-stakes testing across the U. S.* Greenwich, CT: Information Age Publishing.

Kirst, M., & Walker, D. (1971). An analysis of curriculum policy-making. *Review of Educational Research, 41*(5), 479–508.

Lakoff, G., & Johnson, M. (1980). *Metaphors we live by*. Chicago, IL: University of Chicago Press.

National Council for the Social Studies. (1994). *Expectations of Excellence: Curriculum Standards for Social Studies*, Bulletin 89. Washington, DC: National Council for the Social Studies.

Siegfried, J. J., & Meszaros, B. T. (1997). National voluntary content standards for pre-college economics education. *The American Economic Review, 87*(2), 247–253.

Sykes, G., & Darling-Hammond, L. (Eds.). (1999). *Teaching as the learning profession: Handbook of policy and practice*. San Francisco, CA: Jossey-Bass.

Tyack, D., & Cuban, L. (1995). *Tinkering toward Utopia*. Cambridge, MA: Harvard University Press.

Vincent, T. (2008, December). The problem with metaphors. *The Ethical Spectacle, 14*(12). Retrieved from www.spectacle.org/1208/vincent.html.

Social Studies Standards: Too Little for Too Long

Commentary by Tim Slekar, Edgewood College

In the 1930s, George Counts dared schools to "build a new social order" (1978/1932) comprised of an active, critical citizenry, challenging industrial society's inequities through boldly democratic education. In 2016, a supposedly educated population of United States citizens elected Donald Trump as its next president, ushering in what surely will be a new social order. For decades preceding that election, social studies educators, researchers, and leaders have rejected powerful and critical social studies learning efforts in favor of superficial standards setting and accountability talk. I begin this way to address the chapter's prompt about the usefulness of social studies standards. My guess is that Counts would not be very happy with Trump's construct of a new social order, and my point is that standards—particularly in social studies—have been useless as instruments intended to affect how the social order Counts envisioned might be built through public education.

Since 1983, when the "nation was at risk," we have written and implemented and evaluated standards in the social studies (and every other school subject) toward numerous educational ends, including closing the achievement gap and increasing graduation rates; and in over 30 years of standards writing, there has been little to no movement in either of these areas. Perhaps the biggest related policy movement in social studies education has been to adopt mandatory, standards-based tests for graduation, in civics and history. But such graduation requirements steal resources away from critical social studies education, pacifying conservative critics and deflating what interest students might have in social studies as a means of societal reconstruction.

The most commonly agreed upon goal in social studies education is the formation of an active, participatory citizenry; and yet, via the standards movement, the social studies were sucked into arguments about what counts as knowledge and how we measure it. Meanwhile, concerns about whether or not that citizenry will go on to support and participate in our fragile democratic experiment beyond its years of K–12 schooling intensify. Where is the evidence that spending 30 years arguing about, writing, refining, and codifying standards for the social studies has done anything positive to help create a fully engaged, participatory-democratic citizenry? Returning to the election results of 2016, it seems clear that social studies education as an agent of rational thought, democratic action, and social and economic equity has failed. How did this happen?

Phase 1: Arguments About Knowledge

Diane Ravitch (1987) once argued that social studies was nothing more than "tot sociology," suggesting that Paul Hanna's expanding communities model was developmentally ineffectual and demanding that the study of great people and events in American history pervade the elementary classroom. Similarly, E.D. Hirsch (1988) insisted that there was a shared knowledge in modern American culture and that children who do not acquire that common knowledge will always struggle in school. Between Ravitch's critique of social studies as "vacuous" and Hirsch's insistence that all students need a collective memory of quintessentially American content, the attack on the nature and purposes of social studies—particularly in the elementary grades—was engaged.

The response from some scholars who studied how students learn to "do history" was a sharp critique of Ravitch's and Hirsch's patriotic indoctrination principle. Instead of celebrating American exceptionalism, these scholars contended, children were highly capable of critical thought; thus, social studies education should be grounded in the kinds of investigative practices and analytical and inferential thinking found in history as a discipline. These scholars fought vigorously for more interpretive, constructivist ways to learn social studies subject matter, rather than traditional, transmissive approaches. "Thinking like a historian" became a conceptual and practical framework for many in the social studies field—an alternative, grounded in research on children's learning, to the history education supported by people like Ravitch and Hirsch.

Meanwhile, in the mid-1990s, Gary Nash, Charlotte Crabtree, and their colleagues at the National Center for History in the Schools created a set of history standards that demeaned American exceptionalism as a unifying historical narrative and gave birth to the so-called history wars (Nash, Crabtree, & Dunn, 2000). Across the country, conservatives went into a panic when they discovered that traditional American history content, like George Washington's teeth, was absent from the new National Standards for History (NSH). According to these critics, core American values were being written out of the history curriculum to make way for a more inclusive, multicultural approach. Instead of Christopher Columbus "discovering" America, it was now suggested that 1492 alternatively could be seen as the start of an indigenous genocide that continued unchecked through the 19th and early 20th centuries. The NSH opened the door to replace accomplishment stories of great White men with slave narratives and first-person accounts of sweat-shops and child labor. For conservatives, this shift in perspective, and its accompanying emphasis on interrogating rather than accepting narratives of American exceptionalism, was nothing short of treason. For liberals, it was a vindication of the reality that history is a complex, constructed, unfinished domain, and even somewhat "revisionary" in its capacity to reveal previously unheard stories of the past. At about the same time, the National Council for the Social Studies (NCSS) published its first standards, choosing to focus on interdisciplinary thematic strands that educators could use to establish curricular aims and evaluate instructional practices, rather than specific subject matter for students to learn and demonstrate.

Scholars of social studies education likely learned about these disputes and the differences among standards frameworks in graduate school. Simultaneously, third graders still experienced a mix of Hanna's expanding communities model and holiday history. Children talked about the social orders of their families, schools, and localities; and during Thanksgiving, they reenacted peaceful meals between Indians and Pilgrims. Tepees were erected in the corners of classrooms. Young learners created big, yellow belt buckles out of construction paper, and little hands magically became colorful turkeys. The big fear that tradition and exceptionalism were being cut from the fabric of American society was a mythology conservatives deluded themselves into believing; and at the same time, a more pluralistic, disciplinary approach to teaching history was a mythology kept alive by liberal academics presenting to each other at conferences that merely served as echo chambers. In other words, discourses about the nature and purposes of knowledge in the social studies remained isolated in the conference halls of annual academic meetings, and discussions of standards and their social and practical implications remained the property of intellectuals, rather than the property of K–12 educators. Amidst academic discussions about the nature and intended outcomes of social studies education, social studies learning and teaching in America's K–12 classrooms remained virtually unchanged.

Phase 2: Insert Accountability

Then in 2002, George W. Bush gave the nation No Child Left Behind (NCLB) and "accountability." This shift—tethered tightly to proficiency standards mandating specific reading and math achievement outcomes—changed public education classrooms forever. A frenzy of measurement followed, to meet demands for proof that students and educators were mastering these standards. With the resultant change in the culture of schools and classrooms, disputes over the purposes and intended consequences of history and social studies standards lost significance. Reading and math became the main focus—or I should say reading and math testing and test preparation—and the civic mission of the American public school system was suppressed.

This is the moment that could have been. We in social studies education should have pivoted to the left. We should have advocated for a social studies curriculum immersed in critical pedagogy. Instead, we decided to join the argument for proficiency standards and accountability and demanded that our subject matter be tested, too. For example, when New York State set out to create a high-stakes test for fifth graders, the test was sold as standards- and performance-based because of the inclusion of document-based questions and a written synthesis task. In reality, 35 multiple-choice questions that measured reading comprehension of trivial facts predominated the assessment's weighting, rendering the document-based questions and written synthesis impotent. "Doing history"—let alone informed, critical, participatory citizenship—would remain marginalized by high-stakes assessment regimes. The new social order that Counts dreamed of had become a nightmare of standard setting, testing, and compliance.

The NCSS published an extensively updated, post-NCLB standards document in 2004, in response to current research on student learning and demands for increasingly "rigorous" teaching standards among state licensing and teacher education accrediting agencies; yet its effect on civic participation as an outcome of social studies learning and teaching was minimal. While the language used in this new document emphasized powerful, challenging teaching and constructivist learning, past patterns endured, where standards talk remained largely academic talk, while classroom practices comprised a hodgepodge of persistent traditions, test-preparatory exercises, and occasional investigative sidebars. Instead of building a new social order grounded in critical thought and civic engagement, the social studies engaged fully in the frenzy of standards and accountability currently linked with efforts to discredit and dismantle public education across the United States.

What Could Have Been

If social studies scholars and policymakers had paid attention to long-term shifts in the political macro-milieu, they might have recognized the standards and accountability movement as the antithesis of powerful teaching and learning. For the field of social studies education to be impactful at the state, district, and classroom levels, it would have persuasively represented the standards movement as the continuation of an unimaginative vision of public schooling that only works for White, middle-class children. Such a mission would have required the field to take the position that the social studies were never meant to be discretely measurable subject matter and practices. Although this sounds utopian, the social studies ask us to help prepare children for meaningful participation in public life. If studied deeply, the social studies should promote empathy and compassion. It is the only subject matter in the K–12 curriculum that overtly advocates moral imperatives and a never-ending quest for justice. By contrast, standards, accountability, and testing regimes demonstrably are about spelling out and guarding the status quo.

Imagine curricula and pedagogy grounded in the priorities and principles laid out by those who aspire to justice for all students—critical race theorists, culturally sustaining pedagogues, and anti-colonialists, for example. This is what the social studies could have been. Instead, these powerful ways of understanding the world and helping to create the new social order Counts imagined—rather than the one Trump seems to be ushering in—remain at the fringes of academia, also the property of intellectuals, with occasional sightings in classrooms where extremely brave teachers are enlightening and empowering too few students.

These are the true failures of the standards movement, in general, and social studies standards, in particular. At national, state, and district levels, they have done little to shift social studies teaching toward dynamic social critique and democratic participation and away from the status quo. For all of the standards' language of civic knowledge and participation as democratic aims, a president who explicitly ran on undemocratic principles was elected in 2016; it seems unlikely that any new standards, or any intensification of current ones, will change the forces that motivated his election.

So what should be done, on principle? Stop focusing on the transmission of some contested knowledge base; stop filling buckets and arguing over what those buckets should be filled with; reimagine what it means to learn and take public action. Recognize that truly powerful—revolutionary—social studies education should actively resist standardization and embrace the emancipatory powers of curiosity and experience in a quest for social justice. At the same time, we also must be vigilant in guarding against the ways critical social studies might be set in standards and delivered via canned curricula and mind-numbing testing. Social studies is not content; it is a challenge, a critical experience, a public movement.

Dare the social studies build a new social order? How about dare social studies education scholars and policymakers quit trying to fit in with the standards and accountability movement—now inseparably conjoined—and engage with their brothers and sisters in K–12 classrooms, both locally and across the United States? Abandoning old assumptions about "knowledge, skills, and dispositions" that require standards, measurement, and accountability is the only path to a liberating experience with and within the social studies. Perhaps a core problem is the assumption that things must be learned and acquired, rather than experienced through social and political action. Maybe we should move in the direction of civil disobedience toward policies that distort real social studies learning and teaching, rather than conformity. Standards- and assessment-compliant content and stand-and-deliver instruction no more; let us teach critical social studies.

References

Counts, G. S. (1978/1932). *Dare the school build a new social order?* Carbondale, IL: SIU Press.

Hirsch, E. D., Jr. (1988). *Cultural literacy: What every American needs to know.* New York: Vintage.

Nash, G. B., Crabtree, C. A., & Dunn, R. E. (2000). *History on trial: Culture wars and the teaching of the past.* New York: Vintage.

Ravitch, D. (1987). Tot sociology: Or what happened to history in the grade schools. *The American Scholar, 56*(3), 343–354.

Grant's Response to Slekar's Commentary

In his essay, Tim Slekar offers a useful perspective on the potential for schools to play a transformative role in society and on the poor record of educational policies in affecting such reconstruction. In this rejoinder, I offer three reasons for this outcome and then suggest that the *College, Career, and Civic Life (C3) Framework for Social Studies State Standards* (National Council for the Social Studies, 2013) offers George Counts's followers a chance to nod, if not smile.

Critique of U.S. schools in general, and of social studies education in particular, has a long tail. Dissatisfaction with schooling and attempts to reform it trace back to the country's founding. George Counts (1932/1978) dared school folks to "build a new social order"; Skelar rightly notes they have not done so.

One reason is that schools do not do anything by themselves. Reformers of all stripes have nailed their hopes to schoolhouse doors, yet I can think of no social movements initiated, developed, and enacted through educational efforts alone. Teachers and administrators may be able to *support* social transformations, but *building* a new social order seems unfair to ask of any single social institution.

A second explanation is that crafting a vision like Counts's is a far different thing than implementing one. Moving from idea to action is always a challenge; in this case, it involves two particular challenges. One is that Counts's notion of social reconstructionism, while aspirational, yields no single policy prescription. Each of Counts's acolytes (e.g., Bramheld, Rugg, Apple) has offered a slightly different version of the reconstructionist vision. Change is hard enough with a clear directive; any muddying of the waters is likely to promote stasis. An even bigger challenge, however, is the frenzied educational policy landscape. Even if Counts's ideas had emerged today unmediated from the 1930s, they would still face an enormous obstacle: the "steady work" of educational reform (Elmore & McLaughlin, 1988) ensures that a social reconstructionist message would face vigorous competition from the curriculum standards, student assessment, teacher evaluation, and school choice initiatives in play.

One last reason why Counts's directive has not taken hold is that schools seem better able to affect change in individuals than in the collective. Critique of social, political, and economic inequity can find fertile ground in schools, although such critique is unevenly distributed across classrooms and communities (Anyon, 1981). Students may read texts that question prevailing ideas, make arguments that reflect progressive stances, and talk about issues that matter. These and other school-based practices often support individual student efficacy. Finding spots where collective action takes place is far more challenging.

Slekar and I agree that schools have offered rocky ground for innovations of all sorts, especially those of a progressive nature. However, we seem to disagree about the reasons why, about what role policy plays in steering educational activity, and about how school folks should participate in the policy scene.

There are different ways to interpret Slekar's argument. One is that social studies educators simply are not very good at affecting policy because they participate in the wrong conversations and align themselves with the wrong policy actors. Another is that, because of persistent failure, the policy arena itself holds no promising direction, so school folk should consider opting out of it and pursuing a different pathway altogether.

This second interpretation is ironic, as George Counts seemed equally comfortable in policy and academic worlds. Counts did not retreat when his ideas failed to garner immediate support. Instead, he promoted them through his leadership of the American Federation of Teachers and the New York State Liberal Party. It is hard to imagine him reacting to the enactment of poor policies by disengaging.

Slekar and I agree that policies can send mixed messages and undercut teachers' best efforts, yet disregarding the possibilities of policy seems improvident. In fact, one could make the argument that state policies have done nothing to social studies teaching and learning that textbook writers, test developers, state and local curriculum developers, and teachers themselves did not do before the standards and accountability movement. There has never been a golden age of social studies teaching and learning; otherwise, Counts and others would not have advanced their reformist ideas.

Policy, like every other human creation, can create as many problems as it solves. But policy efforts like the *Next Generation Science Standards* (NGSS Lead States, 2013) and the *C3 Framework* suggest that progressive goals can be advanced. Consider the following:

- Both were born from efforts by educators at all levels (i.e., teachers, university faculty, state education department personnel, and professional leaders of cultural institutions) rather than the directive of a central agency.
- Neither standards effort carries a government imprint. The review, revision, and publication of each set of standards was accomplished outside of official

procedures and decision-making. States *may* adopt either set of completed standards, but they are adopting a policy created outside of their individual jurisdictions.

- Both the science and social studies standards place inquiry at the heart of teaching and learning. Educators in both fields have long clamored for a strong commitment to engaging students in close and thoughtful examination of ideas and to enabling students to construct their own meanings.

- The *C3 Framework*, in particular, elevates the practice of taking informed action to the top strata of its standards. Dimension 4 of the *C3 Framework* makes the argument that taking informed action can manifest in various ways, in various venues, and in ways that push toward a more just society.

Schools cannot do everything we want. They *can* do a better job of equipping students to read, write, think, and act in ways that promote the social good. Policies cannot do everything we want either. But they *can* support and extend the best efforts of school folks. I think George Counts could agree with both of these notions.

References

Anyon, J. (1981). Social class and school knowledge. *Curriculum Inquiry, 11*(1), 3–42.

Counts, G. S. (1978/1932). *Dare the school build a new social order?* Carbondale, IL: SIU Press.

Elmore, R., & McLaughlin, M. (1988). *Steady work: Policy, practice, and the reform of American education.* Santa Monica, CA: Rand.

National Council for the Social Studies. (2013). *The college, career, and civic life (C3) framework for social studies state standards: Guidance for enhancing the rigor of K–12 civics, economics, geography, and history.* Silver Spring, MD: National Council for the Social Studies.

NGSS Lead States. (2013). *Next generation science standards: For states, by states.* Washington, DC: The National Academies Press.

Slekar's Response to Grant's Commentary

In his answer to this chapter's central question, S.G. Grant offers three useful metaphors for standards' roles as policy instruments, in addition to the well-known "uncertain lever" metaphor he coined years ago when discussing the implications of state-level testing for social studies education (Grant, 2001). Let me first commend Grant for taking on an important social studies policy question in such an accessible way, with care, precision, and substance—all trademarks of his scholarship throughout his career. In the following rejoinder, I address Grant's three metaphors and suggest a path toward affecting policy activity, from state to classroom levels, in the present.

On the first metaphor—"policy as steady work"—does this imply that reforms are inevitably relentless, changing faster than those who enact them can acknowledge and respond to their intents and effects over time? If so, what are the consequences of this way of conceptualizing what policy is and does? How will policy actually change the work of teachers in social studies classrooms? If there is anything we can be sure of as social studies professionals, it is that, since 1983's *A Nation at Risk*, the amount of work that has been done in the name of standards is monumental. However, that work—as Grant seems to agree—has brought on fatigue in social studies classrooms and little real change in how social studies education is enacted. Therefore, are we really surprised when work being prescribed by policymakers is disconnected from the variables of classroom practice and, thus, has scant, if any, impact on learning and teaching? For many, that expectation for policy has become a default, *because* of its steadiness.

On the second metaphor—"policy as a blunt instrument"—I am struck by the image this conjures in my mind: one of clueless, self-important policymakers who have assumed some degree of prominence with little experience in public education, angrily yelling at subordinates to figure out ways to "make those damn teachers change." I agree with Grant when he points out that top-down approaches to policy often create cultures of incoherence. Running a bit further with this metaphor, blunt instruments deliver blunt forces; and blunt forces cause trauma that affects many parts of the body. This seems appropriate to the ways policies as blunt instruments produce traumatic forces within educational systems. The assumption that blunt force trauma is an effective way to bring forth positive changes to the complex, human activities of teaching and learning speaks to the cluelessness of many policymakers.

On the third metaphor—"teachers' pocket veto"—I agree with this idea, with some reservations. While it is ultimately the teacher who can follow or veto policy mandates, the climate in which teachers now operate has changed dramatically in some places. In the last five years, I have met more teachers who are fearful of using the pocket veto because of the sticks attached to different accountability systems that monitor standards implementation. It may also be time to reexamine the pocket veto phenomenon altogether. We need to remember that our undergraduate teacher education students are products of the pernicious policy war of the last 20 years; when No Child Left Behind passed in 2001, many of today's new teachers were in kindergarten. They have been the ultimate pawns in standards-based accountability games, and consequently, I am not sure this generation of new teachers fully comprehends its own autonomy, especially amidst the blunt force trauma caused by instruments used to enforce today's standards-based reforms.

This leads to a follow-up question: as the trauma of those reforms continues to damage teachers' senses of autonomy, might the "uncertain lever" metaphor also require some fresh reconsideration? In other words, reforms attached to accountability stipulations *certainly* have the ability to *leverage* changes in classroom decisions and alter teachers' actions in the direction of compliance. And it is here that I suggest possible directional shifts in how social studies professionals address the importance or impotence of policies that couple standards with accountability demands.

This shift would be in the directions of public scholarship and public activism among groups of researchers and educators who draw decisively from that scholarship to influence policy activity. Scholars like Grant need to continue providing razor-sharp analyses of policy implications in their work so that others—like me—can take that work and breathe a different kind of life into it; a political life. We can continue to write to each other in echo chambers of traditional scholarship, or we can create, strengthen, and advance less traditional public scholarship venues and trajectories—e.g., blogs, podcasts, media appearances, editorials, and activist networks. While many of us occasionally dip our feet into the waters of public scholarship, "traditional scholarship" remains the only currency accepted in the pursuit of an academic career.

It is time to change that. Grant's helpful metaphors and my critiques of them are not just academic arguments; they are frameworks and guidelines for considering what policy actions to take, how to take them, and why. Those actions must be taken, and taken publicly and collectively. Precedent suggests that the work of social studies professionals is unlikely to leave the pages of academic journals and books if we continue to value such a narrow definition of scholarship as we do currently. Moreover, we are unlikely to change policy without commissioning professional groups who can communicate to new people in new ways about the kind of work being done by folks like Grant and lobbying persistently on behalf of such work. If we are looking for a "more certain lever"—one that social studies professionals control, not respond to—then we need to value activism in social studies education and build an academic reward structure that incentivizes public scholarship in all its different forms.

Reference

Grant, S. G. (2001). An uncertain lever: Exploring the influence of state-level testing in New York State on teaching social studies. *Teachers College Record, 103*(3), 398–426.

3

"HOW MIGHT POLICY TOOLS AND ACTIVITIES CONTRIBUTE TO REPRIORITIZING SOCIAL STUDIES EDUCATION IN ELEMENTARY-LEVEL CURRICULUM AND INSTRUCTION?"

The Promise of Policy and Action for the Reprioritization of Social Studies

Commentary by Tina L. Heafner, University of North Carolina at Charlotte

Many policy mechanisms have the potential to reprioritize social studies. Ironically, these same policy tools have also been associated with the marginalization of the subject area. Nevertheless, recent shifts in policy aims accompanied by grass-roots activities are making strides in positioning social studies as an essential field of study. These trends manifest most notably in the elementary schools.

Time Structures Are Policy Tools

Time that elementary students spend learning social studies is associated with knowledge construction (Nuthall & Alton-Lee, 1993), given that the degree of learning is greatly dependent upon the amount of time students actively engaged in domain-specific learning and authentic intellectual work (King, Newmann, & Carmichael, 2009). Consequently, attention to school and district policies that define elementary school time structures are needed to ensure social studies has designated instructional time. Allocating a specific daily block of time designated for instruction comparable to other core content areas conveys a message that social studies concepts are valued within the curriculum beyond their ability to provide a context for lessons in other subjects, and has the capacity to influence teachers' perceptions of social studies, as well as the time devoted to instruction (Fitchett, Heafner, & VanFossen, 2014).

Adding social studies to accountability structures is a plausible pathway for increasing social studies elementary time. When social studies is included, teachers at the tested grades demonstrate a stronger commitment to teaching social studies than colleagues at non-tested grade levels (Brophy & Alleman, 2008). Moreover, teachers working in states that mandate social studies tests spend significantly more time teaching social studies than teachers who work in non-tested states (Heafner, Libscomb, & Fitchett, 2014). However, testing alone is not an assurance that elementary school daily schedules afford time for social studies. Prioritization of sacred subjects prevails even in districts where (a) social studies was tested and (b) time was added to the instructional day. Despite professed optimal policy circumstances, social studies failed to gain the stronghold accountability promised (Heafner & Plaisance, 2016), suggesting that enacted local curriculum, time schedules, and administrative influence (Heafner & Fitchett, 2015b) emasculate national policy if not directly addressed.

A focus on time without consideration of who has access to social studies will underserve elementary school children. When school schedules couch social studies within the literacy block, social studies is rarely taught and students are more likely to be pulled for remediation and language support (Heafner & Plaisance, 2016). Inequitable learning opportunities correlate with achievement gaps. While glaring differences manifest in cumulate exposure to social studies (Heafner & Fitchett, 2015a), elementary-level learning reveals stark contrasts in foundational content knowledge.

Although a predictor of elementary content knowledge and discipline-specific skills, when accounting for building level context, social studies time is no longer significant (Fitchett & Heafner, 2017). Time may be conflated by school type, and discrepancies in scheduled time allocations across schools suggest a hidden curriculum of elementary social studies, in which affluent schools prioritize the subject in ways that schools serving high poverty, minority communities do not (Pace, 2011; Wade, 2007). Since the degree of learning is greatly dependent upon the amount of time students are actively engaged in domain-specific learning and authentic intellectual work, if students are not afforded the same opportunity to learn social studies in both time and curriculum access, social studies becomes a subject segregated by communities (Salinas, 2006). Policies that ensure instructional time should include demands for equal access to social studies for all students, no matter where they attend school, and establish the discipline as a scheduled priority in elementary curricula. Educators' role as determinates of school schedules, time allocations, and advocates for curricular access should not be overlooked: Teachers and administrators share responsibility in enacting a well-rounded education.

Standards Shift Policy

While not specifically a byproduct of accountability pressures, the marginal role of social studies can be traced to national education policy pushes for curriculum standardization (Heafner & Fitchett, 2012). Privileging literacy, mathematics, and, later, science as key subject areas, No Child Left Behind (NCLB) remained silent on other content, undermining the position of social studies particularly in elementary schools when emergent literacies and foundational math skills are taught (Fitchett & Heafner, & Lambert, 2014a). The sacred subjects were not only protected by policy but also in the enactment of policy (e.g., states and LEAs set requirements for time allocated to ELA and math in elementary schools). NCLB implementation led to administrative positioning of subject hierarchy, as well as the lack of support for social studies and related standards (Fitchett, Heafner, & Lambert, 2014b).

State and local-level enactment of NCLB revealed curriculum constriction and limited opportunities to learn ancillary subjects, particularly for high poverty and minority students, which led to the Whole Child movement and subsequent policy changes. The Every Student Succeeds Act (ESSA) (2015) shifts educational control to states and districts while also emphasizing the development of the "whole student." Provisions within the law allow for the inclusion of civics, and the social studies more broadly, with portions of federal funding to states allocated for history, civics, economics, geography, and government (Title IV, Part A, Sub-part 1, Section 4107, Well Rounded Education Opportunities). The ESSA creates grant programs for American history, civics, and government while also offering potential funding for providing quality social studies instruction for underserved students (Title II, Part B, Subpart 3, American History and Civic Education, Section 2232–2233).

Under the new law, states have the authority to determine how they will ensure all students are offered a "well-rounded education," and these plans may include the social studies; however, social studies appears within a long list of content areas that will ultimately compete for curricular attention. As local education agencies (LEAs) draft plans for use of federal funding for well-rounded education, subject-area competition for limited funding allocations will ensue. The steps professional organizations (e.g., NCSS) and their members take to ask questions and do research will be crucial for safeguarding policy provisions for social studies realized at the state and local levels. Although the winds of policy have shifted from silencing social studies to recognizing social studies and civic life preparation as central to a comprehensive elementary school curriculum and all students' learning, efforts are necessary to not only know who is writing state and local plans, but also to determine who will represent social studies in these policy conversations. The outcomes of advocacy under ESSA are undetermined; however, they hold promise in repositioning social studies.

Policies Privilege, Advocacy Prioritizes

Despite heightened emphases on literacy as a hallmark of prior national policies, Common Core State Standards (CCSS) and its intersection with the College,

Career, and Civic Life (C3) Framework renews and formalizes social studies' shared role in literacy instruction and in civic understanding, particularly during informative and emergent education in the elementary grades. By focusing on the organic and indispensable links between language use and disciplinary knowledge, disciplinary literacy offers social studies teachers an authentic approach to elementary instruction that is more than another layer atop content (Shanahan & Shanahan, 2008). With standards' emphasis of domain specific knowledge, literacy is not a skill but rather a condition teachers create for students to learn content.

Meaningful and sustained engagement with subject matter rooted in discipline-specific information, texts, and literacy are fundamental to successful reading comprehension (Hirsch, 2006). Couched within core knowledge, the dynamic use of literacy to construct personal, figured, and public worlds for citizenship further underscores the intimate connection between literacy and the social studies. The uncertainty and messiness of social studies open dialogue to thinking about texts from social positions and in culturally diverse ways (Epstein & Oyler, 2008; Wade, 2007). This reveals the dual social nature of content literacy, both the way that language is created, used, and understood within specific social contexts and the way that meaning is socially constructed and transmitted largely through academic language. Instead of teaching reading through social studies (e.g., the primacy of integration), the new CCSS and C3 standards' message conveys the need to teach content.

Yet, the real power of standards as a policy tool occurs when states, LEAs, administrators, and teachers enact standards. Numerous states, including New York, Connecticut, Illinois, Nebraska, and South Dakota, who adopted Common Core have also modeled or rewritten their social studies curricula and state standards around the C3 Framework. In the case of Illinois, the state legislature passed House Bill 4025, which required the addition of a civics or government course as a K–12 graduation requirement and created a Civic Education Task Force to revise state social studies standards. Leveraging the C3 Framework to create elementary standards by grade, the task force reinvigorated the social studies, a largely displaced subject area, as the discipline with intense focus on literary skills and citizenship in order to meet the CCSS in English and Language Arts (Healy, 2016). Replicating the model of online teacher practice professional learning networks of the NCSS C3 Literacy Collaborative (C3LC), educators shepherded inquiry-focused civic literacy training throughout Illinois. As proponents of social studies–friendly legislation, guides in the manifestation of standards, and developers of ensuing education for social studies professionals, teachers in Illinois are repositioning social studies in the K–12 curriculum.

Grassroots professional development positions social studies teachers as leaders in standards interpretation (Heafner, Handler, & Journell, 2016). Connecticut leaders engaged teachers in inquiry design while also influencing local curricula enactment though inquiry toolkits targeted for social studies classroom use and professional learning communities. Similarly, in Minnesota, a district-level initiative emphasizing social studies as inquiry and social studies educators as experts in disciplinary literacy has drawn attention from ELA colleagues and administrators across the state. A team of California elementary school teachers engaged in inquiry to create learning episodes integrating geography, literacy, and service learning. Their collaborative model has been replicated with other elementary teams across the district and serves as a national exemplar of teacher-initiated professional learning. Collectively, these grassroots efforts are "bringing social studies back to the center" through literacy-focused standards and affirming unique disciplinary contributions by establishing the "importance of critical literacy in the civic mission of the social studies" (Nelson, 2016, p. 386–387). Teachers leading teachers has far-reaching implications for the social studies. Educators are policy and standards brokers; they play a critical role in determining the role social studies has within the enacted curriculum.

Teacher Agency and Autonomy

As shared stakeholders in the education of children, teachers exercise agency in their gatekeeping of standards and associated curriculum (Thornton, 2005). Policies promoting teacher agency have the capacity to impact social studies particularly in the elementary grades, given there is an established association between national policies and teacher autonomy. Even during the curricular and accountability constraints under NCLB, teacher autonomy was significantly associated with instructional decision-making: autonomous teachers engaged in actions promoting social studies (Fitchett, Heafner, & Lambert, 2014b). However, as standardization and accountability pressures increased, elementary teachers' instructional autonomy decreased, resulting in curricular and time constriction for social studies. As national policies shift educational control to local agencies under ESSA, elementary teachers' increased sense of agency and standards articulation can work in tandem to reprioritize social studies.

Promoting a disposition of greater instructional autonomy within schools can improve the curricular primacy of social studies in elementary classrooms, given that the power of teachers' curricular decision-making (to teach and not to teach social studies) within schools is a product of their perceptions of control (Wills & Sandholtz, 2009). Moreover, educators with a greater sense of agency are more likely to foster students' opportunities to learn social studies and engage learners in dynamic instructional practices (Fitchett & Heafner, 2017). Harnessing opportunities afforded by national policies while also directing attention to increasing teacher autonomy in schools can scale up the impact of teachers as policy brokers.

Conclusion

Although national policy and standards create policy cultures in which social studies is viewed more favorably and positioned as having a seat at the curriculum table, policy alone will not lead to the reprioritization of social studies. Operating within policies to leverage the influence of teachers and administrators to enact policy is equally important. Empowering educators and policymakers with the foundational value of social studies establishes advocates who can work within policy cultures to position social studies as literacy-essential, core knowledge in the elementary grades. Raising awareness of enacted curriculum opportunity gaps and school structure barriers (e.g., time and resources) can create a common credo and social philosophy that all children must acquire fundamental social studies knowledge and skills in the elementary years if they are to become well-rounded, active, and responsible democratic citizens in a globally dynamic, complex, and controversial society. Dichotomous stances on policy (e.g., anti-testing) polarize social studies proponents, undermining the possibilities for social studies that policy and action generate. For policy and action to have their intended results, funded mandates must address the need for additional support and appropriation of resources for development of teachers and teacher agency in the early grades. Working collectively for policies that ensure the teaching of social studies in the elementary grades, accompanied by grassroots activism, stands to make meaningful gains in repositioning social studies.

References

Brophy, J., & Alleman, J. (2008). Early elementary social studies. In L. Levstik & C. Tyson (Eds.), *Handbook of research in social studies education* (pp. 33–49). New York: Routledge.

Epstein, S. E., & Oyler, C. (2008). "An inescapable network of mutuality": Building relationships of solidarity in a first grade classroom. *Equity & Excellence in Education, 41*(4), 405–416.

Every Student Succeeds Act (ESSA). (2015). Washington, DC: U.S. Department of Education. Retrieved from www.ed.gov/ESSA.

Fitchett, P. G., & Heafner, T. L. (2017). Student demographics and teacher characteristics as predictors of elementary-age students' history knowledge: Implications for teacher education and practice. *Teaching and Teacher Education, 67*, 79–92. doi:http://dx.doi.org/10.1016/j.tate.2017.05.012

Fitchett, P. G., Heafner, T. L., & Lambert, R. (2014a). Examining social studies marginalization: A multilevel analysis. *Educational Policy, 28*(1), 40–68.

Fitchett, P. G., Heafner, T. L., & Lambert, R. (2014b). Assessment, autonomy, and elementary social studies time. *Teachers College Record, 116*(10), 1–34.

Fitchett, P. G., Heafner, T. L., & VanFossen, P. J. (2014). An analysis of time prioritization for social studies in elementary school classrooms. *Journal of Curriculum and Instruction, 8*(2), 7–35.

Heafner, T., & Fitchett, P. (2012). National trends in elementary instruction: Exploring the role of social studies curricular. *The Social Studies, 103*(2), 67–72.

Heafner, T. L., & Fitchett, P. G. (2015a). An opportunity to learn US History: What NAEP data suggest regarding the opportunity gap. *The High School Journal, 98*(3), 226–249.

Heafner, T. L., & Fitchett, P. G. (2015b). Principals' and teachers' reports of instructional time allocations in third grade. *Journal of International Social Studies, 5*(1), 64–80.

Heafner, T. L., Handler, L. K., & Journell, W. (2016). Do this, not that: Designing effective professional development. *Social Education, 80*(6), 381–384.

Heafner, T. L., Lipscomb, G. B., & Fitchett, P. G. (2014). Instructional practices of elementary social studies teachers in North and South Carolina. *The Journal of Social Studies Research, 38*(1), 15–31.

Heafner, T. L., & Plaisance, M. P. (2016). Exploring how institutional structures and practices influence English learners' opportunity to learn social studies. *Teachers College Record, 118*(8), 1–36.

Healy, S. P. (2016). Teachers at the center: Recent efforts to strengthen the civic mission of schools in Illinois. *Social Education, 80*(6), 375–377.

Hirsch, E. D, Jr. (2006). Building knowledge: The case for bringing content into the language arts block and for a knowledge-rich curriculum core for all children. *American Educator, 30*(1), 8.

King, M. B., Newmann, F., & Carmichael, D. (2009). Authentic intellectual work: Common standards for teaching social studies. *Social Education, 73*(1), 43–49.

Nelson, C. A. (2016). Designing your own C3 inquiry: Lessons from the C3LC project. *Social Education, 80*(6), 385–387.

Nuthall, G., & Alton-Lee, A. (1993). Predicting learning from student experience of teaching: A theory of student knowledge construction in classrooms. *American Educational Research, 30*(4), 799–840.

Pace, J. (2011). The complex and unequal impact of high stakes accountability on untested social studies. *Theory and Research in Social Education, 39*(1), 32–60.

Salinas, C. (2006). Educating late arrival high school immigrant students: A call for a more democratic curriculum. *Multicultural Perspectives, 8*(1), 20–27.

Shanahan, T., & Shanahan, C. (2008). Teaching disciplinary literacy to adolescents: Rethinking content area literacy. *Harvard Educational Review, 78*(1), 40–59.

Thornton, S. (2005). *Teaching social studies that matters*. New York: Teachers College Press.

Wade, R. C. (2007). *Social studies for social justice: Teaching strategies for the elementary classroom*. New York: Teachers College Press.

Wills, J. S., & Sandholtz, J. H. (2009). Constrained professionalism: Dilemmas of teaching in the face of test-based accountability. *Teachers College Record, 111*(4), 1065–1114.

Promoting Elementary Social Studies Through Policy: Possibilities Within Multiple Contexts of Schooling

Commentary by Judith L. Pace,
University of San Francisco

Social studies has never been a prioritized subject at the elementary level (Stodolsky, 1988). However, the high stakes accountability regime of No Child Left Behind, intended to raise achievement in reading and math, further marginalized social studies, as well as other subjects (Au, 2007), in elementary schools across the nation (Fitchett & Heafner, 2010). The inclusion of science testing under the Every Student Succeeds Act (ESSA) of 2015 and support for STEM education firmly establishes science as the third most important core subject. Though the Common Core State Standards for Literacy in History-Social Science ostensibly promote teaching with informational texts in history and other subjects, the standards send a message that social studies be taught in the service of English-language arts (ELA). More than ever, teachers confront an intensification of curricular-instructional demands that include the traditional subjects as well as differentiation for English-language learners and students with special needs; technology; arts integration; and social-emotional learning.

What policy levers do we have for increasing the visibility and prioritization of social studies education in elementary schools? Consultation with several experts in my own state of California—an interesting case for consideration—helped me identify initiatives that might move this agenda forward. Before presenting these initiatives, I briefly turn to research that should inform policy decisions.

Research on Social Studies Teaching and High Stakes Accountability

There is some convergence of implications from quantitative and qualitative research on social studies under high stakes accountability. Fitchett, Heafner, and Lambert (2014a, 2014b) conducted statistical analysis of teacher self-report survey data that yielded three main findings. First, state testing of social studies was positively associated with more instructional time for the subject. Second, in states that did not test for social studies, teacher autonomy, defined as authority over curricular decisions, was positively associated with instructional time. Third, more time was devoted to social studies in the intermediate grades than in the primary grades. In line with these findings, they suggest that elementary social studies be part of a state assessment system, school leaders cultivate a climate of professional autonomy for teachers, and social studies curriculum for the primary grades be reformulated.

The maxim "What gets tested gets taught" has posed a dilemma for advocates who support social studies but oppose standardized testing. While some researchers found that in states that test, teachers allocate more time for social studies, others found that the impact of testing on social studies teaching is uncertain (Grant, 2001, 2006). The quality of curriculum and instruction may suffer when teachers feel pressured to teach to the test (Au, 2009). Importantly, this depends on the nature of state testing and the ways in which individuals teach to requirements of different tests. Another important finding is that state testing of social studies is associated with lower perceptions of autonomy among teachers (Fitchett, Heafner, & Lambert, 2014a). Thus, two variables associated with increased time for social studies conflict.

The importance of autonomy for social studies teaching is related to teachers' role as curricular-instructional decision-makers, or gatekeepers (Thornton, 1991). Gatekeeping is influenced by teachers' professional agency as well as multiple sources that exert varying degrees of authority (Grant, 1996). Along with teachers' skills, interests, and knowledge, these sources include colleagues and administrators, students, and organizational structures that interact with state and district curriculum policy as manifested in textbooks, standards, and tests.

It is important to identify the influences on gatekeeping that advances social studies learning opportunities. The small-scale qualitative research I conducted found that along with teacher autonomy, professional development, teacher collaboration, and curricular-instructional resources were major supports for social studies teaching (Pace, 2008, 2011, 2012). In fact, teachers enthusiastic about social studies said that "flying under the radar" of high stakes testing helped them teach what and how they wanted. However, the pressure to focus on literacy in social studies detracted from quality teaching and suggested it is crucial to promote those social studies aims that are distinct from those of literacy, as well as those that are linked.

What Opportunities Are Offered by Current Policy Changes?

Federal Policy

To put forward ideas about state, district, and school policy tools, it is necessary to understand how they fit within the larger context of policy changes at the federal level. With the reauthorization of the Elementary and Secondary Education Act, for the first time in fifteen years, authority shifts back from the federal government to state governments for the development of accountability systems. At the same time, testing in three subjects is still mandatory. Student performance in ELA and math is assessed annually in grades 3–8 and once during grades 10–12. Student performance in science is assessed once at each level of schooling (elementary, middle, and high school). Social studies is still left out.

In a 2016 webinar titled "Social Studies in the ESSA: Where do we go from here?" Caltronia Macdonald explained opportunities for strengthening social studies education within the new policy landscape. The ESSA gives states the authority to create their own accountability systems that describe how they will qualify for and use federal funds. States give 95% of these funds to local education agencies (LEAs), or school districts, and describe in their plans how they will support LEAs in reaching goals.

In their accountability systems, states must lay out how all students have access to a "well-rounded education." The notion of a well-rounded education is broadly conceived and may include STEM, music and art, foreign language, social studies (including American history, civics, economics, geography, and government), financial education, and other subjects. At minimum, 20% of federal funding must be used by the state to support this overarching aim.

Federal funding also contributes to well-rounded education through competitive Student Support and Academic Enrichment Grants (SSAEGs). These grants fund Presidential Academies for American History and Civics, which are institutes for teachers, and Congressional Academies for American History and Civics for high school students. Other grants support innovative programs and professional development in American history, civics and government, and geography to address the needs of underserved students, as well as innovation and research in social studies and other subjects.

State Policy

To consider the role of policy in strengthening the status of social studies, I discuss my own state of California, which offers examples of policy initiatives that can shed light on other states. In California, the shift to local control preceded the ESSA. The Local Control Funding Formula (LCFF), promoted by Governor Jerry Brown, was passed by the state legislature in 2013 (Fensterwald, 2016). Designed to allocate more funds to districts with higher needs and broaden accountability measures, it granted authority to LEAs—or school districts—to develop their own Local Control and Accountability Plans (LCAPs). In September 2016, the State Board of Education approved a new school accountability system with eight priorities (California Department of Education, n.d.). These include implementation of the academic content standards adopted by the State Board of Education, pupil achievement, pupil engagement, access to a broad course of study, school climate, and pupil outcomes. Advocates have tried to persuade state officials in the State Board and Legislature to mandate the inclusion of history-social science measurable learning outcomes in LCAPs (Jim Hill, personal communications, December 14 & 16, 2016), but have not been successful thus far.

A significant development in California this year was the approval in July 2016 of the new History-Social Science Framework, after a long, participatory, and contentious process. In a 2016 blog on the California History-Social Science Project's (CHSSP) website, Executive Director Nancy McTygue explained that the new framework responds to the Fair Act (Senate Bill 48) that mandated inclusion of people with disabilities and lesbian, gay, bisexual, and transgender people, as well as new research, historiography, and events, such as the election of President Obama. Also, the revision promotes an inquiry-based approach throughout the K–12 spectrum. According to McTygue, "The new Framework emphasizes the development of student content knowledge, discipline-specific inquiry, student literacy, and citizenship." It aligns with the Common Core State Standards, Standards for English Language Development, and the College, Career, and Civic Life (C3) Framework for Social Studies Standards. It also makes connections with the California Education and Environment Initiative.

The release of the new state framework hopefully calls attention to history-social science. Eight rollout conferences were scheduled at different locations. The new framework offers guidance on interweaving history, civics, economics, and geography in grades K–12 and provides themes for organizing content to help teach for depth over breadth. It also prompts the adoption of new textbooks. Teachers seem very positive about the new framework, but new content and approaches make demands that must be supported by professional development and new curricular-instructional materials (McTygue, personal communication, December 8, 2016).

Another initiative in California was the establishment of the California Task Force on K–12 Civic Learning (www.powerofdemocracy.org/). The Power of Democracy (POD) Steering Committee was formed in 2014 to oversee implementation of the task force's recommendations throughout the state. POD sponsors an annual Civic Learning Award competition open to elementary, middle, and high schools that has energized schools. The Bechtel Corporation funded the development of civic education action plans in six county offices that included materials and stipends for teachers involved in professional development. Districts have written resolutions to include civics instruction beyond the required 12th grade half-year course in government.

Amid these developments, the possibility of new state testing in social studies was a controversial question. California used to test history-social science in grades 8 and 11, but this ended in 2013. State Superintendent of Public Instruction Tom Torlakson proposed in March 2016 that new standardized tests be developed in history-social science and administered in grades 4 and 7 and once in high school (Freedberg, March 9, 2016). But his proposal met with resistance, as

California has reduced standardized testing. For example, the 15-year-old regime of STAR testing—which consisted of mostly multiple choice items—was ended in 2014. It was replaced by the California Assessment of Student Performance and Progress, comprised mainly of Smarter Balance tests that include a variety of item types but only address English-language arts and mathematics. Opponents of testing history-social science argued that it would be regressive to add new tests and too expensive for the state to afford, and Torlakson's proposal was rejected. In sum, California state policy points to the role of new subject-matter documents, professional development, special task forces and organizational collaborations, incentives, and affordance of district decision-making in promoting social studies.

District Policy

Given the shift to local control, school districts have a crucial role to play in deciding on and designing assessments not mandated by the ESSA that could be part of their accountability system. Fred Jones, legislative analyst for the California Council for the Social Studies (CCSS), voiced a widespread view (Jones, personal communication, December 8, 2016): There are three drivers that incentivize what will be taught: (1) what the government requires, (2) what the government measures, and (3) what the government funds. Based on this theory, he and Jim Hill, emeritus chair of the CCSS Governmental Relations Committee, advocate that social studies must be part of the new accountability system. They have worked to integrate measurable student performances in social studies as part of district LCAPs. The California Council for the Social Studies' (CCSS) journal, *The Social Studies Review*, devoted its entire 2015–2016 issue to this cause. The goal is to get districts to report student learning outcomes under LCAP metrics (Hill, personal communication, December 8, 2016). For example, student responses to document-based questions, history projects, civic action projects, or other performances would be assessed, using a rubric, by teams of assessors who have calibrated their scoring for purposes of reliability. Progress on particular skills would be measured. Performances could target standards not just in history-social science but also in English-language arts and even science.

The 2015–16 issue of *The Social Studies Review* explains what districts need to do to include history-social science in their LCAPs (Hill, 2015). It provides examples of social studies units and student performances linked to various sets of standards, frameworks, rubrics, and state accountability plan priorities. It ends with an annotated list of organizations that support social studies teaching. The issue is enormously valuable to schools and districts where educators are motivated to develop assessment systems in social studies that can count towards accountability to the state. A major obstacle is that most administrators are not motivated. Districts still face so many accountability and other demands that it is unlikely to happen. District administrators, under pressure to raise test scores on the demanding Smarter Balance tests in English-language arts and mathematics, are invested in keeping their LCAPs simple and focusing their efforts on what is mandated by the state.

To advance elementary-level social studies, districts can take other policy actions. They can adopt new textbooks that support teaching to the new History-Social Science Framework (this has not occurred since 2005, and many schools use textbooks dating from the late 1990s (McTygue, personal communication, December 8, 2016). Even as curricular integration in teaching is supported, they can distinguish history-social science as a focus distinct from English-language arts, instead of combining the two under humanities. They can dedicate full-time coordinator positions for both secondary and elementary history-social science. Districts can assist coordinators in applying for federally and state-funded grants and organizing high-quality professional development opportunities for teachers. They can write and implement resolutions to support civics education. Thus, districts can promote social studies in a variety of ways, such as including it in accountability plans, supporting teachers, and investing in resources.

School Policy

School administrators and teachers play a crucial role. They can educate themselves about the recent developments outlined here and advocate for social studies at meetings for designing local accountability plans. If the subject is part of a district's plan, school personnel can give input and implement these activities in ways that engage students with diverse sociocultural identities, academic abilities, and interests. Principals can allocate funds for new materials and professional development to support teachers implementing the new History-Social Science Framework in ways that preserve their autonomy while enlarging their expertise. Teachers and administrators can identify action civics, service learning, and other projects that relate to social studies as part of history-social science. The daily/weekly classroom schedule determines to a large extent how much social studies is taught. Principals in collaboration with teaching staff can decide that social studies be taught multiple times during the week, which would be a step forward for many schools.

Lisa Hutton, professor and director of the California History Project at Dominguez Hills, hears teachers say they now have more time for social studies (Hutton, personal communication, December 9, 2016). They realize that history-social science teaches thinking and literacy skills demanded by both the Common Core and Smarter Balance tests. But they may feel unprepared because they haven't taught social studies in a long time and lack the disciplinary knowledge and experience with the inquiry-based approach promoted by the new framework. She sees teacher development of interdisciplinary units in which literacy dominates and several other subjects are pushed in, creating an incoherent and fragmented approach to teaching history. The problem points to the need for professional development for teachers and the importance of collaboration with university faculty.

In addition to professional development, schools can address the need for subject-matter expertise by departmentalizing. There are schools in which teachers specialize in ELA and social studies or math and science, so that teachers can develop knowledge and curriculum in fewer areas. Specialization and increased subject-matter confidence among teachers can lead to more time in the classroom schedule devoted to social studies. Policy tools at the school level are crucial. Classroom scheduling, teacher development, curricular resources and design, collaboration, and teacher autonomy are at the core of strengthening social studies.

Concluding Thoughts

As I conclude, the presidential election weighs on our national conscience. The "charged classroom"—full of challenging tensions and possibilities for democratic education (Pace, 2015)—takes on new meaning in this tumultuous political climate. There is a felt urgency in educating democratic citizens who support political decision-making based on facts rather than fictions, stewardship of the natural environment, and human and civil rights. Whether policymakers at school, district, and state levels—still pressured to raise test scores—are willing to commit to these aims is a key question. In the meantime, creative advocacy, networks, and collaborations among professional organizations, social studies experts, and educators at all levels may influence classroom teaching more than policy tools ever can.

Acknowledgements

Thank you to Jim Hill, Lisa Hutton, Fred Jones, Janet Mann, and Nancy McTygue for their extremely helpful contributions.

References

Au, W. (2007). High stakes testing and curricular control: A qualitative metasynthesis. *Educational Researcher, 36*(5), 258–267.

Au, W. (2009). Social studies, social justice: W(h)ither the social studies in high stakes testing? *Teacher Education Quarterly, 36*(1), 43–58.

California Department of Education. (n.d.). *State priority-related resources.* Retrieved from www.cde.ca.gov/fg/aa/lc/statepriorityresources.asp

Fensterwald, J. (2016, August 11). *The basics of state's new school improvement system.* Retrieved from https://edsource.org/2016/the-basics-behind-states-new-school-improvement-system-essa-lcff/568018

Fitchett, P., & Heafner, T. L. (2010). A national perspective on the effects of high-stakes testing and standardization on elementary social studies marginalization. *Theory and Research in Social Education, 38*(1), 114–130.

Fitchett, P. G., Heafner, T. L., & Lambert, R. G. (2014a). Assessment, autonomy, and elementary social studies time. *Teachers College Record, 116*, 100306.

Fitchett, P. G., Heafner, T. L., & Lambert, R. G. (2014b). Examining elementary social studies marginalization: A multilevel model. *Educational Policy, 28*(1), 40–68.

Freedberg, L. (2016, March 9). *Proposed history-social science tests raise concern about testing burden*. Retrieved from https://edsource.org/2016/proposed-history-social-science-tests-raise-concerns-about-testing-burden/561606

Grant, S. G. (1996). Locating authority over content and pedagogy: Cross-current influences on teachers' thinking and practice. *Theory and Research in Social Education, 24*(3), 237–272.

Grant, S. G. (2001). An uncertain lever: The influence of state-level testing in New York state on teaching social studies. *Teachers College Record, 103*(3), 398–426.

Grant, S. G. (Ed.). (2006). *Measuring history: Cases of state-level testing across the United States* (pp. 249–272). Greenwich, CT: Information Age Publishing.

Hill, J. (2015). Rationale for districts and teachers to use social studies performance for local control accountability plans. *Social Studies Review, 54*, 4–5.

McTygue, N. (2016, July 14). *What you need to know about California's history-social science framework*. Retrieved from http://chssp.ucdavis.edu/blog/what-you-need-to-know-about-california2019s-new-history-social-science-framework

Pace, J. L. (2008). Inequalities in history-social science teaching under high stakes accountability: Interviews with fifth-grade teachers in California. *Social Studies Research and Practice, 3*(1), 24–40.

Pace, J. L. (2011). The complex and unequal impact of accountability on untested social studies across diverse school contexts. *Theory and Research in Social Education, 39*(1), 32–60.

Pace, J. L. (2012). Teaching literacy through social studies under No Child Left Behind. *Journal of Social Studies Research, 36*(4), 329–358.

Pace, J. L. (2015). *The charged classroom: Predicaments and possibilities for democratic teaching*. New York: Routledge.

Stodolsky, S. (1988). *The subject matters: Classroom activity in math and social studies*. Chicago, IL: University of Chicago Press.

Thornton, S. J. (1991). Teacher as curricular-instructional gatekeeper in social studies. In J. P. Shaver (Ed.), *Handbook of research on social studies teaching and learning* (pp. 237–248). New York: Macmillan.

Heafner's Response to Pace's Commentary

Judith Pace and I share similar perceptions of policy tools and activities that have the potential to reprioritize elementary social studies. Fundamentally, national policy establishes the tenor toward content areas, such as the effects noted by Common Core State Standards' elevation of history and the social sciences through increased attention to informational knowledge and disciplinary literacies, as well as the College, Career, and Civic Life (C3) Framework's attention to inquiry and informed action. We acknowledge the possibilities created by the inclusion of social studies in ESSA's well-rounded education and associated funding. These national policies differ from prior legislation by allowing greater flexibility and interpretation, which empower state and local agencies to attend to the unique needs of their constituents. Albeit more positive than NCLB, shifting control of enacted policies to local governments positions social studies at the whim of state policy climates.

While the tone may be set by national policy, we both contend that state and local governments are the real power brokers of educational policy. State and local agencies exercise direct control over social studies regulations, content, resources, and access. For example, state governments have a key role in professional requirements and licenses. Neither of us attempts to address this issue, but it is an important consideration given empirical evidence suggesting that preparation credentials, particularly content and content pedagogical training, are associated with student learning outcomes (Fitchett, Heafner, & Lambert, 2017). Attention to elementary teacher preparation requirements, such as the expectation of content preparation and discipline-specific pedagogy, can improve the overall teaching of social studies and how social studies is perceived as a field. Although revised NCSS National Standards for the Preparation of Social Studies Teachers (Cuenca et al., 2017) provide rigorous expectations that will require rethinking of teacher education, attention to how state agencies interpret and sanction these recommendations will be crucial.

State and local governments determine social studies curriculum; nonetheless, coalitions of educators and citizen groups ensure equity and quality of enacted curriculum. New York, Florida, and Illinois passed legislation to revise standards to require instruction in citizenship and civic education spanning all grade bands (Barrett & Greene, 2017; Kawashima-Ginberg, 2016); however, policy coalitions underscored social studies content as essential reading for ELA and advocated provisions for discussing current and controversial issues, engaging learners in service learning, and utilizing digital tools (e.g., iCivics or Civics in a Snap) to augment democratic process awareness. In each state, collaboration among nonprofit organizations, university researchers, curriculum specialists, and teachers ensured laws were realized with fidelity and excellence. As an example, the McCormick Foundation joined by social studies teachers are strategically leading professional development efforts to provide teachers across the state of Illinois with in-person regional training around the new civics requirement and revised social studies standards (see www.illinoiscivics.org/resources/calendar).

Judith's example of California offers yet another example of the importance of collaboration among governments and stakeholders. The new History-Social Science Framework garnered the attention of the California Council for the Social Studies and was a central focus of the 2017 Annual Conference in Sacramento, CA. The new framework received much attention, as it compels student-initiated inquiry and action in the core content domains of history, geography, civics, and economics, as well as disciplinary literacies that support students' independent reading of complex, informational texts. Districts, such as Glendora, CA, have embraced a model of teacher-led professional development and online learning modules to enact grassroots curricular change (Valbuena & Roy, 2016).

Local governments have a responsibility to ensure access to standards, curricular materials, and professional learning that model nationally recommended practices. Districts can leverage online professional development and teacher mentor models to establish a network of mentors and trainers to support continuing education for all educators. Embracing a grassroots infrastructure for change can address inequities of curricular access for high poverty, minority, and immigrant students while also cultivating teacher agency (Kawashima-Ginberg, 2016). In addition, local governments can adopt newer materials that reflect national policy shifts (e.g., social studies textbooks that emphasize inquiry and align with the C3 Framework) and specialized approaches to content, such as tailored text sets for state-focused curriculum to advance elementary social studies. A bottom-up collaboration rather than a top-down approach is recommended. Collaborating among teachers, community stakeholders, university scholars, and social studies organizations can ensure the relevance of these materials. This shared decision-making approach would be a stark improvement from disconnected top-down decisions, such as purchasing globes for every 2nd-grade classroom and requiring literacy integration without consideration of unrelated ELA content (Heafner & Plaisance, 2016).

Intimate control over day-to-day learning furthers the significance of administrators and teachers. Judith and I agree that administrators and teachers have a critical role in defining how much or how little social studies is taught and the structures for content delivery, e.g., departmentalization of content. We also acknowledge that shared decision-making opportunities empower educators and are essential for promoting teacher agency. Moreover, collaboration between administrators and teachers to set daily time schedules that include standalone time for social studies can go a long way in changing curricular access to social studies in elementary schools. Suggesting that these schedules are outside the purview of teachers implies an unwillingness to accept the responsibility teachers have in ensuring all students have equitable access to social studies.

References

Barrett, K., & Greene, R. (2017). *Civic education: A key to trust in government.* Lexington, KY: The Council of State Governments.

Cuenca, A., Benton, B., Castro, A. J., Heafner, T., Hostetler, A., & Thacker, E. (2017). *National standards for social studies teachers.* Silver Spring, MD: National Council for the Social Studies.

Fitchett, P. G., & Heafner, T. L. (2017). Student demographics and teacher characteristics as predictors of elementary-age students' history knowledge: Implications for teacher education and practice. *Teaching and Teacher Education, 67,* 79–92. doi:http://dx.doi.org/10.1016/j.tate.2017.05.012

Heafner, T. L., & Plaisance, M. P. (2016). Exploring how institutional structures and practices influence English learners' opportunity to learn social studies. *Teachers College Record, 118*(8), 1–36.

Kawashima-Ginberg, K. (2016). *The future of civic education.* Alexandria, VA: National Association of State Boards of Education.

Valbuena, R., & Roy, A. (2016). What's collaboration go to do with it? Setting the table for teacher-led collaborative inquiry. *Social Education, 80*(6), 378–380.

Pace's Response to Heafner's Commentary

Tina Heafner has contributed so much to the field through groundbreaking research, advocacy, and work with teachers. There were several areas of overlap in our essays. The importance of expanding instructional time is paramount, yet teacher development to improve instructional quality also is crucial. We both expressed hope for possibilities offered by the Every Student Succeeds Act (ESSA), with greater state and local control and emphasis on well-rounded education. And we both cautioned that the ways in which the ESSA plays out are unpredictable, given many competing demands for attention and funding. Heafner was more supportive of state testing than I was, but did not strongly advocate for it and noted that local policy decisions can undermine state accountability. Both essays spoke to policy documents such as the Common Core State Standards and the C3 Framework as levers for increasing prioritization of social studies.

I appreciated Heafner's concern with connecting social studies with literacy and inquiry to gain traction in schools and deepen student learning. At the same time, I puzzled over the two first paragraphs under the heading "Policies Privilege, Advocacy Prioritizes." They beg for deliberation on the aims of elementary social studies, and specifically the purposes of citizenship education and content knowledge. Heafner argues that developing disciplinary literacy as highlighted in the Common Core State Standards and C3 Framework generates the need to teach content. She cites E.D. Hirsch to further argue that "engagement with subject matter" is needed for reading comprehension. Heafner continues, "Couched within core knowledge, the dynamic use of literacy to construct personal, figured, and public worlds for citizenship further underscores the intimate connection between literacy and the social studies."

Several questions come to mind as I read and reread these paragraphs. What kind of citizenship does Heafner have in mind (e.g., Westheimer & Kahne, 2004)?

What does she mean by "personal, figured, and public worlds"? And, given the claims about the connection between citizenship and literacy, what constitutes the "dynamic use of literacy"? Another question is whether disciplinary literacy should be an emphasis for elementary social studies, especially in the younger grades. I worry that this has become an unquestioned assumption for many educators, partly because of abundant support from scholars and professional developers. Thornton (2005) asks us to think broadly about aims that drive curriculum and teaching and to not let disciplinary purposes (or standards) override interdisciplinary and real-world concerns. Gardner (1991) reminds us to think about curriculum in terms of child development. In the younger grades, children should have opportunities to explore the world, through different modalities, domains, and intelligences. Later, the focus should be on developing disciplinary understandings. We need to deliberate on where to strike the balance at different grade levels as we interpret, question, and revise policy documents.

A third question centers on utilizing E.D. Hirsch's work on the importance of content knowledge in comprehension of texts. Although not as controversial as he used to be, let us remember that Hirsch developed the infamous construct of "cultural literacy," consisting of long lists that privilege mainstream, hegemonic knowledge, much of which was deemed insignificant. What does Heafner mean by core knowledge? I also worry about social studies being taught in the service of reading and writing, and teachers and students not understanding the multidimensional value of social studies on its own terms.

I was grateful that Heafner's essay addressed disparities in access to social studies. In prior research, I found less instructional time and/or lower quality social studies teaching in lower income schools serving a majority of students of color than in higher income schools serving a majority of White students (Pace, 2008, 2011, 2012). Heafner points out that even within schools, some students are pulled out of social studies for remedial and language support. Her admonition that policy address inequality of learning opportunities is crucial. I also appreciated the emphasis on "grassroots activities," such as curriculum development efforts in various locations. I hope to see empirical studies conducted by outsiders on the teacher teams doing this work.

I think both essays point to the seemingly intractable problem of prioritizing what Heafner refers to as "sacred subjects." I am encouraged that, as she points out, the importance of civics has gained recognition. However, I am discouraged that this past year a number of school districts across the country have either discouraged or prohibited teachers from discussing the 2016 presidential election with their students. The fear of controversy runs deep and works against social studies education that teaches students to explore significant public issues. In advancing elementary social studies, we need to question policies that have a tremendous impact on what is taught and learned.

In these turbulent times, the importance of history education must also be recognized. Our nation, and the world, struggle so much with legacies of the past. In Colum McCann's novel, *Transatlantic*, the epigraph, a quote from Eduardo Galeano, expresses a profound truth: "No history is mute. No matter how much they own it, break it, and lie about it, human history refuses to shut its mouth. Despite deafness and ignorance, the time that was continues to tick inside the time that is." Of course, similar claims could be made about geography, economics, and culture. My hope is that new policies advance an integrated approach to social studies through which elementary school students explore connections between past and present, make meaning of their own and others' lives, and open doorways to the world.

References

Gardner, H. (1991). *The unschooled mind: How children think and how schools should teach*. New York: Basic Books.

Pace, J. L. (2008). Inequalities in history-social science teaching under high stakes accountability: Interviews with fifth-grade teachers in California. *Social Studies Research and Practice, 3*(1), 24–40.

Pace, J. L. (2011). The complex and unequal impact of high stakes accountability on untested social studies. *Theory & Research in Social Education, 39*(1), 32–60.

Pace, J. L. (2012). Teaching literacy through social studies under No Child Left Behind. *Journal of Social Studies Research, 36*(4), 329–358.

Thornton, S. J. (2005). *Teaching social studies that matters: Curriculum for active learning*. New York: Teachers College Press.

Westheimer, J., & Kahne, J. (2004). What kind of citizen? The politics of educating for democracy. *American Educational Research Journal, 41*(2), 237–269.

Perspectives

Disciplinary Viewpoints on Social
Studies Education Policy

4

"CAN EDUCATION POLICIES BE EFFECTIVE TOOLS FOR ENCOURAGING YOUTH CIVIC ENGAGEMENT AND ACTIVISM IN SCHOOLS?"

The Possibilities of Policy Relative to the Purposes of Civic Education

Commentary by Peter Levine, Tufts University

It is useful to ask first whether current education policies influence youth civic engagement and activism—for good *or* ill. Federal policies regarding civic education are limited; the US government allocates no funding for civics, which has been overlooked in major federal reform efforts such as the No Child Left Behind Act and the US Department of Education's Race to the Top grant competition program. Federal policies that emphasize reading, math, and science may actually diminish attention to civics. However, this effect is not obvious from available data. For example, the mean number of course credits that high school students earn in social studies has climbed steadily since 1992 and now surpasses four per student, or one full course per year (Nord et al., 2011, p. 13).

What States Do Now

States currently choose from a menu of policy options to influence civic education within their borders. Every state has standards for the social studies that are meant to determine what is taught in each grade. The content varies, especially because these state documents tend to be long lists of concrete topics that teachers are supposed to cover—for example, in Texas, the influence of "Judeo-Christian (especially biblical law)" and Moses on the US Constitution (Smith, 2011); and in California, the "contributions of . . . lesbian, gay, bisexual, and transgender Americans" (Senate Bill 48, Chapter 81 of the Statutes of 2011). In general, neither students nor teachers face much accountability for meeting civic standards.

Most states require relevant courses with various names and descriptions, but the norm is at least one semester of US government or civics and a minimum of several high school credits in social studies as a whole. Fewer than ten states offer and require a standardized test in civics, and the stakes of these exams vary. States also require various degrees of demonstrated civics knowledge among social studies teachers (Godsay, Henderson, Levine, & Littenberg-Tobias, 2012).

I have been involved in two studies to investigate whether the variation in these state laws and policies is related to what and how students learn about civics and what they know and do as citizens. In both studies, young people who reported that they had personally experienced interactive civic education—moderated discussions of controversial issues, collaborative projects in the school or community, and/or shared experiences with civically active adults—were more interested in politics and civic life and participated at higher rates than those without similar educational opportunities. However, what the state required was not related to what they experienced in the classroom or what they knew, either for better or for worse. For example, the existence of a state civics test did not raise students' factual knowledge of civics, nor did it lower their likelihood of experiencing interactive civics as a result of "teaching to the test." The effect was null for almost all outcomes (Lopez, Levine, Dautrich, & Yalof, 2009; Kawashima-Ginsberg & Levine, 2014). Reanalyzing the data from our latter study, Campbell (2014) did find that state tests raised levels of knowledge for disadvantaged students, but this is the sole impact found so far.

Districts and schools also set policies that affect civics. To my knowledge, there have been no large studies comparing the impacts of variations in districts' policies on civic outcomes. Most evaluations in the field of civic education have focused on programs delivered by nonprofits rather than on strategies or policies adopted by districts, although McIntosh, Berman, and Youniss (2010) infer positive results from an ambitious approach in one small district that built its new high school with the goal of enhancing civic education. In that school—the only high school in the district—the whole student body was organized into representative clusters of between 100 and 150 students who met weekly for discussions of school issues and performed community service together.

Options for More Substantial Reforms

A second question is whether districts, states, and the federal government *could* change civic education by adopting different policies than the ones they have chosen so far. One explanation for the lack of impact of current policies is that they are quite modest. There may not be much difference between requiring or not requiring one semester of civics, especially if most students take related content anyway. For instance, my state, Massachusetts, does not require a course on civics or government but weaves a great deal of civics into its history and social studies standards. It may not be surprising that the difference between that approach and a required course is too subtle to show up in any survey of student outcomes. One could imagine that requiring several civics courses or imposing several high-stakes tests might change student outcomes—again, for better or worse.

My colleagues at CIRCLE (The Center for Information & Research on Civic Learning & Engagement) and I are pursuing a different hypothesis. We suspect that the impact of state policies depends heavily on how they are implemented. It may matter less whether a state requires a test than whether the test is well designed, whether teachers are supported to handle the material, how the test data is used, and what happens to students, teachers, or schools that perform badly.

With that in mind, we have been working closely with organizations and networks that are implementing recent reforms in Florida and Illinois. In Florida, a coalition composed of districts' social studies coordinators, academic specialists, and state representatives meets regularly to review current civics test score data and other evidence and to plan strategies. At the heart of the coalition is the Florida Joint Center for Citizenship, which has received state funding for on-site and online professional development, curriculum development, and research. In Illinois, an essential aspect of the reform is an ambitious professional development program for teachers, linked to a new state-required high school course. The professional development is supported by private philanthropy.

Although we do not yet have quantitative outcome data that I can report, our impression is that attention to implementation in Florida is gradually improving instruction. At first, when Florida imposed a new 7th-grade civics test, student outcomes could be predicted reliably by their socioeconomic status and performance on the state's English/language arts tests. But a considerable number of civics classes are now beating these predictions, and we think this is because instruction is improving. I would judge the test to be substantive and reasonably valid. Illinois's reforms are more recent and focus on a course rather than a test, but the implementation effort there is serious as well.

Thus, one might argue that states *can* improve civics by choosing the right combinations of mandates, assessments, and supports—but only if they invest in robust and lasting efforts to implement these policies equitably and well. Although a course or a test is insufficient as an isolated mechanism for change, it may be helpful if states follow through with the right combinations of mandates and supports.

What Is Civics For?

Of course, much depends on what you think civic education should accomplish. The intended outcomes of a reform like Florida's are very conventional: increased knowledge of laws and political systems, increased interest in voting and participating in civil society, and perhaps increased support for the existing political system. If you want students to *change* the existing political order, that is unlikely to become a state policy. Even though I have my own critical views of our political economy, I am not sure that I would advocate for states to depart from a mainstream view of politics and civic life in their standards and in the other ways they influence curricula. After all, public schools shape young children's hearts and minds. Parents face strong incentives and pressures to enroll their own kids in these powerful institutions. If a whole state decides that its schools will inculcate or encourage a controversial understanding of politics, not only would that court political conflict, but the implications thereof strike me as intrinsically dangerous.

The content of social studies does change as broad public opinion shifts (e.g., witness how Reconstruction is presented in today's history textbooks versus those of a generation ago). Also, there may be controversies about what is controversial. For instance, I think that schools must teach that climate change is largely caused by human consumption of carbon, and I think that view should not be controversial. Others disagree. In general, though, I would expect statewide policies to follow changes in majority opinion, not to cause such changes.

Community-based activists who take a critical stance toward current policies and institutions could consider endorsing a division of responsibilities. The schools teach a baseline of valuable knowledge about how our systems work; activists add a critical lens of their own choice and offer youth opportunities for social change.

To be sure, no view of politics and civic life is neutral, and a description of the regime that captures the support of a majority of a state's adult population can alienate disadvantaged youth and even oppose their political interests. For example, a favorable depiction of the state's government can estrange students who have experienced that very government as discriminatory. In a study of youth civic identities in four distinctly different public secondary schools in New Jersey, Beth Rubin finds that:

> Some students experienced disjunctures between ideals [taught in class] and realities of life and were negative in their attitudes toward the utility of civic participation. These students expressed a sense of discouragement about working to rectify inequalities they personally experienced and a sense of hopelessness about using established channels of civic participation to bring about change
>
> *(2007, p. 473)*

I consider this a serious problem and would urge states to address it, at least by encouraging all students to consider diverse perspectives on controversial issues. I doubt that any state's framework for understanding civic life can fully match the experience of its least advantaged young people, but it can aim for intellectual pluralism. That means that, by policy, state standards and widely used textbooks and materials should be reviewed with an eye to whether they reflect diverse opinions and experiences—including perspectives that may not be common in the state.

Perhaps more importantly, a state can strive to reduce the "disjuncture" between the ideals present in civics textbooks and the realities of students' lives by combating actual discrimination and injustice. For instance, being suspended has been found to lower the odds that a student will vote or volunteer in adulthood (Kupchik & Catlaw, 2014). That means that disciplinary policies that achieve reasonable order in schools *without* suspension—let alone arrest—are preferable from a civic perspective. Many students will be permanently alienated from government and civil society if they perceive education to be undermined by discrimination. Therefore, reforming school discipline policies, protecting free speech rights for students and teachers, and providing equitably excellent public education to all may be more important ways to improve civics education than strengthening civics classes.

References

Campbell, D. E. (2014). Putting civics to the test: The impact of state-level civics assessments on civic knowledge. *American Enterprise Institute for Public Policy Research*. Retrieved from http://files.eric.ed.gov/fulltext/ED558007.pdf

Godsay, S., Henderson, W., Levine, P., & Littenberg-Tobias, J. (2012). *State civic education requirements*. Medford, MA: Center for Information and Research on Civic Learning and Engagement. Retrieved from www.civicyouth.org/wp-content/uploads/2012/10/State-Civic-Ed-Requirements-Fact-Sheet-2012-Oct-19.pdf

Kawashima-Ginsberg, K., & Levine, P. (2014). Policy effects on informed political engagement. *American Behavioral Scientist, 58*(5), 665–688.

Kupchik, A., & Catlaw, T. J. (2014). Discipline and participation. *Youth & Society, 47*(1), 95–124.

Lopez, M. H., Levine, P., Dautrich, K., & Yalof, D. (2009). Schools, education policy, and the future of the First Amendment. *Political Communication, 26*(1), 84–101.

McIntosh, H., Berman, S., & Youniss, J. (2010). A five-year evaluation of a comprehensive high school civic engagement initiative. *CIRCLE Working Paper# 70*. Center for Information and Research on Civic Learning and Engagement (CIRCLE). Retrieved from http://civicyouth.org/PopUps/WorkingPapers/WP_70_McIntosh_Berman_Youniss.pdf

Nord, C., Roey, S., Perkins, R., Lyons, M., Lemanski, N., Brown, J., & Schuknecht, J. (2011). *The nation's report card: America's high school graduates (NCES 2011-462)*. U.S. Department of Education, National Center for Education Statistics. Washington, DC: U.S. Government Printing Office.

Rubin, B. C. (2007). "There's still not justice": Youth civic identity development amid distinct school and community contexts. *Teachers College Record, 109*(2), 449–481.

Smith, M. (2011, February 16). Texas social studies standards receive failing grade. *Texas Tribune*. Retrieved from www.texastribune.org/2011/02/16/texas-social-studies-receive-failing-grade/

Legislate Conditions, Not Curriculum and Pedagogy

Commentary by Beth Rubin, Rutgers University

Can education policies be effective tools for encouraging youth civic engagement and activism in schools? This question is constructed out of seemingly simple terms that, in their unpacking, give rise to a host of interpretations and further questions. What sorts of policies are we talking about? How do we know if something is an "effective tool"? What counts as "civic engagement and activism"? Does "in schools" mean that schools should be the sites of or the training grounds for this engagement and activism . . . or perhaps both? For the purpose of this essay, I am interpreting educational policy as legislated attempts to engineer particular forms of education in school settings. I hope to contribute to this discussion with descriptive examples to problematize the idea that learning can be directly shaped by policy initiatives, and by suggesting areas where I think policy might be helpful in ensuring that schools can provide educational practices that we know encourage youth civic engagement.

Learning to Teach for Civic Engagement

In March 2016, I led a professional development session for middle-level and secondary social studies teachers at a New Jersey school district. The topic was a familiar and favorite focus of mine—integrating discussion of controversial issues into the classroom. The district's social studies supervisors wanted to expose their teachers to a variety of methods for facilitating discussion on controversial topics in their classrooms.

We know that such discussions are of critical importance for civic learning and engagement. In a diverse democracy, the ability to listen and communicate across differences of all sorts is essential. Discussion of controversial issues is "arguably the centerpiece of democratic education because it engages students in the essential practice of democratic living" (Larson & Parker, 1996, p. 110). The Civic Mission of Schools report, written and endorsed by leading scholars and practitioners in the field, recommends that educators "incorporate discussion of current, local, national, and international issues and events in the classroom, particularly those that young people view as important" (2011, p. 6).

As I generally do in my work with teachers, I led the group through a series of activities, so that they would be able to immediately use those activities with their own students if they so chose. Each activity was followed by a debriefing session to engage the educators in thinking about why, when, and how they might integrate these new practices into their teaching. In these sessions, we discussed how it felt to participate in the activity, when the method might be used, what preparation students needed to participate effectively, and what types of instruction could profitably follow and build on discussion activities.

I moved the teachers into the three different discussion activities that I had selected to share with them. We started with a "deliberation" on Hammurabi's code: was the code cruel or a step forward? Teachers worked in pairs to read a short passage, recorded evidence for different sides of the question, partnered with an opposing pair, and proceeded through a series of steps designed to build active listening skills. We moved on to an "A/B" writing activity, in which I presented them with two strong and opposing statements on a topic, they wrote in response, and then I facilitated a discussion. The final demonstration activity was a "take-a-stand" discussion in which participants moved to different parts of the room based on their stances on a controversial statement, spoke from their physical locations on a spectrum to explain their stances, listened to each other, and moved as their opinions shifted.

As I led the activity, the room filled with a familiar energy—the physicality of moving around the room; the novelty of speaking from a standing position; the visual depiction of the group's stance on an issue provoking interest; sometimes humor. I drew the problem statements from current issues, embedded in larger civic themes, that could be adapted to students of different ages: "The US should change from a system where the presidency is decided by the electoral college to one with straight majority rule"; "There are not enough political parties in the United States"; "US immigration laws are not enforced strictly enough"; "Everyone is treated equally by the legal system in this country."

With time running short, I posed the final statement, one inspired by a recent proposal by the Joe Foss Institute (http://joefossinstitute.org) that state policies require high school students to pass the test for US citizenship for high school graduation. Their efforts have been successful in 14 states to date. "Students should be able to pass the citizenship test given to new citizens before they can graduate high school," I proclaimed. Teachers flocked to opposite ends of the room, a large clump standing by the "agree" sign I had taped to one wall, and another group taking up residence by the "disagree" sign on the facing wall.

The ensuing discussion was one of the most heated I have ever facilitated, with some teachers passionately insisting that high school students be required to pass the same test that immigrants must pass to become citizens, and others issuing angry warnings about how such a requirement would further narrow the social studies curriculum, in which teachers would drill students on civic facts rather than engaging them in high-quality instruction. Of all of the controversial topics we had discussed during the session, the question that asked, in effect, if civic education could be achieved through a policy edict was the most provocative.

In sharing this detailed example, I aim to draw attention to potential problems with using policy to directly influence civic education. These teachers' conflict over the question is revealing. They were torn between the implementation of a policy that they knew would do little to improve instruction and the allure of mandating that some degree of attention be paid to civic education. Having personally experienced how mandates for particular types of learning could result in narrowed classroom approaches, they also knew that their field was suffering for attention amid the national focus on the assessment of math and literacy skills.

This vignette also illustrates the complexity of civic education and of learning to teach for civic engagement. The complex theoretical and practical preparation that goes into actualizing powerful teaching in this area is not immediately visible to the general public, or even to policymakers who are concerned with civic education. Discussion of controversial issues, along with the other practices known for developing active civic engagement, requires students to learn to think in complex, rigorous, and open-minded ways; it requires them to listen carefully and to voice and support their own opinions—new skills for many students that call for deft instruction. Civic education policies should support such instruction, yet be attentive to the ways that mandates can take shape within schools and classrooms.

Using Policy to Mandate New Forms of Civic Engagement

The notion that questions of civic learning and engagement might be addressed through policy solutions hinges on a particular understanding of how change occurs in educational settings. Policymakers believe, to some extent, that policy has an "irrevocable influence on orders of being and practice down the chain of command" (Levinson & Doyle, 2008, p. x). Yet, as anthropological investigations of educational policy enactment reveal, the reality is far more complex.

In a recent qualitative research project investigating civic education policy and practice in Guatemala, I saw first-hand the difficulties of using policy as a lever for democracy promotion. A Central American country of around 15 million people, Guatemala's recent history is marked by a 36-year-long internal armed conflict between army and guerilla forces, during which the country's large Indigenous population suffered disproportionately; of the estimated 200,000 people killed in this conflict, over 80% were Indigenous. The conflict ended in 1996 with the signing of the UN-brokered *Firm and Lasting Peace Accords*. The Accords included a promise by the government to "design and implement a national civic education programme for democracy and peace, promoting the protection of human rights, the renewal of political culture, and the peaceful resolution of conflicts" (Sieder & Wilson, 1997, p. 55).

These agreements placed the task of civic reconstruction at the feet of Guatemala's educational system, responsible for fostering democratic citizenship, developing a culture of peace, promoting human rights, and inculcating the value of multiculturalism. These policy edicts were instantiated in the *Currículum Nacional Base* [CNB], Guatemala's new national curriculum. In this curriculum, specific discussion of historical and contemporary violence toward Indigenous Guatemalans was subsumed by an emphasis on "democratic life and a culture of peace, unity in diversity, sustainable development, and science and technology" (Ministerio de Educación, 2013).

Transforming civic identity through educational policy, however, was no simple task. The civic learning proposed by Guatemala's globally framed educational policy was embedded (as is all policy, when manifested) within particular contexts and practices. In my study, for example, teachers in a rural public school serving Indigenous students, whose community had suffered at the hands of the military during the civil war, had a much different approach to the federally mandated study of history and civics from that taken by educators in an urban private academy serving affluent Ladino (the term commonly used in Guatemala to refer to Spanish-speaking Guatemalans with European or mixed ancestry) students.

In El Básico, a village school serving an Indigenous population, the social studies teacher critiqued the national curriculum for its glaring silence on questions of violence and cultural annihilation:

> Now here in Guatemala it is said that Rios Montt [former president and general who was, at the time of the study, on trial for genocide during the armed conflict] committed genocide against . . . our Indigenous culture. Our Mayan culture. . . . But we all don't know this because they don't explain it, they don't tell it. We are here, we come to form ourselves bit by bit, and this is what this course is about.

For this teacher, the nation was divided into an Indigenous "we" and a powerful "they" that had perpetuated violence on their "Mayan culture" and refused to acknowledge it. Policies legislating a focus on the inculcation of liberal democratic values did not speak to this teacher's desire to help his students understand the specific history of their community, and in his teaching, this commitment eclipsed adherence to educational policy aims.

In this case, local policy "appropriation" (Levinson, Sutton, & Winstead, 2009) revealed the complexity of using education as a means of building a "new Guatemalan nation," (Ministerio de Educación, 2013), calling into question the role of civic education initiatives in post-conflict settings. Young Guatemalans' locally constructed notions of citizenship and belonging—developed amid the disparately felt legacies of conquest, colonization, exploitation, and repression—competed with a national civic education policy designed to promote democracy through an emphasis on human rights and multiculturalism. Within the classrooms, schools, and communities that educational policy intends to address, teachers and students take in policies and (re)make them as their own, appropriating policy to the varied historical, cultural, economic, and political contours of local settings.

How Policy Might Contribute to Civic Education for Engagement and Activism

In my work, I have had the opportunity to see a lot of effective teaching for civic engagement: discussions of civic issues in which young people engage passionately with each other about questions of personal and national importance, mock election debates in which students study and then voice a wide array of political positions, and participatory action research projects in which students investigate local civic problems and work for change. These examples are all in line with the policy recommendations outlined in a report by the Education Commission of the States, which include discussion of current events, "particularly those that young people view as important to their lives" (Guilfoile, Delander, & Kreck, 2016, p. 10).

These practices require empowered, well-prepared teachers who have the discretion to build relevant classroom activities that connect their students to civic life in meaningful ways. They require that schools place a premium on learning beyond the achievement of math and literacy proficiency scores, supporting creative curricula and instruction that invigorate young people and prepare them for complex, critical thinking by linking classroom deliberation to civic participation in their communities. They require that schools be adequately resourced, teachers have enough time to plan, and stipends are available for teachers to supervise afterschool activities. To engage all young people, such practices need to be available in every school, not only those in well-resourced districts serving affluent students.

These preconditions could be addressed through policy initiatives that support high-quality, equally accessible public education and a well-prepared, professionally empowered teaching force. I do not believe they can be directly mandated: the first example I presented in this chapter shows the complexities embedded in teaching for civic engagement; the second example shows how context can powerfully shape civic teaching and learning, despite policy mandates. Yet policymakers have a vital role to play in ensuring that our schools are well resourced and provide equitable access to civic learning opportunities.

The types of teaching and learning necessary for cultivating engaged citizenship and activism in schools cannot flourish amid a climate of fear. The rhetoric of the 2016 presidential election was marked by threats to young people from marginalized communities in the form of proposed policies—toward immigrant, Muslim, and transgendered youth, and youth of color. Fundamental aspects of the US political system—freedom of the press, civil liberties, trust in federal agencies—were frequently questioned, denigrated, and undermined. The new federal agenda toward public education is a matter of grave concern, with indications that policy may be coming that would destabilize the public school system. In a time in which learning to exchange ideas across difference of all kinds is more critical than ever, we potentially face a policy landscape in which our capacity to develop youth as engaged, activist citizens may be drastically undermined.

Although the cultivation of educational practices to inspire civic participation may defy direct policy edicts, policy can help ensure the preconditions necessary for such learning. Now, more than ever, we as citizens need to voice our support for policy-making that promotes our public schools as democratic, accessible institutions that have the resources and latitude necessary to support educators in creating meaningful civic learning opportunities for students, among others.

References

Campaign for the Civic Mission of Schools. (2011). *The guardian of democracy: The civic mission of schools.* Silver Spring, MD: Campaign for the Civic Mission of Schools.

Guilfoile, L., Delander, B., & Kreck, C. (2016). *Guidebook: Six proven practices for effective civic learning.* Denver, CO: Education Commission of the States. Retrieved from www.ecs. org/citizenship-education-policies

Larson, B. E., & Parker, W. C. (1996). What is classroom discussion? A look at teachers' conceptions. *Journal of Curriculum and Supervision, 11*(2), 110–126.

Levinson, B., & Doyle, S. (2008). *Advancing democracy through education? U.S. influence abroad and domestic practices.* Charlotte, NC: Information Age Publishing.

Levinson, B., Sutton, M., & Winstead, T. (2009). Education policy as a practice of power: Theoretical tools, ethnographic methods, democratic options. *Educational Policy, 23*(6), 767–795.

Ministerio de Educación, Guatemala. (2013). *Ejes de la reforma educativa y su relación con los ejes del curriculum.* Retrieved from http://cnbguatemala.org/index.php?title=Ejes_de_la_ Reforma_Educativa_y_su_Relaci%C3%B3n_con_los_Ejes_del_Curr%C3%ADculum

Sieder, R., & Wilson, R. (Eds.). (1997). Negotiating rights: The Guatemalan peace process. *Accord: An International Review of Peace Initiatives, 2.* Retrieved from www.c-r.org/ accord/guatemala

Levine's Response to Rubin's Commentary

On the question of whether education policies can be effective tools for encouraging youth civic engagement and activism in schools, Beth Rubin and I agree on many important points, which is not surprising since I have learned a great deal from her work. We agree that the most important way to improve civic education would be to enhance the general climate of our schools for both teachers and students. If the government provided all young people with equitable, respectful, and inclusive schools in which they not only learned academic material but also contributed their ideas and values, our students would develop into more confident, committed, and responsible citizens.

However, it is not clear what social policy or policies would make most schools resemble that description. More money alone will not suffice, as is clear from school districts that have relatively high per-pupil expenditures and yet maintain some dehumanizing school climates and practices.

We also agree that the teacher is the most important ingredient in civics and that no governmental policy will accomplish excellent and equitable civic education, unless teachers are supported and their values align reasonably well with the policy. Reform cannot, and should not, simply come from the top down. Still, I would note that governments *inevitably* adopt policies that regulate courses and curricula for civics.

In the United States, for example, every state has civics standards, and most states require at least one course in government or civics. But suppose that a given state adopted neither standards nor a course requirement; that would still be a policy, albeit one that probably would reduce the amount of classroom time and the number of instructors focused on civics.

Therefore, it is important to get the policy recipe right, even as we also pursue two strategies that should complement any policy: (1) organizing interested teachers from the bottom up to support one another and innovate and (2) providing official help, such as professional development, to accompany any requirements imposed from the top down.

I also would try to set reasonable expectations for the contribution of schools to the overall civic and political development of youth. I think both Rubin and I would like to see youth equipped with concepts, tools, skills, and inspiration that they can use to make their world more just. But I do not believe we should expect public schools to devote themselves to social change understood in any particular way. Public schools must strive for a kind of ideological neutrality (elusive as that goal is) and answer to the majority population that rules any democracy. Schools can be spaces in which students develop their own ideas and skills but not drivers of political agendas.

Meanwhile, families, networks of teenagers, community organizations, and the media outlets from which they draw can share whatever ideas they like, including highly controversial and critical ones. The First Amendment enables them to perform this function. A school can teach in some detail and complexity how the First Amendment is used (and contested), while social groups outside of school employ free speech to discuss and spread ideas that the students will encounter in and beyond school. The First Amendment is just an example; the rest of the Constitution, how it has evolved and been used for a variety of ends, and the social/political order that the Constitution governs also should be taught in schools.

Thus, the main aim of public policy for civics should be to create time and space for students to encounter the kinds of ideas, skills, and values that are broadly endorsed by the public that supports public schools. What they learn in school should be useful as they develop and express their own views.

The policy recipe I would recommend is a combination of:

1. Thoughtful standards that are relatively few, broad, and essential, and that encourage experiential civic learning instead of memorizing large bodies of information. The *College, Career, and Citizenship (C3) Framework* (National Council for the Social Studies, 2013) offers guidelines for states. (In full disclosure, I chaired the civics writing team for that document.)
2. Course requirements that create time for explicit focus on civics.
3. Reforms in school discipline policies that reduce the frequency of penalties that are known to suppress civic engagement.
4. Tests, as long as they are well designed and do not devolve into batteries of multiple-choice items about disconnected facts. When students fail the tests, they should receive attention that helps them succeed rather than simply face penalties. Tests that assess students' ability to work together would be very welcome but would take substantial resources to develop.
5. An ongoing mechanism for supporting teachers with professional development, ancillary materials, opportunities to learn from each other, and feedback based on tests and other data. Creating and sustaining such mechanisms requires annual state appropriations.

I do not believe this combination of policies, by itself, will produce a capable and responsible citizenry or give all our people equal voice and influence. I do believe these policies would help toward those ends. Put another way, getting policy right does not answer the question, "How should all our students learn to be effective citizens?" But it does answer the question: "What is the role of a state or local government in improving civic education at large scale?"

Reference

National Council for the Social Studies. (2013). *The College, Career, and Civic Life (C3) framework for social studies state standards*. Silver Spring, MD: National Council for the Social Studies.

Rubin's Response to Levine's Commentary

Peter Levine is right to start his essay with the question of whether current educational policies have any influence at all on civic education. As he points out, it is state rather than federal policy that has direct bearing on civic learning and, even at the state level, "what the state required was not related to what [students] experienced in the classroom or what they knew, either for better or for worse." Furthermore, while we do have an indication that "interactive civic education" correlates with higher interest and participation in civic life, there is no research that posits a connection between particular policies and requirements and the use of more engaging pedagogies.

With this being the current state of affairs, how are we to go about improving civic education? I very much agree with Levine and his CIRCLE colleagues that improving civic education depends more on how policies are implemented than on the content of a particular policy. While the evidence mounts that interactive, creative, and highly engaged learning activities are more effective for civic education, the climate in schools for the past several decades, in response to powerful policy edicts, has in many ways encouraged a move in the opposite direction. Teachers and administrators feel pushed to focus on preparing students aggressively on a narrow band of competencies, the result being that social studies often is given less time in the curriculum; and the types of discussions, activities, and instruction described by many advocates, as well as in state curricular frameworks, are de-emphasized. The promising coalitions to support and encourage educators to provide high-quality civic education that Levine describes are all the more essential today.

The question Levine raises—"what is civics for?"—and his answer to that question provide us with a rich issue for discussion. Should civics education be trying to change the existing political order? Levine says no, suggesting that schools should teach "a baseline of valuable knowledge about how our systems work" while "activists add a critical lens of their own choice." In some ways, this seems a reasonable approach, given the lack of political consensus.

Complicating such an approach, however, is the assumption that there really can be a politically neutral "baseline of valuable knowledge" that exists apart from historical and structural inequalities linked to race, class, and other dimensions. As Levine notes, "no view of politics and civic life is neutral." Abowitz and Harnish assert in their review of contemporary citizenship discourses that the historical and civic content of social studies courses is dominated by "Enlightenment-inspired citizenship discourses of civic republicanism and liberalism" presenting a "pallid, overly cleansed, and narrow" view of political life (2006, p. 654). My own research and that of other scholars shows that many students, particularly those from historically disenfranchised communities, disconnect from a version of civic education that leans heavily on these narrow discourses of progress and patriotism and avoids the critical approaches that can help to explain those students' personal and community experiences of persistent injustice and inequality (Rubin, 2007; Levinson, 2012).

More affluent, White, and Asian American students have greater access to high-quality civic education practices than low-income African American and Latino students have (Kahne & Middaugh, 2009). Beyond this well-documented "civic opportunity gap" (Levine, 2009), there is an argument to be made that "neutral" approaches to civic learning do not directly speak to the needs and experiences of a sizeable and growing demographic of students hoping to make sense of a "lived curricula of citizenship" that does not cohere with traditional discourses (Abowitz & Harnish, 2006, p. 657). A critical approach is essential to helping historically underserved students understand the current circumstances of their communities.

A relevant civic education, I believe, would help students understand how the present civic context connects to past policies and practices. This goes beyond the suggested "baseline of valuable knowledge about how our systems work" and ventures into the territory of helping students to develop a "critical lens." Without such a lens, particular populations are left without answers about how their citizenship has taken shape. As Abowitz and Harnish write,

> much of our schooling in citizenship fails to reflect the continual struggles of democratic politics. In short, the lived curricula of citizenship and the lively debates among activists, scholars, and thinkers are ideologically diverse and suggest multiple forms of democratic engagement, while the current formal, taught curriculum of citizenship produces a relatively narrow scope and set of meanings for what citizenship is and can be. This difference suggests that, rather than blaming democratic disengagement on the apathetic choices of young people, we should perhaps be looking at how we reduce, confine, diminish, and deplete citizenship meanings in our formal and taught curriculum.
>
> (p. 657)

Approaches that engage with the multiple meanings, struggles, and ambiguities of citizenship are already drawing our diverse, young population into new forms of democratic engagement, such as online organizing and vigorous political and activist discourse utilizing social media platforms.

Our within-school civic education practices could benefit from a look at the new forms of civic engagement and activism that speak to today's youth. However, while such approaches could be allowed for through broadly and non-restrictively written educational policies, they are too politically contentious to be directly embedded within policy directives. Educational policies that require teachers to be well educated and robustly supported and that uphold schools as sites of free expression may increase the likelihood of an engaging, challenging, critical civic education for this country's diverse new generation.

References

Abowitz, K., & Harnish, J. (2006). Contemporary discourses of citizenship. *Review of Educational Research, 76*, 653–690.

Kahne, J., & Middaugh, E. (2009). Democracy for some: The civic opportunity gap in high school. *CIRCLE Working Paper 59*.

Levine, P. (2009). The civic opportunity gap. *Educational Leadership, 66*(8), 20–25.

Levinson, M. (2012). *No citizen left behind*. Cambridge, MA: Harvard University Press.

Rubin, B. C. (2007). "There's still not justice": Youth civic identity development amid distinct school and community contexts. *Teachers College Record, 109*(2), 449–481.

5

"HOW AND TO WHAT EXTENT DOES EDUCATION POLICY UNITE THE DISCIPLINE OF HISTORY TO THE ACADEMIC SUBJECT OF SOCIAL STUDIES, AND IS THIS A FRUITFUL UNION?"

Finding Possible Policy Directions in the Shared Purposes of History and Social Studies Education: A Canadian Perspective

Commentary by Alan Sears, University of New Brunswick

There is an aphorism that states, "A camel is a horse designed by committee." This saying, of course, pokes fun at both camels as strange animals and committees as less than effective at producing sensible outcomes. Social studies, like the camel, was designed by committee and often looks like a strange creature compared to other school subjects with narrower foci and clearer links to traditional academic disciplines. Although subjects like history and geography had been in the American curriculum for some time, social studies was introduced in 1916 by the Committee on Social Studies, within the National Education Association's Commission on the Reorganization of Secondary Education (Dunn, 1916). From the beginning, it was designated an area of the curriculum and a subject in its own right, and in both manifestations, its relationship with the discipline of history has been integral and fractious.

In its seminal report, the Committee on Social Studies laid out a six-year cycle of courses for secondary schools alternating among American and European histories, geography, civics, and a culminating course focused on "problems of democracy—social, economic, and political" (Dunn, 1916, p. 12). In this arrangement, we see both manifestations of social studies. First, like science, it delineates an area of the curriculum containing different subjects like history, geography, and civics. More recently, these have been expanded to include economics, sociology, anthropology, and psychology, among others.

Second, social studies also is a distinct subject, focused on bringing to bear a combination of disciplines to study and, in some cases, to propose solutions to social problems. The "problems of democracy" course suggested by the Committee on Social Studies was an early example of this, and the current approach to social studies in the Alberta provincial curriculum is a contemporary instance. Alberta defines social studies as:

> the study of people in relation to each other and to their world. It is an issues-focused and inquiry-based interdisciplinary subject that draws upon history, geography, ecology, economics, law, philosophy, political science, and other social science disciplines. Social studies fosters students' understanding of and involvement in practical and ethical issues that face their communities and humankind.
>
> *(Alberta Education, 2005, p. 1)*

Social studies relates differently to the discipline of history depending on which way we use the term. As a curriculum category, it is simply a place where history courses show up in school organizational charts and graduation requirements. As a subject in the curriculum, it offers a different approach to social education than history does and is often seen as a rival for educational priority and curricular space.

Social Studies and History in Canadian Policies and Curricula

Writing about Canadian education policies and curricula is tricky because legislative authority for education lies with the provinces and territories rather than with the federal government, and this jurisdictional power is fiercely protected. Canada has no federal department of education that might do things like sponsor educational research or the development of national standards. Political realities in Canada, particularly with regard to the two official language communities, would never allow for such an overt federal role in public education, and consequently, there is considerable variation across the country.

One of the manifestations of siloed provincial jurisdiction is the persistent concern that children learn very different things about the history, politics, and social affairs of the nation depending on where they live. In the early 20th century, the Dominion Education Association sponsored a contest to develop a history textbook to be used nationwide, but that went nowhere; subsequent attempts to develop national approaches to history education largely have failed to bring any sense of national coherence to the field (Osborne, 2001). The Historical Thinking Project (HTP) (http://historicalthinking.ca/), discussed in more detail below, might be offsetting that trend.

Curricular organization across the Canadian provinces illustrates a range of ways in which history and social studies are linked, or not, in policy. As the above quote indicates, Alberta holds the most thorough commitment to social studies as a synthetic subject. The entire compulsory social education curriculum in that province, K–12, is oriented around an interdisciplinary, issues-based social studies approach (Alberta Education, 2005). By contrast, in Québec, learners from elementary through secondary school study history, geography, and civics as discrete subjects (Gouvernment du Quebec Ministere de l'Education, 2001; Gouvernment du Quebec Ministere de l'Education du Loisir et du Sport, 2007). One secondary course, "The Contemporary World," focuses on interdisciplinary studies of current global issues, but otherwise, disciplinary study carries the day. Ontario offers an approach partway between these two, with social studies as the organizational framework for elementary school and more disciplinary courses permeating the secondary curriculum—a fairly common pattern in jurisdictions across North America (Ontario Ministry of Education, 2013a, 2013b).

These variations are partly explained by political, cultural, and linguistic differences among the provinces. For example, in the mid-20th century, during the emergence of education as a unique academic field in Canada, most of its leaders received their doctorates in the United States (Clark, 2004). This substantially influenced policy in Alberta, where

> convergence between the interests of the governing party and Alberta's educational leaders, several of whom had done graduate work at Teachers College, Columbia, and the University of Chicago where they were influenced by the pantheon of American progressivists, resulted in the decision to bring progressive education to Alberta.
>
> *(Coulter, 2005, p. 684)*

Simultaneously, in 1940, Alberta teacher educator Donalda Dickie published the seminal book *The Enterprise in Theory and Practice*, which built on the project method developed by William Kilpatrick in the U.S. and shaped approaches to social studies teacher education at institutions in most of English Canada.

French Canada, particularly the province of Québec, has always taken its own approach to social studies and history education. In that province, history education is seen as a force for building a sense of Francophone solidarity and nationhood. Changes to the history curriculum in Québec usually involve wide public consultation and always generate vociferous debate. In recent years, the provincial government moved to reform the history curriculum with the aim of making it less ideological, focusing on historical thinking practices that are becoming more common in English Canada and beyond. The reforms passed, but not without considerable public opposition (Letourneau, 2011).

Elsewhere, I detail other Canadian examples of the variable relationships between history and social studies, suggesting "the ongoing conflicts are largely built on false premises, have been destructive for both sides, and undermine social education's already tenuous place in the school curriculum" (Sears, 2011, p. 346).

While it is true that school history sometimes is more akin to what Seixas (2014) calls "celebratory heritage" as opposed to "critical history" (p. 14) and some manifestations of social studies really do offer, in Neatby's (1953) devastating phrase, "so little for the mind," these are not the mainstream positions of policy documents or formal curricula. In 2013, for example, Ontario became the latest province to embed the HTP's model of historical thinking into its curriculum, a development that inevitably impacts teaching and teaching materials, assessment practices, and demand for professional development. The HTP model shares considerable common ground with the subject of social studies in terms of its foci on developing important conceptual and procedural understandings rather than accumulating static content knowledge. These are valuable bases from which to forge productive directions for policy, practice, and research in social education, generally.

Moving Forward: A New Synthesis

Productive policy directions begin by acknowledging common fundamental purposes of history and social studies education: those of engaged and critical citizenship. Recently, Hess and McAvoy (2015) made a compelling case that schools and classrooms "ought to be political sites" where "students develop their ability to deliberate political questions" (p. 4). The best social studies classrooms, they argue, are characterized by thoughtful, "best practice discussion" (p. 47), where students address controversial issues, encounter views different from their own, and "learn to see disagreements as a normal part of democratic life" (p. 54). Their research led them to the conclusion that

> students in classes with rich and frequent discussion of controversial political issues describe these courses as engaging, become more confident in their ability to participate competently in discussions, demonstrate increased political knowledge, and display more interest in politics.
>
> *(p. 46)*

This bears striking similarity to the deliberative approach to history education advocated by Barton and Levstik (2004), who argue that learning history can contribute to democratic practices that are "participatory, pluralist, and deliberative" (pp. 34–35). It is possible, they say, to teach history in a way that both develops a sense of national identity and explores the contested and complex nature of that identity, emphasizing discussions of difference, exclusion, and inclusion. They posit that national histories should focus, in part, on struggles by various groups over time to be included, legally, politically, and sociologically. More traditional approaches to teaching history in multinational states like Australia, Canada, and Britain regard multinationalism as a problem that can be fixed through the presentation of singular, often heroic versions of the nation's past. The history education that Barton and Levstik propose opens this multinationalism up for investigation by asking questions like these: How have certain groups or nations been included in the state, and are members of those groups or nations satisfied with that inclusion? What issues do the state and its people face because of the complex social and legal tensions between inclusion and autonomy? Such questions and deliberations are completely consistent with the political social studies classroom advocated by Hess and McAvoy.

Not only are contemporary approaches to history and social studies compatible, the two subjects need each other. All of the important issues social educators want to explore have a history, and it is impossible to do any contemporary issue justice without detailed explorations of the historical roots of controversy and conflict. How could one study contemporary multicultural policy in Britain, for example, without some understanding of colonialism and how it contributes to both the make-up of the society and injustices faced by particular ethnic and racial groups? On the other hand, historical studies of colonialism that do not explore questions about its contemporary implications—what Seixas and Morton (2013) call "the ethical dimension of history" (p. 168)—is clearly deficient. Neither an ahistorical social studies nor an apolitical history serves students or society very well.

Further, because social education policy is situated in broader public policy contexts, it makes sense to consider how the former should relate and respond to the latter. In Canada, there may be new space for creative thinking and policy making in social education with the recent release of the Truth and Reconciliation Commission of Canada's report on Indian residential schools (Truth and Reconciliation Commission of Canada, 2015). The Commission called for restructuring education to foster understanding and reconciliation between and among Canada's indigenous and non-indigenous peoples. Several jurisdictions have taken up the Commission's work, moving forward with Treaty Education and other approaches to indigenous studies in ways that require attention to both history and contemporary circumstances—fertile ground, in other words, for linking history and social studies.

Conclusion

Social studies and history have been inextricably linked since the former broke onto the scene in 1916. They share, and compete for, space as subjects within the segment of the school curriculum dedicated to social education. I have argued here that there is great potential for their relationship to be fruitful; yet, for the most part, it has been marked by "turf wars among competing camps, each with its own leaders, philosophy, beliefs, and pedagogical practices" (Evans, 2004, p. 1). This happens while social education generally suffers from low priority vis-à-vis math, English, and other subjects perceived as more practically oriented to future employment. A recent illustration of this is found in a special issue of the journal *Citizenship Teaching and Learning*, including studies from European Union nations about the place of citizenship education after the economic crisis of 2008–2009. In the introduction, the issue's editors wrote that since the downturn:

> Active and participatory citizenship policies received major cuts to funding as part of the austerity drive, and were no longer considered a policy priority at both the European and the national level as concerns about mounting unemployment and a skills crisis took over. In addition, there was a general policy shift from cosmopolitan European citizenship to a more nationalistic and reactive citizenship, driven by responses to pressing social issues such as extremism, radicalization, migration, and violence.
>
> *(Hoskins, Kerr, & Liu, 2016, pp. 249–250)*

Even more recently, the province of Ontario considered cutting its compulsory high school civics course to make way for an expanded career education class. The province backtracked on this proposed change in the face of opposition generated largely by the Ontario History and Social Science Teachers' Association, which organized a letter writing and public awareness campaign about the proposal. In the face of such policy challenges, continued fighting between social studies and history advocates is akin to fiddling while Rome burns.

Researchers and practitioners in both fields have expanded the base of knowledge about historical and civic understanding and provided effective pedagogical strategies for fostering those things. In Canada, the HTP also had extensive influence on policy and curricula by warranting its proposals with empirical research on how students think about and learn history, by building early and substantial connections with ministerial officials across the country, by involving teachers in the creation and dissemination of materials, and by working with publishers to ensure that educational materials reflected the latest approaches to teaching history. This model of influence—based in engaged and critical citizenship and responsive to developments in public policy, more broadly—has considerable potential to enhance social education on the whole.

References

Alberta Education. (2005). *Social studies K–12*. Retrieved from www.education.gov.ab.ca/k_12/curriculum/bySubject/social/sockto3.pdf.

Barton, K., & Levstik, L. (2004). *Teaching history for the common good*. Mahwah, NJ: Erlbaum.

Clark, P. (2004). Social studies in English Canada: Trends and issues in historical context. In A. Sears & I. Wright (Eds.), *Challenges and prospects for Canadian social studies* (pp. 17–37). Vancouver: Pacific Educational Press.

Coulter, R. P. (2005). Getting things done: Donalda J. Dickie and leadership through practice. *Canadian Journal of Education, 28*(4), 669–699.

Dunn, A. W. (1916). *The social studies in secondary education: A six-year program adapted both to the 6-3-3 and the 8-4-4 plans of organization*. Retrieved from http://files.eric.ed.gov/fulltext/ED542444.pdf

Evans, R. W. (2004). *The social studies wars: What should we teach the children?* New York: Teachers College Press.

Gouvernment du Quebec Ministere de l'Education. (2001). *Quebec education program, approved version: Preschool education, elementary education.* Retrieved from http://www1.education.gouv.qc.ca/sections/programmeFormation/primaire/pdf/educprg2001/educprg2001.pdf

Gouvernment du Quebec Ministere de l'Education du Loisir et du Sport. (2007). *Quebec education program, secondary cycle two* (06-00283). Retrieved from http://www1.education.gouv.qc.ca/sections/programmeFormation/secondaire2/index_en.asp

Hess, D., & McAvoy, P. (2015). *The political classroom: Evidence and ethics in democratic education.* New York: Routledge.

Hoskins, B., Kerr, D., & Liu, L. (2016). Citizenship and the economic crisis in Europe: An introduction. *Citizenship Teaching and Learning, 11*(3), 249–265.

Letourneau, J. (2011). The debate on history education in Quebec. In P. Clark (Ed.), *New possibilities for the past: Shaping history education in Canada* (pp. 81–96). Vancouver: UBC Press.

Neatby, H. (1953). *So little for the mind.* Toronto: Clarke, Irwin.

Ontario Ministry of Education. (2013a). *The Ontario curriculum grades 9 and 10 Canadian and world studies: Geography, history, civics (politics).* Toronto: Ontario Ministry of Education.

Ontario Ministry of Education. (2013b). *Social studies grades 1–6 history and geography grades 7 and 8.* ISBN 978-1-4606-0403-8. Retrieved from www.edu.gov.on.ca/eng/curriculum/elementary/sshg18curr2013.pdf.

Osborne, K. (2001). Public schooling and citizenship education in Canada. In R. Bruno-Jofré & N. Aponiuk (Eds.), *Educating citizens for a pluralistic society* (pp. 11–48). Calgary: Canadian Ethnic Studies.

Sears, A. (2011). Historical thinking and citizenship education: It is time to end the war. In P. Clark (Ed.), *New possibilities for the past: Shaping history education in Canada* (pp. 344–364). Vancouver: UBC Press.

Seixas, P. (2014). History and heritage: What's the difference? *Canadian Issues (Thèmes Canadiens), 10*, 12–16.

Seixas, P., & Morton, T. (2013). *The big six historical thinking concepts.* Toronto: Nelson Education.

Truth and Reconciliation Commission of Canada. (2015). *Honouring the truth, reconciling for the future: Summary of the final report of the Truth and Reconciliation Commission of Canada.* Retrieved from www.trc.ca/websites/trcinstitution/File/2015/Findings/Calls_to_Action_English2.pdf

Building Consensus Around a Roadmap for Inquiry in the United States

Commentary by John K. Lee, North Carolina State University, and Kathy Swan, University of Kentucky

In this essay, we consider how and to what extent education policy unites the discipline of history to the academic subject of social studies, and whether this is a fruitful union. The reality is that education policy in this area is slim. With the end of the US Department of Education's Teaching American History grant program in 2012, no single federal program has directly affected policy related to the discipline of history. The Teaching American History program generated curriculum materials and related professional development, and those efforts certainly impacted history education and, by extension, social studies (Ragland & Woestman, 2010). But the program, in many ways, reinforced a longstanding distinction between history and social studies—the notion that social studies is a school subject intended to integrate content from disciplines like history (Lee, 2005; Thornton, 2008). The value of social studies as an academic field has been sidelined as issues around history education have dominated scholarly activity. No better example of this phenomenon can be seen than in the work of Wineburg (2001), who created a cottage industry around historical thinking, rarifying school-based history as rigorous and, in the minds of many teachers, where the *real* academic work takes place. This has only deepened the distinction between the discipline of history and the academic subject of social studies.

We are entering a new and perhaps unprecedented period in the history of social studies. The 2013 publication of the *College, Career, and Civic Life (C3) Framework for Social Studies State Standards* brought together factions in social studies that have otherwise engaged in internecine conflict (National Council for the Social Studies, 2013). Ron Evans (2004) used the term "social studies wars" to describe the "continuing battles over the purposes, content, methods, and theoretical foundations of social studies curriculum" that marked much of the 20th century (p. 1). Despite those disagreements, or perhaps in spite of them, the C3

Framework offers promise in forging consensus around what and how to teach social studies.

How did we get to a place where leaders and organizations in all the major disciplines that make up social studies, as well as organizations that support the missions of those disciplines, were willing to put aside their long-held disagreements to agree on the central aims of the C3 Framework? And, what special role did the discipline of history play in that process? These questions frame this essay. Herein, we suggest that the C3 Framework is a de facto education policy led by state social studies leaders, teacher educators and scholars, and national content and social studies organizations. We argue that the role of history in the C3 Framework is situated academically alongside other disciplines to accomplish the long-held goal that social studies might represent multiple disciplines while maintaining a unique interdisciplinary nature. We argue that inquiry is the glue that holds the disciplines together, as represented in the C3 Framework's Inquiry Arc, and that efforts to develop inquiry models are thus policy initiatives to advance the C3 Framework. Furthermore, inquiry-related policy initiatives actually unite the discipline of history with the academic subject of social studies in a productive manner. Finally, education policy in social studies is bereft without considering the civic mission of schooling. Ultimately, there is a civic nature to social studies education policy. This functions as the driving force behind initiatives to extend and support social studies and shapes the experiences we would expect students to have in schools. The net effect is that school should balance disciplinary experiences in areas such as history with civic experiences that enable students to learn and practice living in the world as productive citizens.

The C3 Framework as Education Policy

It was no accident that brought together so many varied interests to work on the C3 Framework. In January of 2011, leaders of 15 professional organizations, along with social studies leaders from 23 states, met in Savannah, Georgia, to discuss the storm clouds that loomed over social studies, brought on by current educational reform forces (Swan & Griffin, 2013). When this project began, the Common Core State Standards (CCSS) were sweeping the country. The majority of states had formally adopted new standards in English language arts (ELA) and mathematics emphasizing a "fewer, higher, clearer" approach to K–12 education. The momentum of the CCSS created tremors within the social studies community: without a framework for state social studies standards, our domain could be squeezed out of the curriculum further. Many in the social studies community feared that the effect of the CCSS would be to subsume the social studies within English language arts, making the ELA standards de facto standards for social studies as well. It was essential to reassert the importance of social studies subjects, especially as the CCSS acknowledge the necessary contributions of history and other social studies subjects to literacy in grades 6–12. Where once disciplinary quarrels and boundary disputes might have sunk any attempt at building social studies standards, the potential elimination of social studies as a viable school subject created a more constructive environment.

From *A Nation at Risk* in the 1980s, to the "back to the basics" movement that followed, and through No Child Left Behind, social studies was pushed to the sidelines in federal education policy initiatives. Social studies was excluded from the testing regime that emerged from No Child Left Behind; because school districts panicked over the prospects of being labeled as failing, they took instructional time from social studies to remediate in the tested areas of literacy and math (Heafner & Fitchett, 2012). The publication of the CCSS and its almost universal adoption similarly excluded social studies from the national education policy discussion. Although social studies was mentioned in the CCSS's ELA standards, it was relegated to just five pages (64–69) and presented as if social studies ought to be in service of larger and more seemingly important aims associated with general literacy. Many social studies leaders thought the day was near when social studies as a school subject would wither away, at least in the elementary grades, leaving middle-level and secondary social studies to specific academic disciplines, particularly history.

It was in this moment of relative gloom for the field that social studies leaders convened in Savannah, where aims and design of the C3 Framework emerged. As the framework moved toward its final form in the spring of 2013, additional voices representing K–12 educators, university faculty, state education personnel, professional organization representatives, educational publishers, and cultural organizations were asked to weigh in during a series of targeted reviews. By May 2013, more than 3,000 social studies educators had reviewed the C3 Framework draft and found the document compelling. The project was up against great odds—a dearth of funding, a history of incivility amongst the disciplines within social studies, a knack for ending up in media battles over what should be taught in a social studies curriculum, and a lack of disciplinary and interdisciplinary coherence within previous social studies standards documents. In the first couple of months, one of the more optimistic participants in the C3 project gave the work about a 30 percent chance of success.

The voluntary, state-led effort to develop what would become the C3 Framework faced long odds because it hinged on professional collaboration between and among a loosely arranged coalition of state departments of education and professional organizations. If the past is any kind of predictor (e.g., the "history wars" of the 1990s), social studies educators seemed like the last group of subject-matter specialists that should bet on a cooperative movement. Further, while the Council of Chief State School Officers (CCSSO)—the CCSS's sponsor—initially had agreed to host C3 planning meetings, that organization was clear that its commitment to the Common Core initiative did not extend to a leadership role in the development of state social studies standards. Against this tenuous backdrop, the group forged ahead; and despite the odds, the C3 Framework was published in September 2013. What the C3 Framework represents is a shared policy vision for what disciplines like history, relative to the academic subject of social studies, should consist of in the schools.

History Relative to the Civic Nature of Social Studies in the C3 Framework

One of the key characteristics of the C3 Framework is that it clearly defines the roles of the disciplines in social studies. For perhaps the first time, a consensus document, approved by virtually all of the major organizations that make up the field, represented four core disciplines as similarly positioned in the social studies. While curricula may provide students with more time to learn about topics in one discipline than another—a commensurate division of time on topics is as arbitrary as it is difficult to implement—the general policy implication of the C3 Framework is that civics, economics, geography, and history have equitable roles to play in the practices of teaching and learning social studies.

At the same time, history plays an important and unique role in social studies education, as evinced in the C3 Framework. Research on thinking and learning in the discipline provides a powerful means to articulate what the structures and consequences of students' learning experiences, in social studies, ought to be (Barton & Levstik, 2004; Hicks, van Hover, Doolittle, & VanFossen, 2012; VanSledright & Limón, 2006). We now talk regularly about thinking in the disciplines—in *all* the disciplines—due to the groundbreaking research on learners' interactions with history that began in Britain in the 1960s and continued through the next four decades (Monte-Sano & Reisman, 2016). Today, such research impacts policy and practice—for example, resources and pedagogies built around students' interpretation of documentary evidence—in programs like Advanced Placement histories, taken by millions of students.

The discipline of history also provided a roadmap for inquiry, setting forth a broad outline for what inquiry looks like when applied with disciplinary rigor in K–12 settings. We see this in the 17 indicators that make up the history strand in the C3 Framework; 12 of these indicators are focused on disciplinary inquiry skills. The other three disciplines of civics, economics, and geography are far more conceptual in focus, with each discipline including just three or four process-oriented indicators—almost the reverse of the emphasis on historical inquiry. We think this is a reflection of the research base in history informing the writers of the history standards in the C3 Framework. Historians and history educators know, with a higher degree of confidence than do those in other social studies disciplines, what thinking in their field looks like and were able to express that in the standards.

We would be remiss if we did not take into consideration the unique place of civics in US schools. Social studies exists, in large part, for the purpose of preparing young people to experience an active and productive civic life. Perhaps now more than ever we see the possibilities and complications associated with holding together the experiment of democracy in the United States. As a policy document, the C3 Framework makes a clarion call for a new sort of social studies that uses what we know from the disciplines, perhaps most importantly from the discipline of history, to deliberately inform civic action. Levinson and Levine (2013) described civic action as "essential to the inquiry arc—and even more fundamentally, to the social studies as a whole—because, as Aristotle first argued, learning to be an active and responsible citizen requires experience" (p. 339).

Inquiry as the Glue

Inquiry is a central feature of the C3 Framework. It holds the potential to fundamentally alter how social studies is taught and learned, assuming that the C3 Framework represents the predominant social studies education policy tool of our era. Inquiry is the glue that connects the discipline of history with the academic subject of social studies, with at least two important policy implications. First, it sets the expectation that educators and scholars in civics, economics, and geography would clarify what disciplinary inquiry entails and suggest how unique forms of inquiry in their disciplines might shape inquiry in social studies. Second, inquiry provides a powerful, well-substantiated basis for building and implementing curricular models and pedagogical instruments in K–12 settings.

Over the last three years, we have worked with leaders in states and professional organizations that curate social studies content to develop such a curricular model (Swan, Lee, & Grant, 2015). The Inquiry Design Model (IDM) is one approach to enacting social studies education policy. In this model, students work toward constructing arguments and taking informed civic action by responding to compelling, open-ended questions, participating in learning tasks that draw from sources and practices in the academic disciplines. Our IDM work pinpoints an immediate need for new funding, through organizations both public and private, national and local, to invigorate inquiry-based designs for learning, teaching, and assessment, and to extend our understanding of the consequences of those designs.

Conclusion

As daunting as this process seems, the publication of the C3 Framework really was just the beginning. Project participants knew, from the framework's inception, that ushering in an ambitious new era in social studies education would require more than standards. Statewide and classroom-based assessments need to evolve to overcome current shortcomings; instructional materials and resources need to be developed to assist teachers in promoting inquiry and supporting students' informed action; new teacher learning standards are needed to impart the framework's approach to teaching and learning; and to realize these changes, funding for professional development around the C3 Framework needs to be plentiful. In other words, like any education policy, the success of the C3 Framework lies in its *implementation effects*.

Education policy serves to channel educators' discourses and directions. As a social studies policy tool, the C3 Framework presses educators to construct social studies as an inquiry process, whereby the disciplines of civics, geography, economics, *and* history comparably allow students to uncover questions about our social world. While enactments of policy could vary, the C3 Framework's intentions are clear: to provide a fruitful union of the four social studies disciplines that honors the integrity and uniqueness of each of them.

References

Barton, K. C., & Levstik, L. S. (2004). *Teaching history for the common good*. Mahwah, NJ: Erlbaum.

Evans, R. W. (2004). *The social studies wars: What should we teach the children?* New York: Teachers College Press.

Heafner, T. L., & Fitchett, P. G. (2012). Tipping the scales: National trends of declining social studies instructional time in elementary schools. *Journal of Social Studies Research*, *36*(2), 190–215.

Hicks, D., van Hover, S., Doolittle, P., & VanFossen, P. (2012). Learning social studies: An evidence-based approach. In K. R. Harris, S. Graham, & T. Urban (Eds.), *APA educational psychology handbook: Vol. 3. Application to learning and teaching* (pp. 283–307). Washington, DC: American Psychological Association.

Lee, J. K. (2005). Reconsidering the debate: Social studies, history, and academic disciplines. *International Journal of Social Education*, *20*(1), 61–63.

Levinson, M., & Levine, P. (2013). Taking informed action to engage students in civic life. *Social Education*, *77*(6), 339–341.

Monte-Sano, C., & Reisman, A. (2016). Studying historical understanding. In L. Corno & E. M. Anderman (Eds.), *Handbook of educational psychology* (3rd ed., pp. 281–294). New York: Routledge.

National Council for the Social Studies. (2013). *College, Career, and Civic Life (C3) framework for social studies state standards: Guidance for enhancing the rigor of K–12 civics, economics, geography, and history*. Silver Spring, MD: National Council for the Social Studies.

Ragland, R. G., & Woestman, K. A. (2010). *The teaching American history project: Lessons for history educators and historians*. New York: Routledge.

Swan, K., & Griffin, S. (2013). Beating the odds: The College, Career, and Civic Life (C3) framework for social studies state standards. *Social Education*, *77*(6), 317–321.

Swan, K., Lee, J., & Grant, S. G. (2015). The New York state toolkit and the inquiry design model: Anatomy of an inquiry. *Social Education*, *79*(6), 316–322.

Thornton, S. (2008). Continuity and change in social studies. In L. S. Levstik & C. A. Tyson (Eds.), *Handbook of research in social studies education* (pp. 15–32). New York: Routledge.

VanSledright, B., & Limón, M. (2006). A review of cognitive research in history and geography. In P. A. Alexander & P. H. Winne (Eds.), *Handbook of educational psychology* (pp. 545–570). Mahwah, NJ: Erlbaum.

Wineburg, S. (2001). *Historical thinking and other unnatural acts*. Philadelphia, PA: Temple University Press.

Sears's Response to Lee and Swan's Commentary

I want to begin by thanking John K. Lee and Kathy Swan for an interesting response to our common question that stimulated my thinking in a number of areas. I found myself agreeing with most of their central points, in particular, their argument that "inquiry is the glue that holds the disciplines together" in the area of social studies. I also agree that scholars in history and history education have led the way in working out a detailed and pedagogically useful model of how inquiry works in a single discipline. That is certainly the case in Canada, where the model of historical thinking developed by Seixas and Morton (2013) has been a major driver of curriculum reform. In recent revisions to its social studies curriculum, the province of Ontario extrapolated from that model to propose "concepts of disciplinary thinking across subjects" including, in addition to history, social studies, geography, politics, economics, and law (Ontario Ministry of Education, 2013, p. 13). The disciplinary models provided for these other subjects, however, are at best nascent and need much further elaboration.

While I could go on to detail other areas of agreement with Lee and Swan, I want to focus the rest of this response on how their piece pushed me to think in more complex ways about the factors influencing policy making related to history and social studies education, and education more generally. Their description of the development and publication of the *College, Career, and Civic Life (C3) Framework for Social Studies State Standards* illustrates the importance of several contextual factors in curriculum development and implementation. A better understanding of these, I argue, is essential to effectiveness in influencing policy making and practice.

The political structures of educational jurisdictions have significant influence on how policy is developed and implemented. A substantial part of my own scholarship has been comparing how these processes work in Canada with other jurisdictions, most particularly, Australia, England, and the United States (Hughes, Print, & Sears, 2010). That work consistently laments Canada's lagging behind the other countries in terms of both collaborative processes of policy and curricular reform and the implementation of new programs and approaches. As one of our article titles succinctly put it, "Citizenship Education: Canada Dabbles While the World Plays On" (Hughes & Sears, 2006).

Across those four countries there are three significantly different sets of political structures with regard to educational policy making: a unitary state where jurisdiction for education lies with the federal or central government (England); a federation where jurisdiction for education lies with the states but where the federal government and national civil society organizations play a key role (Australia and the United States); and a federation where jurisdiction for education lies with states or provinces, the federal government has virtually no overt role, and educational civil society organizations are generally weak and/or provincially focused (Canada).

Our work shows these structures have had a very significant impact on policy development related to history and social studies. One factor, for example, is the ability to have national conversations about policy and practice that result in using academic and applied resources to lay a foundation for change. Lee and Swan illustrate how just such a conversation, fostered largely by professional and academic civil society organizations, laid the groundwork for *C3*. One could also point to similar public deliberations in the U.S. around the development of standards documents in history, civics, geography, and social studies in the 1980s and 1990s, as well as the publication of *The Civic Mission of Schools* (Gibson & Levine, 2003).

Both Australia and England have had many of the same sorts of conversations—in their cases, more government directed—but such conversations almost never take place in Canada. There has not been a serious and well-thought-out national proposal of any kind for history and social studies education reform in Canada in almost 50 years. Our work demonstrates these kinds of broad public discussions are fundamental for laying the groundwork for policy and curricular reform and the implementation of new programs. Lee and Swan point out that many "voices" representing stakeholder groups and teachers participated in the development and vetting of *C3* "and found the document compelling." These will become necessary allies in the next and more difficult stage of reform: implementation of the report's recommendations.

There are at least two other elements of policy-making contexts illustrated in Lee and Swan's article. Unfortunately, space prohibits me from elaborating on them in detail, but they deserve a mention. The first is temporality—or the general tenor of the times. Lee and Swan make the point that the pressure on social education created by the push for Common Core Standards made collaboration between and among disparate groups possible where it had not been before. The second factor is agency. The times being right is not enough; reform also requires that individuals and organizations step up to take advantage of windows of opportunity provided by the temporal context. Lee and Swan detail some of the organizations that led the way on the development of C3.

Reading Lee and Swan's article, I was struck by our common conclusion that social studies and history share a commitment to fostering the kind of inquiry essential to effective democratic citizenship. Success in moving that shared commitment into policy and programs that work depends on deep understanding of the contexts in which those are made and implemented.

References

Gibson, C., & Levine, P. (2003). The civic mission of schools. A Report from Carnegie Corporation of New York and CIRCLE: The Center for Information and Research on Civic Learning and Engagement. Retrieved from http://www.civicmissionofschools.org/site/campaign/cms_report.html

Hughes, A. S., Print, M., & Sears, A. (2010). Curriculum capacity and citizenship education: A comparative analysis. *Compare, 40*(3), 293–309.

Hughes, A. S., & Sears, A. (2006). Citizenship education: Canada dabbles while the world plays on. *Education Canada, 46*(4), 6–9.

Ontario Ministry of Education. (2013). *The Ontario curriculum grades 9 and 10 Canadian and world studies: Geography, history, civics (politics).* Toronto: Ontario Ministry of Education.

Seixas, P., & Morton, T. (2013). *The big six historical thinking concepts.* Toronto: Nelson Education.

Lee and Swan's Response to Sears's Commentary

We enjoyed writing with Alan Sears about the ways in which education policy unites the discipline of history and the academic subject of social studies. Astute readers will pick up on some key differences in how we situated this task and thought through the implications for social studies education policy. While we diverge in some areas, the confluence in our thinking is remarkable. Here, we examine areas of agreement and disagreement and suggest some ways forward in conversation about the roles of educational policy in uniting history and social studies.

Like us, Sears views social studies and history as being often at odds. He wrote, "As a subject in the curriculum, [social studies] offers a different approach to social education than history does and is often seen as a rival for educational priority and curricular space." We described recent policies as "reinforc[ing] a long-standing distinction between history and social studies." Similarly, Sears sees the potential for a new synthesis among history and social studies through "engaged and critical citizenship." We also see a new policy horizon where history and social studies policy serves our collective civic interests. Moreover, Sears draws effectively from the work of Seixas and Morton (2013) to argue that history "shares considerable common ground with the subject of social studies in terms of its foci on developing important conceptual and procedural understandings rather than accumulating static content knowledge." We could not agree more. In our telling, "we now talk regularly about thinking in the disciplines—in all the disciplines—due to the groundbreaking research on learners' interactions with history that began in Britain in the 1960s and continued through the next four decades (Monte-Sano & Reisman, 2016)."

Our agreement with Sears on these issues is to be expected. Decades of curricular marginalization and a consistent flow of scholarship about learning in the disciplines, coupled with a consensus view of the purposes of social studies, make for sturdy ground upon which to stand when crying out for policy changes.

We need more time on social studies.

That time ought to focus on building disciplinary habits.

Such time well spent will pay dividends in our democratic lives.

We are in agreement about these underlying policy ideas. Now what? Now begins the hard work of policy. We view that work as curriculum building, seeding the changes we seek by working with teachers and nurturing habits and pedagogies that bring to life our policy aims.

Here, we just might part ways with Sears—not necessarily in a pedagogical or intellectual manner, but in terms of tactics. To be sure, our approaches share some underlying tendencies. Sears sees the value of teachers as curriculum innovators involved in the "creation and dissemination of materials" that reflect the "latest approaches to teaching history." We take those approaches to be the disciplinary approaches outlined by Sexias and others. Sears hopes to use the broader public policy context to advance these goals. Specifically, Sears sees opportunities within socially just policy actions, such as the Truth and Reconciliation Commission of Canada (2015). At the same time, Sears is skeptical that any coordinated national efforts in Canada will affect change in social education. We share his concern about the prospects of federal action in the United States and doubt seriously that policy recommendations for agencies, both federal and state, will move the needle far in the direction of new disciplinary approaches.

Where we see potential is in the activation of teacher networks, as a grassroots movement, to take action on the policy ideas we share about social studies. The *C3 Framework* offers a context to do just that. In four short years since the publication of the *C3 Framework*, we have worked to develop an inquiry-based instructional model that merges the disciplinary instincts of history with the civic aims of social studies. This curriculum approach, the Inquiry Design Model (IDM), and a network behind the model, C3 Teachers, aim to empower teachers with the tools they need to enact policy through curriculum action. C3 Teachers is a network of over 6,000 teachers who are developing inquiry materials and using them in the classroom (see www.c3teachers.org). More than 20 states and hundreds of districts are using the model to support teachers as they seek out ways to enact the C3 Framework in their classrooms.

IDM supports students as they respond to compelling questions by completing learning tasks that integrate resources from the academic disciplines, by working toward constructing arguments, and by taking informed civic action. The model draws upon the long history of inquiry-based instruction in social studies and carefully brings forward newer ideas about thinking and learning in the disciplines, specifically the discipline of history.

But from a policy perspective, the power of IDM is in its utility as a curriculum-making model. In the hands of a skilled teacher, IDM is a tool to create curriculum, with grounding in the C3 Framework. In this regard, IDM functions as a policy tool by enabling teachers to take control of the teaching and learning in their classrooms. Drawing on Thornton's notion of teacher as "curricular-instructional gatekeeper" (1991), we would argue that teachers employing IDM are enacting the standards perhaps even more robustly than if standards alignment was mandated by rule. Different from more traditional regulatory policy tools, IDM draws upon the strength of a public, professional network of these gate-keepers, all of whom use the model to enact new instructional approaches while responding simultaneously to the perpetual motion of other policies in educational situations both common and unique. IDM and the C3 Framework carry no enforcement mechanisms. Instead, the effectiveness of the model rests with the judgment of teachers who are mostly free to use or not use IDM.

By teaching with inquiry, C3 Teachers are creating educational opportunities that forge ahead where formal policy often fails. The history of social studies, like other subject areas, is littered with policy reforms that disempower teachers and students and confuse parents and the general public. We think most would agree that there is no formal policy substitute for a good teacher and engaging lessons. Accordingly, we remain skeptical that policy recommendations and actions from national, provincial, and state governments, and think tanks and commissions that are disconnected from practitioners, will make much of a difference in practice.

References

Monte-Sano, C., & Reisman, A. (2016). Studying historical understanding. In L. Corno & E. M. Anderman (Eds.), *Handbook of educational psychology* (3rd ed., pp. 281–294). New York: Routledge.

Seixas, P., & Morton, T. (2013). *The big six historical thinking concepts.* Toronto: Nelson Education.

Thornton, S. J. (1991). Teacher as curricular-instructional gatekeeper in social studies. In J. P. Shaver (Ed.), *Handbook of research on social studies teaching and learning* (pp. 237–248). New York: MacMillan.

6

"WHAT IS THE POTENTIAL IMPACT OF THE C3 AS A POLICY TOOL ON CURRICULUM DEVELOPMENT IN TRADITIONALLY UNDERREPRESENTED SOCIAL STUDIES DISCIPLINES?"

Economic Education: Social Studies' "Marginal" Discipline

Commentary by Phillip J. VanFossen, Purdue University

Economics is the social science that investigates the choices people make about how to use their scarce resources in order to satisfy their unlimited wants, and has been described as the science of decision-making (Atkinson, 1982). Because citizens in a democratic society are engaged in decision-making all the time, one can make a strong case that economics is an essential part of effective citizenship education. Noted economists claim that basic economic literacy is an "important goal for a democratic society that relies heavily on informed citizen and personal economic decision-making" (Walstad, 1998) and that economic literacy actually enhances the functioning of both a market system *and* democracy (Rivlin, 1999). Economics also seeks to develop in students an *economic way of thinking* that highlights how incentives affect behavior in all areas of life and that describes the costs and benefits of current and alternative policies. This economic way of thinking provides a "unique way of thinking about social issues" (Winter, 2005, p. xi) by identifying the "trade-offs—that is, the costs and benefits—of whatever issue is at hand" (p. 1).

The Economics Curriculum

While economics is occasionally taught in the business studies curriculum, or sometimes as consumer economics, it is typically taught as a senior-level, 18-week, concept-based economics course in the social studies curriculum (Walstad & Watts, 2015) defined by the 12th-grade benchmarks in the *Voluntary National Content Standards in Economics* (CEE, 2010). These 20 foundational standards are the discipline of economics' best 'short list' of what economics content should be covered in the high school course (Walstad & Watts, 2015).

Recent financial crises (e.g., the sub-prime mortgage debacle, the 'Great Recession') have brought a call for more personal finance and consumer education. Morton (2005) argued that such personal finance concepts should be 'part of' what constitutes economic literacy and that economic education and personal finance education can be complements rather than substitutes, because "economics and personal finance are ultimately about choices and the consequences of those choices" (pp. 66–67).

The Place of Economics in the Social Studies Curriculum

Economics appears in the social studies standards of all 50 states and the District of Columbia, and 45 of those states—and DC—required those standards to be implemented (Council on Economic Education, 2016). However, only 20 states require a course in economics for high school graduation. Moreover, economics is tested—at any grade level—in only 16 states, and, of these, only three states have explicit testing of economic content at the high school level (Education Commission of States, 2015a). Thus, economics only accounts for approximately 7.5% of the mandated social studies curriculum.[1] In contrast, history[2] is required for graduation in 40 out of 50 states[3] and accounts for more than 41% of the mandated Carnegie units in states where social studies is a graduation requirement.[4] The most recent High School Transcript Study indicated that while 94% of high school students had taken a course in U.S. history, only 56.7% had taken a course in economics (Walstad & Rebeck, 2012).

Why isn't economics mandated in more states? Obviously, this is a complex question with complex answers. As the data above show, one answer may lie in the 'history-centric' nature of the mandated social studies curriculum. Indeed, economists would say this illustrates the scarcity identity nicely. If states only mandate (on average) 2.9 Carnegie units of social studies, and students are taking mandated courses in U.S. government, U.S. history, and world history, there is very little space for economics. A second reason may be that economics was not part of the testing scheme in No Child Left Behind, and states allocated more curricular space to subject areas where such high-stakes testing occurred (Grimes & Millea, 2003).

Why focus on mandating economics in the curriculum? Grimes and Lee (2000) suggested that there is evidence that mandated economic education is important "at the aggregate level" because "states with mandated economic education . . . experienced significantly greater rates" of economic growth (p. 4). Urban, Schmeiser, Collins, and Brown (2015) found that students who took a mandated financial education course had significantly higher credit scores, all else being equal. These results are especially important to note because, as Grimes and Millea (2003) found, states with higher poverty rates among children were less likely to have mandated economic education. This may be a case of correlation and not causation, but if economic education leads to improved economic literacy, and economic literacy has the potential to impact economic growth, then it is possible that mandating economic education may be able to "promote economic growth through investments in economic human capital" (Grimes & Millea, 2003, p. 14).

The C3 Framework

The College, Career, and Civic Live (C3) Framework for the Social Studies was developed to provide states with "voluntary guidance for upgrading existing social studies standards" and is only suggestive and designed to "support states in creating standards" (NCSS, 2013, p. 6). Rather than defining precise content knowledge, the C3 focuses on the pedagogical content knowledge—drawn from the four major disciplines that undergird the social studies in U.S. schools (history, civics, economics, and geography)—that future citizens will require. At the heart of this focus on process is what the authors have called the 'Inquiry Arc.'

The C3 Framework describes 'economic thinking' as distinct from other disciplinary knowledge and states that the goal of economic education is to develop the degree of economic literacy necessary to analyze and understand economic activity, such as the recent Great Recession, for example. This economic literacy depends on "understanding and employing key concepts such as supply and demand . . . and the application of theories that describe the interconnections among concepts and how they play out in market structures" (p. 85). Such literacy, the authors argue, is essential to citizens' ability to think economically and to solve economic problems. There are clear similarities between the C3 Framework and the long-held rationale for economic education; in fact, the C3 Framework makes a very similar case concerning the need to promote economic literacy in our citizens. In this, the C3 would appear to add little to the long-held rationale for economics in the school curriculum outlined earlier in this chapter.

The C3 provides examples of the Inquiry Arc at work. Among the compelling and supporting questions the authors selected was "What were some of the causes of the Great Recession?" In order for students to explore this compelling question within the discipline of economics, they would need a deep understanding of some very sophisticated economic content. This disciplinary knowledge is further divided into four areas (economic decision-making, the global economy, exchange and markets, and the national economy) which serve as a de facto scope and sequence of key economic knowledge that students will need in order to address such compelling questions. This also raises an issue concerning social studies teachers' knowledge of this sophisticated economics content.

The Potential of the C3 Framework for Impacting Policy

If more states are to mandate economics, and students are to have greater opportunities to become economically literate, then state (and in some cases local) policies will need to be changed by advocating for a more prominent place for economics within the social studies curriculum. The Council for Economic Education (CEE) defines such advocacy as "educating the public, including elected officials" (CEE, 2016, n.p.). How best to advocate to change state graduation requirements? The CEE has designed an Advocacy Tool Kit for economics educators and advocates to inform policymakers that includes suggestions to focus on clear message points and to define communication activities that include, for example, the *Voluntary National Content Standards in Economics*.

How does the C3 Framework contribute to such advocacy? A clear strength of the C3 is that it reiterates the case that both economic education and economic literacy are central to the mission of citizenship education, which can be useful for policy advocates making a case for more mandated economics in the curriculum. However, C3 offers little that extends this case beyond what currently exists (as noted earlier), and it adds little to the already robust and long-held argument for including economics in the curriculum. Even the Inquiry Arc, for example, is not an entirely new idea within economic education. In fact, economic education has a long history of developing curriculum that requires inquiry on the part of students to answer compelling questions; one example is *The Great Economic Mysteries Book: A Guide to Teaching Economic Reasoning in Grades 9–12* (Council on Economic Education, 2000). Examples of other compelling questions around which economics curriculum has been developed include, "If we have so many poor people, why don't we just print more money?" and "If trade is such a good thing, why are so many people against it?"

The focus of C3 on process and not explicit content may also be a weakness in terms of advocacy. The focus on process may leave open to political winds the question about what content—indeed, what *disciplines*—to include in standards. The authors note as much in the preamble to the C3 when they state the purpose of the Framework is for 'guidance' and the Framework is merely 'suggestive.' This puts decision-making in the hands of state legislators, boards of education and others who may not value the inquiry process when deciding which content to privilege. As one reviewer of the C3 noted, "social studies content will be left up to the individual states and thus the politically charged hot potato of 'what to teach' is effectively passed on" (Stuart, 2016, n.p.).

Has the C3 Framework Had Measurable Impact on Policy or Implementation?

Perhaps it is too early to tell, and I have not conducted a detailed review of changes to state standards that have occurred since C3 was released in 2013. However, I can point to two informal data sources that suggest there has been little to no impact thus far. In 2011, 22 states required an economics course (or economics content) for high school graduation, and 25 states required that a high school course be offered. The C3 Framework was released in 2013. In 2016, 20 states required an economics course or economic content for high school graduation, and 23 states required that a high school economics course be offered (CEE, 2016). While policy changes in education, especially in state standards, may take years to manifest themselves, it appears that C3 Framework has yet to impact on economics' position at the bottom of the 'big four' pile.

I also conducted an unscientific content analysis of the online program for the 2016 National Council for the Social Studies annual meeting. Searching by subject area generated the total number of sessions cataloged under that subject area, and while there are certainly errors in key word assignment and labeling, it is unlikely these are systematic errors. Search results indicated that 290 sessions were classified as 'history' (213 United States; 77 world); 160 as 'civics/government'; 41 as 'geography'; and 27 as 'economics'. Not only is economics still last of the four key disciplines, but there were almost 11 times as many history sessions. There were nearly six times as many civics/government sessions; this is concerning given the fact that the civics/government course is often paired with the one-semester economics course.

Final Thoughts

Grimes and Millea (2003) found that whether a state has mandated economic education is a function of (1) the infrastructure in place to implement the economics course, as measured by the number of Centers for Economic Education (see http://councilforeconed.org/resources/local-affiliates/) in the state, (2) the state's testing scheme, and (3) the degree of parental involvement (as measured by PTO membership). What these results suggested was that engaging in successful advocacy is a complex, multifaceted task that can benefit from all of the tools outlined above (including C3, of course), but it also requires both relationship and capacity building. To this last point, research indicates that, in general, social studies teachers do not have the background or the capacity to successfully teach the key disciplinary knowledge in economics outlined in the C3.[5] This may also mean that teachers are unable to see the necessary role that economics plays in citizenship education or the connections between economic literacy and effective citizenship. Perhaps one place to start, in terms of building capacity, would be to examine the economic content preparation of future social studies teachers. While certainly no panacea, it may be a first step in creating new advocates for economics' place in the curriculum.

Notes

1 0.5 Carnegie units × 20 states = 10; 134 = total number of mandated Carnegie units in socials studies; 10/134 = 7.46%.

2 Refers to a course in US, world, or state history, but does not include 'history and geography of the world.'
3 Four states have no state level graduation requirements; six states have requirements, but require no explicit content (e.g., history).
4 States mandated a total of 55 Carnegie units in 'history'; 134 = total number of mandated Carnegie units in socials studies; 55/134 = 41.04%.
5 See Miller and VanFossen (2008) and Schug, Dieterle, and Clark (2009) for literature review. Research reveals that, on average, teachers with broad-field social studies licenses take fewer than two college-level economics courses. Schug and Western (2003) found that 72% of these teachers had taken no college-level economics.

References

Atkinson, L. (1982). *Economics, the science of choice.* Burr Ridge, IL: Irwin Professional Publishing.

Council on Economic Education. (2000). *The great economic mysteries book: A guide to teaching economic reasoning in grades 9–12.* New York: Author.

Council on Economic Education. (2010). *Voluntary national content standards in economics.* New York: Author.

Council on Economic Education. (2016). *Survey of the states.* Retrieved October 20, 2016, from http://councilforeconed.org/policy-and-advocacy/survey-of-the-states/

Education Commission of the States. (2015a). *50-State comparison: High school graduation requirements.* Retrieved October 15, 2016, from www.ecs.org/high-school-graduation-requirements/.

Education Commission of the States. (2015b). *State summative assessments: 2015–16 school year.* Retrieved October 15, 2016, from www.ecs.org/state-summative-assessments-2015-16-school-year/.

Grimes, P. W., & Lee, D. O. (2000). Economic education and economic growth. *Atlantic Economic Journal, 28*(4), 490–490.

Grimes, P. W., & Millea, M. J. (2003). Economic education as public policy: The determinants of state-level mandates. *Atlantic Economic Journal, 28*(4), 490–490.

Miller, S. L., & VanFossen, P. J. (2008). Recent research on the teaching and learning of precollegiate economics education. In L. Levstik & C. Tyson (Eds.), *Handbook of research in social studies education* (pp. 284–304). New York: Routledge.

Morton, J. (2005). The interdependence of economic and personal finance education. *Social Education, 69*(2), 66–69.

National Council for the Social Studies. (2013). *College, Career, and Civic Life (C3) framework for social studies state standards.* Retrieved September 1, 2016, from www.socialstudies.org/c3

Rivlin, A. (1999, May). On economic literacy. Speech presented at the *Economic Literacy Conference,* Federal Reserve Bank of Minneapolis, MN. The speech was retrieved from www.federalreserve.gov/boardDocs/speeches/1999/199905132.htm.

Schug, M. C., Dieterle, D. A., & Clark, J. R. (2009). Are high school economics teachers the same as other social studies teachers? The results of a national survey. *Social Education, 72,* 71–75.

Schug, M. C., & Western, R. D. (2003). *Wisconsin public schools: An economics free zone.* Thiensville, WI: Wisconsin Policy Research Institute.

Stuart, D. (2016). *What's the C3 framework, and how does it affect your social studies class?* Retrieved November 3, 2016, from www.davestuartjr.com/c3-framework-common-core-social-studies/

Urban, C., Schmeiser, M., Collins, J. M., & Brown, A. (2015). *State financial education mandates: It's all in the implementation.* Washington, DC: FINRA Investor Education Foundation.

Walstad, W. B. (1998, December). Why it's important to understand economics. *The Region,* 22–26.

Walstad, W. B., & Rebeck, K. (2012). Economics course enrollments in US high schools. *The Journal of Economic Education, 43*(3), 339–347.

Walstad, W. B., & Watts, M. (2015). Perspectives on economics in the school curriculum: coursework, content, and research. *The Journal of Economic Education, 46*(3), 324–339.

Winter, H. (2005). *Trade-offs: An introduction to economic reasoning and social issues.* Chicago, IL: The University of Chicago Press.

Best of Times, Worst of Times: Geography Education Today

Commentary by Sarah Witham Bednarz,
Professor Emerita, Texas A&M University

Poor, Poor Pitiful Me

When I first thought about writing this essay, I kept hearing in my head the refrain "Poor, poor pitiful me." As a geographer working in a social studies world, it has been a challenge to see my discipline represented, respected, or even *included* in a history-dominated domain. The litany of sorrows is long. Geography's position in the curriculum as a strand (at best) of the social studies has always been one of the key challenges in gaining traction for geography in the United States. The subject is just not taught. Perhaps more challenging has been public perception of the discipline as focused on the "principle products of Peru" and knowing capitals. It is more—much more—than trivia or what Gersmehl (2005) called "categorillas," the term coined for knowing the longest, deepest, smallest, or otherwise most exceptional feature in a category, although the National Geographic Society Bee does not do much to allay this impression. We geographers have failed to excite the public imagination or to contribute in significantly open and transparent ways to public policy.

Finally, in terms of education policy, geography was the only discipline not provided any financial resources in the No Child Left Behind (NCLB) legislation in 2001. Geography in the National Goals (passed into Public Law 103–227 as Goals 2000: The Educate America Act) did lead to the development of the National Assessment of Educational Progress (NAEP) assessment in geography and the National Geography Standards (1994, 2012). Unfortunately, the NAEP test has been given sporadically; this has not allowed educators to measure meaningful changes or trends in geographic knowledge. The Standards have provided teachers and curriculum developers with a rich resource and allowed a tighter alignment between academic geography and the school subject. However, it has been loosely and selectively incorporated in state social studies documents. I could continue to list grievances and slights, but in the end, I really think this is not how I feel now. I don't feel pitiful.

Instead, I turn to Dickens who began *A Tale of Two Cities* with the famous line, "It was the best of times, it was the worst of times." Even after the abysmal presidential election of 2016, I feel cautiously optimistic about the discipline of geography and its position in education in the United States. This may be magical thinking on my part, but let me explain. First, I will discuss opportunities for geography right now, then talk about some of the challenges we continue to face.

Best of Times

Geography as a discipline is increasingly valued and respected, particularly because of its two main perspectives, the spatial perspective and the environmental perspective. The spatial perspective drives geographers to document, analyze and explain, "the location, organization, and character of physical and human phenomena on the surface of Earth" (NRC, 2010) and to recognize the importance of spatial variability across a range of scales (Hanson, 2004). The environmental perspective leads geographers to explore relationships between humans and the environments in which they live. Due to the traditional separation of social and physical sciences, other disciplines tend to focus on either human or physical systems. Because geography straddles the social sciences, the humanities, and the physical sciences, the subject brings to bear intellectual frameworks that can help stakeholders address problems facing the world today, notably climate change and ways individuals and societies can develop resiliency and survival strategies in the face of significant environmental changes. In addition, geography offers educators perspectives to teach effectively about some of the key "grand challenges." Not surprisingly, membership in the American Association of Geographers, the major professional association for geographers, currently exceeds 12,000, up from 6,000 in 2000, about 30 percent of whom are international members.

The duality of geography as both a social and physical science (as well as a humanity) is a real niche for geography in the social studies from my perspective. Science teachers are not well prepared or inclined to teach about humans and societies; most history-trained social studies teachers do not have the deep understanding of physical processes that geography-trained teachers do. Exploring the interactions of the world's human and environmental systems at local, regional, and global scales is embedded in the nature of the discipline of geography. Geography, better than any other discipline, can explore the spatial relationships of social and physical phenomena at diverse scales and suggest solutions to significant and persistent problems. Therefore, geography education has a great potential to provide the next generation with the understandings, attitudes, and behaviors required to work for solutions to global problems. This should be an advantage for geography.

Geography was once termed "the art of the mappable" (Haggett, 1990). There is now wide and growing interest in maps, mapping, and visual communication in popular and social media; people increasingly are communicating through spatial representations. Just open the website for any major news outlet like the *New York Times*, CNN, or *The Guardian* to see rich, visually sophisticated presentations on issues ranging from shrinking ice caps (www.cnn.com/2016/11/18/world/sea-ice-arctic-antarctic-lows/index.html) to the best ways to display election results (www.nytimes.com/interactive/2016/11/01/upshot/many-ways-to-map-elec tion-results.html?_r=0). The Atlantic website CityLab even has a section entitled Maps (www.citylab.com/posts/maps/) filled with articles featuring spatial analysis of topics that range from the location of Latinos to the ways climate change is relocating fish populations.

Perhaps the key reason these are good times for geography is the explosion of location-based technologies like geographic information systems (GIS), GPS, and remote sensing. The US Department of Labor has forecast a 29 percent growth in jobs in geography as a consequence (US Department of Labor, 2016). The numbers of majors in geography and geographical information sciences and technology is growing in US colleges and universities. These geospatial technologies, along with the concurrent growth of social media, are changing how we live. As Downs (2014) makes clear, the ubiquity of GIS and associated technologies, particularly mapping technologies, has affected the relationships people have with each other and the world in which they live. Enormous amounts of geographic data are available digitally in real time. We are tracked on closed circuit television systems; we check in to let friends know where we are through Facebook and Four Square; our smartphones track our physical activities and locations. We express our opinions on a range of issues frequently through Twitter, Instagram, and other sharing applications. We report on traffic patterns, complain about neighbors who don't pick up their garbage, and alert authorities about suspicious activities through place-oriented social media. Who we are, where we are, what we do, and how we feel is all shared in geographic contexts. The world is at everyone's fingertips, all the time (Downs, 2014). How does this brave new world affect us as members of society? How is it affecting our roles as citizens and at what scales? What are the challenges and opportunities for geographers in taking a leadership role in preparing the next generation of geospatially literate citizens? These are important questions for social studies educators to consider and best addressed by geography educators.

And lest my enthusiasm and optimism lag, I suggest that another opportunity for geography education exists in the C3 Framework (NCSS, 2013). The framework focus on practices of inquiry moves social studies education away from a transmission model of instruction. It offers geography educators at least two distinct advantages. First, the emphasis on *compelling questions* provides so many opportunities for powerful, integrated instruction that highlight a range of disciplinary perspectives. We can't really understand the world today or become effective citizens by just thinking like a historian or taking an economic perspective or even assuming the spatial and environmental perspectives of geography. Addressing important ideas from a trans-social studies perspective offers an authentic approach to real-world problem solving; this is how we genuinely come to understand things. All too often in education and life we approach topics from only one point of view and miss deepening comprehension as a result. But using compelling questions to drive inquiry offers opportunities to look at a range of factors that affect events, including geography. C3 gives social studies teachers the framework they need to truly teach all the social sciences as well as to explore new and important questions, such as how geospatial technologies and social media affect our roles as participants in a civic society. This may give geography a better chance to be taught and open up the social studies curriculum to truly 21st-century issues and concerns.

A second advantage of the C3 Framework is that it brings social studies education more in line with the practices of inquiry that geography teachers have been following for a number of years. Since the publication of the *Guidelines for Geographic Education* (1984), geography education has focused on helping students acquire skills and emphasized *doing* geography through inquiry, including as often as possible through field work. These skills were then adapted in the *National Geography Standards: Geography for Life* (1994) and continued with additional elaboration in the second edition of the Standards (2012). The skills describe a process of inquiry, asking and answering geographic questions through a process of acquiring, organizing, and analyzing geographic information. One of the key innovations offered in the *Road Map for 21st Century Geography Education* (2013) was a shift in focus from an emphasis on *skills* to an emphasis on the *practices* of geography. The term *practice* better captures the complexity of the behaviors that comprise authentic geographic inquiry and problem solving. Now is an ideal time for geography educators to reach out to our social studies colleagues under the guise of the C3 Framework to help them understand our practices, the ways a geographic perspective can contribute to addressing significant issues, and how to conduct inquiries. This change in educational policy is an entry point for geography education and the practices of geography, including the use of geospatial technologies.

Worst of Times

While there are many opportunities for geography education in general and through implementation of the C3 Framework, there are also significant challenges and growing concerns. In 2015, two United State senators, Patty Murray (D-Washington) and Roy Blunt (R-Missouri), asked the Government Accountability Office (GAO) to investigate "whether K–12 students' skills and exposure to geography are adequate for current and future workforce needs." The results, based on NAEP data and other information, were sobering: about three-quarters of 8th graders are not proficient in geography. The report (www.gao.gov/prod ucts/GAO-16-7) also identified challenges to geography education that were discussed previously: misconceptions about what geography is; a lack of teacher preparation and professional development in geography education; poor-quality geography instructional materials; and limited use of geospatial technologies in the classroom.

The C3 Framework may actually exacerbate some of these concerns and questions. Its implementation appears to be spotty and hit or miss. I have seen high-quality implementation efforts in some places, notably in California and New York, but in my own state of Texas, very little. Of course, there is almost no public-sponsored professional development in the social studies in many states anymore, let alone any coherent, focused drive to help teachers understand key aspects of the framework. This lack of guidance and leadership could make C3 irrelevant, taking away all the positives I noted. Further, the longtime route for social studies teachers to gain professional development in geography, a national alliance network sponsored by the National Geographic Society, is in a period of change. There appears to be almost no activity to support C3 through that source. In such a period of unrest with the Common Core under attack and no clear "next thing," I fear social studies teachers will simply revert to tried and true teaching methods and traditional curriculum, dismissing geospatial technologies, social media, inquiry, or trans-social studies instruction; that is, ignore geography.

Moving Forward

I suggest that we need to seize opportunities to ensure the health of the social studies, but particularly geography education. Geography educators must create a clear vision of what *we* need to do to flourish, working within existing educational policies while meeting the needs of society and the workplace in terms of geographic literacy. We may have to change and look forward and think about what we do in very different ways. Two ways to change may be through collaborations with science teachers and more subversive initiatives within the social studies. Collaborating with our colleagues in the sciences, particularly earth and environmental sciences, may strengthen our abilities to teach in an inquiry-based style. Science educators are more accustomed to asking a question, collecting data, and making evidence-based summaries based on that data than are many classically trained social studies teachers. Science teachers are more comfortable with data-collection and geospatial technologies and can offer assistance to social studies teachers in managing students in technology-rich environments, that is, help them to develop their technological pedagogical content knowledge (Mishra & Koehler, 2006).

A second way to move forward is through what I term subversive initiatives. Too many teachers have ceded the curriculum and ways we teach to higher authorities—the latest educational guru, favored method, ism, or fad. We have lost our ability to connect authentically with students and to be curriculum developers and meaning-makers on our own. It would behoove those of us able to work within the educational system to find ways to subvert it and to return to teachers what should be theirs. Of course, this would mean finding ways to empower educators to take ownership and to lead. More than ever, we need leaders.

Finally, we need partners. A hallmark of the National Geographic Society's Alliance Network when first established was the partnership between classroom teachers and higher education faculty. Through collaboration to promote the quality and quantity of geography education, a synergy developed between the two groups. Faculty had a deeper understanding of the content and practices of geography, but classroom teachers knew how to teach. Together with the National Geographic Society, these allies for geography made (and continue to make) a positive difference. Now we need even more partners, particularly among social science brethren as well as private entities like the business community. Geography has an opportunity through its geospatial technology connections. A collaborative effort, GeoMentors, is a partnership between the American Association of Geographers and Esri, the world's largest geospatial technology company. The program supported the Obama administration's ConnectED Initiative to provide every school in the United States with high-speed wireless connections. To support ConnectED, Esri donated ArcGIS Online access to all K–12 schools. But teachers and curriculum supervisors need support to use this powerful geographic tool. GeoMentors (http://geomentors.net) volunteer to provide this support, working with their community's schools. It is an opportunity to develop a new and enthusiastic cadre of supporters and allies to promote the practices of geography.

In summary, it is the best and worst of times, although from the perspective of writing in the opening weeks of the Trump administration, only the worst is apparent. I am a member of a listserv of geography educators. They are struggling with how to teach their assigned curricula and at the same time help students understand the tumultuous events taking place. In conclusion, the C3 Framework could offer teachers grappling with "truthiness" a solution to the problem. By taking an inquiry approach, looking at facts—real facts, not alternative facts—asking questions, drawing reasoned conclusions, and integrating historical, economic, political, and geographic perspectives, our young people may develop the critical perspectives needed to move us forward as a nation.

References

Bednarz, S. W., Heffron, S. M., & Huynh, N. T. (2013). *A roadmap for 21st century geography education: Geography education research.* Washington, DC: Association of American Geographers.

Downs, R. M. (2014). Coming of age in the geospatial revolution: The geographic self re-defined. *Human Development, 57*, 35–57.

Downs, R. M., & Heffron, S. M. (2012). *Geography for life: National geography standards.* Washington, DC: National Council for Geographic Education.

Geography Education Standards Project. (1994). *Geography for life: National geography standards.* Washington, DC: National Geographic Society.

Gersmehl, P. (2005). *Teaching geography* (2nd ed.) New York: Guildford Press.

Haggett, P. (1990). *The geographer's art*. Oxford: Basil Blackwell.

Hanson, S. (2004). Who are "we"? *Annals of the Association of American Geographers*, 94(4): 715–722.

Joint Committee for Geographic Education. (1984). *Guidelines for geographic education*. Washington, DC: Association of American Geographers and National Council for Geographic Education.

Mishra, P., & Koehler, M. J. (2006). Technological pedagogical content knowledge: A framework for teacher knowledge. *Teachers College Record, 108*(6), 1017–1054. doi:10.1111/j.1467-9620.2006.00684.x.

National Council for the Social Studies (NCSS). (2013). *The College, Career, and Civic Life (C3) framework for social studies state standards: Guidance for enhancing the rigor of K–12 civics, economics, geography, and history*. Silver Spring, MD: NCSS.

National Research Council. (2010). *Understanding the changing planet: Strategic directions for the geographical sciences*. Washington, DC: National Academies Press.

U.S. Department of Labor, Bureau of Labor Statistics. (2016). *Occupational outlook handbook: Geographers*. Retrieved from www.bls.gov/ooh/life-physical-and-social-science/geographers.htm

VanFossen's Response to Bednarz's Commentary

> They appear to take as little note of one another, as any two people, enclosed within the same walls, could. But whether each evermore watches and suspects the other, evermore mistrustful of some great reservation; whether each is evermore prepared at all points for the other, and never to be taken unawares; *what each would give to know how much the other knows* . . .
>
> (Charles Dickens, *Bleak House*)

Sarah Bednarz's informative, and delightfully pithy, outline of the struggle geography education to find a foothold in the American K–12 social studies curriculum turns on the Dickensian literary reference *A Tale of Two Cities*. Indeed, she frames her chapter using the (in)famous opening line: "It was the best of times, it was the worst of times." In this, economics education (my discipline) and geography education are connected in that both share similar struggles for a place at the social studies curriculum table.

However, I'm not so sure the correct Dickens reference isn't *Bleak House*. As the quote above implies, while geography and economics live in the same social studies 'house,' both seem to be hidden—in a way—from a history-centric social studies curriculum. In all honesty, I was surprised to find out that geography, and not economics, was at the bottom of the social studies pile, with approximately half as many students having taken a course in geography as had taken a course in economics.[1]

Second, while all 50 states include geography in their state social studies standards, only 13 mandate a course in geography, or geography content (e.g., in a combined world history/geography course) for high school graduation. Moreover, geography content is tested—at any grade level—in only 12 states, with only

Virginia explicitly testing geography content at the high school level (Brysch, 2014).

A third similarity lies in a misunderstanding of the 'fit' within citizenship education of the two disciplines. Bednarz points out that "geography straddles the social sciences, the humanities, and the physical sciences" and that geographic literacy can "help stakeholders address problems facing the world today, notably climate change." Seems a powerful rationale, yes? And yet, because geography is still often seen as "the art of the mappable" or as simplistic map reading—much as economics is misunderstood as only the study of money and banking—its position within the social studies, and it's role in the preparation of future citizens, remains misunderstood. While Bednarz addresses this issue to some extent when she writes about the "challenges and opportunities for geographers . . . in preparing the next generation of geospatially literate citizens," it still begs the question, *why* must citizens be 'geospatially literate' to be effective citizens in a modern, representative democracy such as ours? In economic education, this has been at least partially addressed by focusing on economic tools for analyzing *all* decisions and developing an 'economic way of thinking.' Perhaps developing students' analog 'geographic way of thinking' might help build this case. Bednarz suggests a list of "geographic data (that) are available digitally in real time . . . Facebook and Four Square; our smartphones track our physical activities and locations," and while I would agree that for geographers the immediate relationship of these examples to 'citizenship' *writ large* is quite evident, I doubt that is true for most people, and particularly for millennials. In this, geography education misses an opportunity to close this loop and make this connection to citizenship explicit and foundational.

Fourth, advocates of both disciplines are concerned with the low level of content preparation of K–12 social studies teachers who teach these courses. Geography (or geography-focused) courses are often taught by teachers with little geographic content knowledge, resulting in "a lack of understanding among teachers into the nature of geography and what best techniques can be put in place to teach the subject" (Brysch, 2014, p. 23). Facilitating the kind of integrative, inquiry-oriented activities suggested by C3 requires *deep* content knowledge. A lack of content knowledge may also mean that teachers are unable to see the necessary role geographic literacy plays in citizenship education and make explicit the connections to effective citizenship. Without such an understanding, geography teachers may lack the capacity to advocate effectively for the discipline. In addition, geography educators without deep content knowledge are less likely, as Bednarz states, "to connect authentically with students and to be curriculum developers and meaning-makers on (their) own"; and advocate for geography (and economics) education. One place to focus attention, then, would be the geographic content preparation of future social studies teachers.

Bednarz and I both have somewhat mixed views on C3's impact on our disciplines' seat at the social studies table. We agree on the potential of C3 for increasing inquiry-oriented teaching (i.e., the 'best of times') within our respective disciplines. As Bednarz writes, the C3 Framework:

> brings social studies education more in line with practices of inquiry that geography teachers have been following for a number of years . . . a process of inquiry, asking and analyzing geographic questions through a process of acquiring, organizing, and analyzing geographic information.

To what degree has C3 impacted geography education? Bednarz places this answer in the 'worst of times'—a characterization I tend to agree with, especially in economic education—because "implementation appears to be spotty and hit or miss" and "there is almost no public-sponsored professional development . . . to help teachers understand key aspects of the framework." This lack of coherent "guidance and leadership could make C3 irrelevant" for geography education. Indeed, as with economics, C3 has had little or no impact on state social studies standards or geography requirements for high school graduation. However, it is also possible that much more is happening in quiet, behind-the-scenes efforts that are not being well publicized. Indeed, it is possible that, to paraphrase Dickens in *Bleak House*, there are two classes of geographic (and economic) educators: "one, the people who did a little and made a great deal of noise; the other, the people who did a great deal and made no noise at all."

To conclude, let me offer one final similarity. I wholeheartedly agree that the disciplines of economics and geography can provide a bulwark within our current political climate by employing the C3's emphasis on data and analysis as a response to questions of 'truthiness.' "By taking an inquiry approach, looking at facts—real facts, not alternative facts—asking questions, drawing reasoned conclusions . . . our young people may develop the critical perspectives needed to move us forward as a nation." What greater charge for future citizens?

Note

1 Walstad and Rebeck (2012) reported that students were much more likely to have taken a course in US history (94%), government (84.3%), world history (81.4%), or economics (56.7%) than geography (28.8%).

References

Brysch, C. (2014). *Status of geography education in the United States: A report for the National Geographic Society Education Foundation*. Washington, DC: National Geographic Education Foundation. Retrieved May 5, 2017, from http://gato-docs.its.txstate.edu/jcr:42d98ff7–42d2–418c . . . /State_of_Geography_Report.pdf

Walstad, W. B., & Rebeck, K. (2012). Economics course enrollments in US high schools. *The Journal of Economic Education, 43*(3), 339–347.

Bednarz's Response
to VanFossen's Commentary

Some of my best friends are economists. My husband is an economic geographer who took many economics courses for his PhD. Paul Krugman, Nobel Laureate in Economics, is a demi-god in my household; we religiously read his columns in the *New York Times* each week and follow him on Twitter. I subscribe to *The Economist*. All of this leads me to believe that geography and economics are very similar—both are "model"-based, conceptual, and theoretical disciplines with strong empirical aspects. Both stand squarely in the realm of science (dismal or not). Both economics and geography have benefitted from borrowing ideas from other disciplines, especially each other, but also from psychology and history. And in terms of status in K–12 education, both economics and geography struggle for the attention of educational decision makers at all levels—from state legislatures and state boards of education who set graduation requirements and approve curricula, to teacher preparation institutions that require only minimal course work in the subjects, to the school districts who refuse to hire subject specialists, preferring teachers with broad preparation able to teach across the social studies. The only advantage we have, as disciplines, is that we are "core" academic subjects while the social studies are not.

My esteemed colleague, Phillip VanFossen, has documented this well for economics. What strikes me as interesting is the way public perception of both of our disciplines appears to keep us marginalized in the curriculum. The general public appears to value economics to inform personal finance decision-making and has come to equate economic literacy with knowing how to obtain your credit score and balance a checkbook. Why else would it be taught frequently in "business" courses? Similarly, the public perceives that the role of geography is to teach students where places are—state capitals and so forth. You just have to follow the cycles of alarm each time someone surveys Americans about their geographic knowledge, measured in terms like, "Where is Afghanistan?" and we turn out to be amazingly (and frighteningly) ignorant. Editorials bemoan the situation; there are calls for improved geography education, and then nothing much happens. And the public watches the annual National Geographic Bee and thinks this is what geography is.

The question then is, How can we break out of these public perceptions and build a deeper understanding of the absolute value of our disciplines with the public and influential decision-makers? Clearly, economics has done a better job of producing public intellectuals than geography has, but I am unclear how that has worked to the benefit of economics education. Have notable economists lobbied for the subject? What is the status of economics educators within the discipline? I know geography educators feel undervalued by the discipline we seek to reproduce. And, I do not think the general public buys into the idea that the purpose of the social studies is to create an educated citizenry prepared to participate in a democratic society. Consequently, this means that the argument linking economic literacy with economic growth may not hold much persuasive value. I have no answer here but think that economists and geographers could benefit from thinking through this dilemma together in order to enhance our status.

And this is where I think that the C3 Framework has something to contribute. It acknowledges the separate modes of thinking of the social sciences in a fresh way. It emphasizes inquiry, a life skill that we should be able to support and encourage through social studies. While VanFossen is not enthusiastic about this aspect of C3, I think it presents a real opportunity for the social studies to become relevant, meaningful, and exciting to young people. It means, however, preparing teachers who know how to conduct inquiries, how to think economically and geographically, and who are not totally history driven. As in all such discussions, it comes back to teacher preparation, both pre-service and in-service, as VanFossen notes. It is unclear to me who is taking responsibility for the dissemination of the C3. But we social studies educators must take responsibility and focus on a plan for how to proceed. Do we need a focused research agenda; a small consortium of teacher preparation institutions to prepare exemplary materials and programs to lead; new forms of online master's degrees or alternative professional development programs for in-service teachers to hone their teaching skills and practices; or a high-level taskforce across disciplines to carry dissemination forward?

I recently reviewed proposals for the National Council for the Social Studies annual meeting. Submissions had to link to an aspect of C3 and it was clear to me that it was not on the radar in any meaningful way of the 15 proposals I read. Perusing these proposals reinforced in me the value of C3 and inquiry. Almost all identified their content as geography but the focus was more on language arts, featured some form of historical thinking, and promised PowerPoint slides to participants. It struck me that the social studies has become a handmaiden of language arts. Where does that leave any disciplinary thinking?

In his final thoughts, VanFossen notes the "complex, multifaceted" nature of advocacy and the relationship between resources and the status of economics education. For geography this is doubly true, especially as our long-time benefactor, the National Geographic Society, is searching for how to move forward in advocacy. I end this response with more questions than answers but with a renewed enthusiasm for the struggle to educate youth to understand their world.

SECTION III

Practices

How Policy Impacts the
Enactment of Curriculum and
Instruction in the Social Studies

7

"SHOULD A STRONGER POLICY EMPHASIS BE PLACED ON DOMAIN-SPECIFIC HIGH-LEVERAGE PRACTICES OR CORE PRACTICES IN HISTORY/SOCIAL STUDIES TEACHING?"

From Defining Content to Supporting Instruction: A Case for Core Practice Policy

Commentary by Brad Fogo, San Francisco State University

For decades, education policy for history-social studies has focused largely on defining what students should know and be able to do, with less attention to how teachers might support student learning. Similarly, as several researchers note, teacher education has prioritized what teachers should know about teaching, rather than preparing teacher candidates to enact teaching practice (e.g., Ball & Forzani, 2009; Grossman, Hammerness, & McDonald, 2009). Recent research on practice-based teacher education calls for greater attention to instructional practice in the training of teachers. At the same time, as part of an academic push for disciplinary approaches to teaching history-social studies, teachers are now tasked to engage students in disciplinary literacy and inquiry-based learning as detailed, respectively, in the Common Core Standards and the C3 (College, Career, and Civic Life) Framework. A stronger policy emphasis, therefore, should be placed on supporting teachers in such ambitious forms of teaching practice.

With that said, it is important to note the pitfalls of endorsing any particular set of instructional practices for history-social studies. For one, the field is well characterized by protracted arguments within and across its various disciplines regarding teaching and learning. There is little agreement about what should be taught in history-social studies classrooms, let alone how it should be taught. Moreover, for many, a focus on teaching practice is suspect, suggesting teacher-dominated, direct instruction and one-size-fits-all practice that disregards context and the diverse learning needs and styles of students. Finally, even within recent practice-based literature, which features promising yet emerging research, there is no strong consensus over what exactly are core teaching practices (see, for example, Peercy & Troyan, 2017).

Nonetheless, in this paper I consider types of teaching practice that might support the literacy- and inquiry-based approaches to learning history-social studies detailed in the Common Core Standards and C3 Framework. To navigate this contested terrain, I first draw from literature on practice-based teacher education to define core teaching practices and discuss them within the framework of pedagogical content knowledge (PCK) (Shulman, 1987). I then focus, in particular, on PCK and instructional practice for the teaching and learning of history. While there is no doubt overlap between effective teaching in history, civics, economics, and geography, the scope of this paper is too limited for a detailed discussion on instruction across the social studies disciplines. Rather, I draw largely from the research on history education, a field that has grown steadily over the past 30 years. Finally, I suggest four possible core practices, grounded in the literature, which might support literacy and inquiry-based history teaching and learning.

Frameworks for Disciplinary Teaching Practice

Practice-based teacher education holds that instructional practice should be the focal point of pre- and in-service teacher education and development. According to the Core Practice Consortium (CPC), a group of educational researchers from leading schools of education, core practices are empirically based "components" of instruction that "teachers enact to support learning." These "consist of strategies, routines, and moves that can be unpacked and learned by teachers" and considered at different grain sizes (CPC, 2016). Core practices can be both generic and subject-specific, with the latter largely determined by disciplinary content and concepts. A fundamental assumption of core practice work is that a "common language" of instruction is necessary to improve teacher education, which, unlike other professions, lacks shared definitions of effective practice (CPC, 2016).

Pam Grossman and colleagues' (2009) model of adult learning encapsulates practice-based teacher education. This model holds that teachers learn best when presented with research-based "representations" of core teaching practices—for example, case studies, model lessons, or video analysis—along with "decompositions" or opportunities to analyze different components of practice. Further, teachers benefit from structured opportunities to practice and receive feedback on different types of instructional practice. These "approximations" might include rehearsals of instruction, such as launching a lesson, or opportunities to practice offering feedback to students.

The core practice literature does not promote one-size-fits-all, generic teaching practice. Rather, advocates for practice-based teacher education stress the complexity and variability of classroom instruction. Pedagogical content knowledge (Shulman, 1987) is a useful framework for this conceptualization of practice. Core teaching practices are, in large part, grounded in the domains of PCK. They are manifestations of a teacher's subject matter knowledge; a teacher's awareness of how different types of students understand disciplinary content, concepts, and skills; and a teacher's ability to select, develop, use, and adjust different instructional strategies and materials to support student learning. In a practice-based approach, teacher education focuses on instances of the latter. Here, novice teachers consider and practice specific instructional strategies to engage students in developing critical and conceptual disciplinary thinking skills. A fundamental assumption of practice-based teacher education is that instances of instruction provide not only a fruitful thought space for considering the interrelationships of subject matter and student learning, but are also connected directly to what teachers actually do in classrooms and set up opportunities for teachers to learn and practice parts of instruction.

One of the central issues of practice-based research is the need to identify and define what instructional practices teacher education and professional development programs should feature. A considerable body of research from the past 30 years informs the different components of PCK for historical literacy and provides rationale for some suggested core practices. As several researchers have noted, subject matter knowledge for such teaching goes beyond knowing historical actors and events to include sophisticated types of historiographical content knowledge for how historical accounts are created, debated, and revised (Bain & Mirel, 2006; Harris & Bain, 2011; Monte-Sano & Budano, 2013). Literature on the teaching and learning of history has also provided detailed descriptions of historical concepts across grade levels, such as cause and effect, continuity and change, and significance (Lee, 2005; Morton & Seixas, 2012), and definitions of critical historical thinking, reading, and writing skills (Wineburg, 2001). This work has helped to define the types of disciplinary literacy detailed in the Common Core Standards. It has also directly influenced the C3 Framework's call for inquiry-based instruction. Moreover, significant research has shed light on how students develop critical historical thinking—namely, how they process historical texts, engage in historical inquiry, understand and misconstrue historical concepts, and demonstrate historical empathy (Davis, Yeager, & Foster, 2001; Lee, 2005; Seixas, 1993; Shemilt, 2000; Voss, Wiley, & Kennet, 1999; Wineburg, 1991). Finally, educational researchers, teacher educators, and teachers have developed telling portraits of disciplinary history teaching (Bain & Mirel, 2006; Fogo, 2014; Stearns, 2000; VanSledright, 2011; Wineburg, 2001). These accounts detail, for example, instruction for engaging students in historical inquiry, using historical questions, modeling historical reading and writing skills, and facilitating historical discussions (Monte-Sano, 2008; Reisman, 2012, 2015).

Possible Core Practices for Teaching History

This work, along with research on literacy development in other disciplines, suggests some possible core teaching practices for history-social studies education. For example, given the policy focus on reading and analyzing primary and secondary texts, evaluating evidence, and developing and presenting argumentation both in writing and speaking, history teachers would benefit from learning teaching practices for *explicit strategy instruction*. These include, for example, cognitive modeling and guided practice (Duke & Pearson, 2002; Kucan & Beck, 1997; Fisher & Frey, 2013). In history classrooms, explicit strategy instruction might involve how a teacher models source analysis when reading a historical document and provides feedback to students as they develop the skill. In a practice-based approach to teacher education, teachers would have opportunities to see examples of modeling, to identify component parts of the practice, consider them in relation to other components of PCK (i.e., student understanding and subject matter), and have opportunities to practice and receive feedback on different components of explicit strategy instruction.

Another possible core practice for teaching history is *facilitating historical discussions*. For one, research across disciplines indicates the value of classroom discussion in student learning. For another, both the Common Core Standards and the C3 Framework call for students to engage in disciplinary discussion across grade levels. And yet, research suggests that discussions are rare in secondary classrooms (Cazden, 2001; Nystrand, Wu, Gamoran, Zeiser, & Long, 2003). Indeed, facilitating discussion is difficult and involves a complex orchestration of helping to elicit and respond to student thinking and supporting student-to-student talk around disciplinary concepts. It is exactly this type of instruction that proponents of practice-based teacher education identify as in need of exemplary representations and opportunities for practice to support teacher learning. A growing body of research on discussion in social studies and history classrooms informs what these representations might involve (Parker, 2003; Hess, 2009; Reisman, 2015; Reisman, Kavanagh, Monte-Sano, Fogo, McGrew, Simmons, & Cipparone, 2017). This work, for example, sheds light on practices for planning discussions and moves involved in eliciting and responding to student thinking while facilitating a discussion.

Given the C3 Framework's focus on inquiry-based learning and research indicating the value of small group instruction, another core practice for history teachers could be *organizing and supporting group work*. Here, one might look to research on complex instruction for a set of instructional practices (Cohen & Lotan, 2014). These could include, for example, how to create heterogeneous groups of students, design group-worthy tasks, create clear and concise task cards for group work, and monitor and provide feedback to group members. In a history classroom, this might feature instructional practices involved in planning, explaining, launching, and facilitating a structured academic controversy (Johnson & Johnson, 1988; Parker & Hess, 2001), where students work in groups of four to analyze, discuss, and attempt to reach consensus around a historical debate or a contentious contemporary issue.

Finally, educational research across grade levels and subject areas indicates the importance of *formative assessment* in supporting student learning (Black &

Wiliam, 2006; William, 2011). While in part embedded within the instruction described above, core practices for formative assessment can be identified, described, and practiced on their own. Such practices involve establishing clear learning objectives, designing and strategically using a variety of assessments that gather relevant and reliable data about student learning, and interpreting and using the data to inform instruction. In a history-social studies methods course, a practiced-based focus on formative assessment might focus on practices for designing reliable assessments of historical thinking, analyzing sample student work to identify student understanding and misconceptions, and using that analysis to plan instruction to support further student learning. Like other core teaching practices, skilled design and use of formative assessment calls for well-developed PCK. Formative assessment practices involve clear understanding of focal content, concepts, and skills; ability to identify and interpret student thinking about disciplinary content; and knowledge of appropriate instruction to address student misconceptions and support further learning.

It is important to stress that these are suggested core teaching practices. The field of core practice research, although promising, is emerging. More work is needed to identify and define core teaching practices and build tools to assist teachers in taking them up. Here, policy might help by supporting such research in history-social studies. Additionally, state policy could go beyond simply identifying content for history-social studies classrooms to also focus resources and credentialing requirements on supporting the development of teachers' pedagogical content knowledge. The new History-Social Science Framework for California Public Schools, adopted in July 2016, marks a promising step in this direction. The new framework, in addition to descriptions of course content, includes new chapters on student learning, instructional strategies, and assessment in history-social science. Such a focus on teaching practice, and the component parts of pedagogical content knowledge, illustrates a departure from lists of content to a policy document more supportive of actual teaching.

References

Bain, R., & Mirel, J. (2006). Setting up camp at the great instructional divide educating beginning history teachers. *Journal of Teacher Education, 57*(3), 212–219.

Ball, D. L., & Forzani, F. M. (2009). The work of teaching and the challenge for teacher education. *Journal of Teacher Education, 60*(5), 497–511.

Black, P., & Wiliam, D. (2006). *Inside the black box: Raising standards through classroom assessment.* West Palm Beach, FL: Learning Sciences International.

Cazden, C. B. (2001). *Classroom discourse: The language of teaching and learning* (2nd ed.). Portsmouth, NH: Heinemann.

Cohen, E. G., & Lotan, R. A. (2014). *Designing groupwork: Strategies for the heterogeneous classroom* (3rd ed.). New York: Teachers College Press.

Core Practice Consortium. (2016). What do we mean by core practice? Retrieved from http://corepracticeconsortium.com/core-practice

Davis, O. L., Yeager, E. A., & Foster, S. J. (2001). *Historical empathy and perspective taking in the social studies*. Lanham, MD: Rowman & Littlefield.

Duke, N., & Pearson, P. D. (2002). Effective practices for developing reading comprehension. In A. E. Farstrup & S. J. Samuels (Eds.), *What research has to say about reading instruction* (3rd ed., pp. 205–241). Newark, DE: International Reading Association.

Fisher, D., & Frey, N. (2013). *Better learning through structured teaching: A framework for the gradual release of responsibility*. Alexandria, VA: ASCD.

Fogo, B. (2014). Core practices for teaching history: The results of a Delphi panel survey. *Theory & Research in Social Education, 42*(2), 151–196.

Grossman, P., Compton, C., Igra, D., Ronfeldt, M., Shahan, E., & Williamson, P. (2009). Teaching practice: A cross-professional perspective. *Teachers College Record, 111*(9), 2055–2100.

Grossman, P., Hammerness, K., & McDonald, M. (2009). Redefining teaching, re-imagining teacher education. *Teachers and Teaching: Theory and Practice, 15*(2), 273–289.

Harris, L. M., & Bain, R. B. (2011). Pedagogical content knowledge for world history teachers: Bridging the gap between knowing and teaching. *American Educator, 35*(2), 13–16.

Hess, D. E. (2009). *Controversy in the classroom: The democratic power of discussion*. New York: Routledge.

Johnson, D. W., & Johnson, R. T. (1988). Critical thinking through structured controversy. *Educational Leadership, 45*(8), 58–64.

Kucan, L., & Beck, I. L. (1997). Thinking aloud and reading comprehension research: Inquiry, instruction, and social interaction. *Review of Educational Research, 67*(3), 271–299.

Lee, P. (2005). Putting principles into practice: Understanding history. In M. S. Donovan (Ed.), *How students learn: History, in the classroom* (pp. 31–79). Washington, DC: The National Academies Press.

Monte-Sano, C. (2008). Qualities of historical writing instruction: A comparative case study of two teachers' practices. *American Educational Research Journal, 45*(4), 1045–1079.

Monte-Sano, C., & Budano, C. (2013). Developing and enacting pedagogical content knowledge for teaching history: An exploration of two novice teachers' growth over three years. *Journal of the Learning Sciences, 22*(2), 171–211.

Nystrand, M., Wu, L. L., Gamoran, A., Zeiser, S., & Long, D. A. (2003). Questions in time: Investigating the structure and dynamics of unfolding classroom discourse. *Discourse Processes, 35*(2), 135–198.

Parker, W. (2003). *Teaching democracy: Unity and diversity in public life* (Vol. 14). New York: Teachers College Press.

Parker, W. C., & Hess, D. (2001). Teaching with and for discussion. *Teaching and Teacher Education, 17*, 273–289.

Peercy, M. M., & Troyan, F. J. (2017). Making transparent the challenges of developing a practice-based pedagogy of teacher education. *Teaching and Teacher Education, 61*, 26–36.

Reisman, A. (2012). Reading like a historian: A document-based history curriculum intervention in urban high schools. *Cognition and Instruction, 30*(1), 171–211.

Reisman, A. (2015). Entering the historical problem space: Whole-class text-based discussion in history class. *Teachers College Record, 117*, 1–44.

Reisman, A., Kavanagh, S. S., Monte-Sano, C., Fogo, B., McGrew, S. C., Cipparone, P., & Simmons, E. (2017). Facilitating whole-class discussions in history: A framework for preparing teacher candidates. *Journal of Teacher Education*, 1–16. doi:10.1177/0022487117707463

Morton, T., & Seixas, P. (2012). *The big six historical thinking concepts*. Scarborough, Canada: Nelson Education Ltd.

Seixas, P. (1993). The community of inquiry as a basis for knowledge and learning: The case of history. *American Educational Research Journal, 30*(2), 305–324.

Shemilt, D. (2000). The Caliph's coin: The currency of narrative frameworks in history teaching. In P. N. Stearns, P. Seixas, & S. Wineburg (Eds.), *Knowing, teaching, and learning history: National and international perspectives* (pp. 83–101). New York: New York University Press.

Shulman, L. (1987). Knowledge and teaching: Foundations of the new reform. *Harvard Educational Review, 57*(1), 1e23.

Stearns, P. (2000). Getting specific about training in historical analysis: A case study in world history. In P. Stearns, P. Seixas, & S. Wineburg (Eds.), *Knowing, teaching, and learning history: National and international perspectives* (pp. 419–436). New York: New York University Press.

VanSledright, B. (2011). *The challenge of rethinking history education: On practices, theories, and policy*. New York: Routledge.

Voss, J. F., Wiley, J., & Kennet, J. (1999). Student perceptions of history and historical concepts. In M. Carretero & J. Voss (Eds.), *Learning and reasoning in history* (pp. 307–330). London: Woburn.

Wiliam, D. (2011). *Embedded formative assessment*. Bloomington, IN: Solution Tree Press.

Wineburg, S. S. (1991). On the reading of historical texts: Notes on the breach between school and academy. *American Educational Research Journal, 28*(3), 495–519.

Wineburg, S. S. (2001). *Historical thinking and other unnatural acts: Charting the future of teaching the past*. Philadelphia, PA: Temple University Press.

"High-Leverage Practices in the Social Studies? Not So Fast": Cautious Considerations for Teaching and Learning Policy

Commentary by Stephanie van Hover,
University of Virginia

My brief response to this question would be: "a *policy* emphasis—no, not yet . . . perhaps never." That before we even begin to consider a policy emphasis, the field has to engage in careful, collaborative (perhaps contentious) discussion about learning outcomes in history/social studies and to identify and research the practices that contribute to student learning. We also have to agree (or disagree) as to what makes a teaching practice discipline-specific or ask whether practices empirically demonstrated to enhance student learning across subjects could be applied to social studies. But before I get too far, my slightly longer response involves pausing to explore the complex—and contested—terms in the question (high-leverage practices/core practices, history/social studies teaching, policy) and to reflect on how the question posed for this chapter surfaces issues and raises questions that should and could lead to generative dialogue about core practice in social studies/history.

High Leverage Practices or Core Practices

Let's say you walk into a classroom where student learning is happening (as measured by multiple, high-quality indicators of student learning). The teacher is engaging in certain practices—instructional actions that are appropriate for the context and that attend to the content learning of students, the skill learning of students, and the socio-emotional/relational needs of students. How do you parse out what is happening? And how do you name those practices? If you invite five people to watch a video of that teacher teaching, will they name that practice, describe that practice, assess that practice in similar ways? How do you 'decompose' or break down the work of the teacher so you can teach someone else how to approximate those practices that are proven to enhance student learning? How can you ensure that the teacher educators (or providers of professional development) possess sufficient expertise to decompose, model, teach, and assess those practices? These complex, important, and difficult questions are being raised (and debated) in the broader field of teacher education and professional development.

The national emphasis on core practices—or high-leverage practices—reflects a shift in the field of teacher education from "what teachers know and believe to a greater focus on what teachers do," (Ball & Forzani, 2009, p. 503) the "core tasks that teachers must execute to help pupils learn (Ball & Forzani, 2009, p. 497). Yet the definitions of these terms continue to be debated—any number of articles and book chapters have been dedicated to conceptualizing, philosophizing, problematizing, and unpacking definitions of 'practice,' 'core practices,' 'ambitious teaching practice,' and 'high-leverage practices.' The Core Practices Consortium (a group of teacher educators from multiple institutions engaging in collaborative research in this area), for example, defines *core practices* in teaching as "identifiable components fundamental to teaching that teachers enact to support learning" and "consist of strategies, routines, and moves that can be unpacked and learned by teachers." These general and content-specific practices are not "a checklist of competencies" or "techniques divorced from principles and theory" (http://core practiceconsortium.com/core-practice). The University of Michigan's *Teaching Works* website identifies *high-leverage practices* as practices that are "used constantly to help students learn important content . . . [and] are central to supporting student development." These practices are high leverage "because they matter to student learning" and are "basic for advancing skill in teaching" (www.teaching works.org/work-of-teaching/high-leverage-practices).

Both definitions highlight the importance of identifying and describing instructional practices that are essential to enhancing student learning and development. Examples include such practices as discussion, eliciting student thinking, and modeling. Proponents of core practices call for rethinking teacher education by shifting to a practice-based curriculum in which preservice teachers are given opportunities to "rehearse and enact discrete components of complex practice in settings of reduced complexity" (Grossman, Hammerness, & McDonald, 2009, p. 283). The idea certainly has power—breaking down a practice proven to enhance student learning and providing preservice and inservice teachers the opportunity to learn the parts of a practice, see it modeled, practice it in/out of context, and receive targeted feedback on quality of implementation.

Yet, some caution that the field of teacher education needs to tread carefully as the work on core practices continues. Zeichner (2012), for example, argues that there is a "danger of scripting of instruction that provides teachers no freedom" (p. 379), a need to attend to the complex contexts in which teachers work, and to be careful not to "imply that all is necessary in teacher education is the mastery of a set of teaching practices" (p. 380). Zeichner also references Pianta's (2011) call for "more rigorous standards for assessing the quality of evidence supporting various models of effective teaching" (Pianta, 2011 cited in Zeichner, 2012, p. 378). It's also evident that a shift to focusing on core practices and practice-based teacher education would require enormous changes in the field, including but not limited to creation of new curricula; generation of a video bank of enacted, high-quality instruction; development of supporting materials; and training for teacher educators so they can engage in and teach these core practices. All who write about this work recognize the complexity and the challenges inherent in this shift from a knowledge-based model of teacher education to a practice-based model. But has the history/social studies field weighed in? What are the core practices or high-leverage practices in our field?

History and Social Studies

While ongoing debates and competing definitions about the term 'social studies' have plagued the field since its inception, the recently published *College, Career, & Civic Life (C3) Framework for Social Studies Standards* (2013) represents an important attempt by the field to coalesce around a shared set of principles to guide instruction. The *C3 Framework (2013)* centers on

> a set of interlocking and mutually reinforcing ideas that feature the four dimensions of informed inquiry in social studies: 1) developing questions and planning inquiries; 2) applying disciplinary concepts and tools; 3) evaluating sources and using evidence; and 4) communicating conclusions and taking informed action.
>
> *(p. 17)*

These goals for student learning are built from research on how students learn but are not core practices. If, however, the field of social studies could agree that these *are* the goals for student learning and could agree on valid assessment(s) that measure whether and what students learn, then these goals could serve as a starting point for (difficult) questions about what instructional practices (supported by research) help students learn the content, skills, and dispositions articulated in the framework.

I would argue, however, that it's an open question as to whether history/social studies requires discipline-specific core practices, or whether the field could look at and adapt core practices identified and researched in the larger world of educational research. For example, one might argue that in order to teach a student to develop a question, a teacher would *model* the process. So we could potentially adopt modeling as a core practice. But then, does modeling how to pose a question in geography, history, or civics look different? If so, in what ways? What are good inquiry questions? How do we know? How do we teach a novice teacher to teach his/her students to create a strong question and plan an inquiry? Do we have a high-quality video library that shows teachers doing this? What are assessment metrics that demonstrate high-quality inquiry teaching practices? These are open questions that need to be discussed by the field, and can lead either to positive, productive conversation or to the potential to fall down the rabbit hole of endless debate and disagreement.

It could be argued that history education, which falls under the umbrella of social studies, is further along with grappling with these questions. History educators Brad Fogo, Chauncey Monte-Sano, and Abby Reisman are participating in the *Core Practices Consortium*. And Fogo (2014) conducted a Delphi study in which researchers, teachers, and teacher educators came to some agreement around a set of teaching practices for historical inquiry:

> use historical questions; select and adapt historical sources; explain and connect historical content; model and support historical reading skills; employ historical evidence; use historical concepts; facilitate discussion of historical topics; model and support historical writing; assess student thinking about history.

> *(p. 176)*

Fogo cautions that identifying these practices is just the beginning, and carefully addresses (and raises) a number of thoughtful and complex questions.

Identification of core practices in history is moving forward but is (much like social studies writ large) hampered by disagreement over the question of student learning outcomes. Seixas and Ercikan (2015) assert that there are three problems confronting the field: (a) lack of clarity about the goals of history education (what knowledge, skills, concepts, competencies, and/or dispositions students should learn) and about the "paths through which students might achieve" those goals; (b) lack of agreement over *how* educators will "know what students know" and "what kinds of tasks and tests" that would allow teachers to know what students know; and (c) questions over what constitutes a valid "indicator of progress" in history education (p. 1). This, I argue, is essential to the field developing core practices—we can list all the instructional practices we want to and engage in endless debates about best practice, but we have to move the field forward by providing high-quality evidence that certain practices are tied to student learning.

We also have to, as noted earlier, debate what makes a core practice specific to history. I had to confront this question when, as part of a Teaching American History (TAH) grant, the project director asked me if I could develop a history-specific observation measure. Working with an employee on the project, Stephen Cotton, and my colleague at Virginia Tech, David Hicks, I spent over a year working to break down research-based history practice into observable behaviors and developing what we called the *Protocol for Assessing the Teaching of History* (PATH). To do this, we exhaustively reviewed the extant literature in teaching history and then watched and pulled apart hundreds of hours of videos collected through the TAH project. We sought input from measurement experts and colleagues in history education. After multiple (as in, I totally lost count) iterations and drafts, we identified six separate dimensions: Lesson Components, Narrative, Interpretation, Sources, Historical Practices, and Comprehension. Under each dimension, we generated indicators and behavioral markers, the specific instructional behaviors or interactions that trained observers look for.

The great challenge in crafting PATH was to take words and concepts that are fundamental to history education—historiography, significance, inquiry, narrative, discussion, chronology, causation, empathy, evidence—and break them down into observable teaching behaviors. As part of the grant, we were able to train coders to reliability. But the instrument is not validated—that is, we haven't conducted sufficient research to claim that if you engage in the practices outlined in this instrument, student learning is enhanced. Why? Because I work in a state that measures student learning with high-stakes, fact recall, multiple-choice tests—assessments that do not reflect best practice in history. And, per state and district policies, we couldn't access teacher-level results, only aggregated school pass rates. And . . . the list is really long but highlights the challenges facing our field. Fundamentally, until we have some agreement on the goals of history education and some agreement on how to assess learning in history education, we might be a bit stuck in terms of core practices. We need goals, assessments, and then a whole lot of research that helps us parse out what teaching practices contribute to student learning in history classrooms.

Do I think PATH includes the core practices necessary for learning in history? Maybe. Maybe not. I'm not entirely convinced that we need a history-specific or social studies–specific list of practices. I'm actually becoming more and more interested in the idea that our field "adopts" the core practices articulated by the *Teaching Works* group of the Core Practices Consortium and then discusses what it means to make them subject specific. In other words, I would caution our field not to talk about core practices in an insular fashion and ignore the larger context. I'm not sure we will move forward as a field or be able to advocate for the core practices we view as essential to teaching and learning history/social studies. And, at the same time, I think our field is ahead of the game in research on the core practice 'discussion' thanks to the work by Diana Hess, Paula McAvoy, Walter Parker, and others. The broader field of education should look at our evidence base as they engage in the hard work of identifying and describing core practices.

Policy

So why not a policy emphasis? In our research on the teaching and learning of history within the standards-based setting of the Commonwealth of Virginia, David Hicks and I often turn to Stephen Ball's work on education policy to frame our work. Ball (2008) defines "big-P policy" as "constructed within the government . . . formal and usually legislated policy" but also notes that "policies are made and remade in many sites, and there are many little-p policies that are formed and enacted within localities and institutions" (p. 7). Education policies are often viewed as a means of positive change, or reform. Ball argues that policies should not be treated as a product, or a stable object, but rather as something that is

> contested, interpreted and enacted in a verity of arenas of practice and the rhetorics, texts, and meanings of policy makers do not always translate directly and obviously into institutional practices. They are inflected, mediated, resisted and misunderstood, or in some cases simply prove unworkable.
>
> *(p. 7)*

My concern? That we do not have a sufficient evidence base to thoughtfully inform policy decisions on core practices, so well-meaning policymakers might try to enact (or impose) their own interpretations and, thus, an unstable or unworkable policy will have been born.

A Brief Conclusion

So, I'm going to pause here and return to the question: Should a stronger policy emphasis be placed on domain-specific high-leverage practices or core practices in history/social studies teaching? My response: no, not yet. Perhaps not ever. Why?

a. Core practices are an interesting idea with the potential to transform teacher preparation so long as we attend to the interactional, contextual, and improvisational nature of teaching and don't lose sight of cultural competencies; but …
b. History/social studies would have to engage in long, difficult, possibly contentious discussions about the goals of the subjects, what student learning outcomes look like, how we measure them in a valid and thoughtful way, and then identify (and research) what core practices contributes to student learning; and
c. As we haven't engaged in those conversations, a policy emphasis might try to push our field down a certain path, one we're not ready for, or to impose a good intention on the field that becomes unworkable and/or unstable.

But it's an important conversation for the field to engage in and should we avoid it, we risk becoming irrelevant, and meaningful change might happen in teacher education without our voice at the table.

References

Ball, D. L., & Forzani, F. M. (2009). The work of teaching and the challenge for teacher education. *Journal of Teacher Education, 60*(5), 497–511. doi:10.1177/0022487109348479

Ball, S. J. (2008). *The education debate.* Bristol: The Policy Press.

Fogo, B. (2014). Core practices for teaching history: The results of a Delphi panel survey. *Theory & Research in Social Education, 42*(2), 151–196. doi:10.1080/00933104.2014.902781.

Grossman, P., Hammerness, K., & McDonald, M. (2009). Redefining teaching, re-imagining teacher education. *Teachers and Teaching: Theory and Practice, 15*(2), 273–289. doi:10.1080/13540600902875340

National Council for the Social Studies (NCSS). (2013). *The College, Career, and Civic Life (C3) framework for social studies state standards: Guidance for enhancing the rigor of K–12 civics, economics, geography, and history.* Silver Spring, MD: NCSS.

Pianta, R. C. (2011). *Teaching children well.* Washington, DC: Center for American Progress.

Seixas, P., & Ercikan, K. (2015). Introduction: The new shape or history assessments. In K. Ercikan & P. Seixas (Eds.), *New directions in assessing historical thinking* (pp. 1–14). New York: Routledge.

van Hover, S., Hicks, D., & Cotton, S. (2012). "Can you make 'historiography' sound more friendly?": Towards construction of a reliable and validated history observation instrument. *The History Teacher, 45*(4), 603–612.

Zeichner, K. (2012). The turn once again toward practice-based teacher education. *Journal of Teacher Education, 63*(5), 376–382.

Fogo's Response to van Hover's Commentary

In reading van Hover's piece, it strikes me that we may share notable common ground regarding core teaching practices. First and foremost, we are both wary of classroom instruction being reduced to narrowly conceptualized scripted practice that does not account for the complexities of teaching and learning. Further, we acknowledge that practice-based teacher education requires a departure from business as usual and calls for, amongst other things, high-quality representations of teaching practice across the social studies disciplines, new curriculum tools for teacher educators to support teacher learners in experiencing and reflecting upon practice, and better assessments of ambitious learning in history-social studies. I agree that such necessities present challenges to the field, and I consider them worthy of the work they demand.

We also agree that the history-social studies community needs to engage in "generative dialogue" about instructional practice. However, and here is where some of our agreement seems to split, I question the need for the field "to engage in long, difficult, perhaps contentious discussions about the goals of the subjects" as a prerequisite for policy supporting practice-based teacher education. Such conversations have characterized the field of history-social studies education through eras of educational reform. Protracted arguments over content have arguably undermined, or at least not supported, quality teaching and learning in history or social studies classrooms (Evans, 2004; Nash, Crabtree, & Dunn, 2000). Moreover, I submit that we are already flush with standards that define "what students should know and be able to do" across history-social studies disciplines. Between the Common Core, the C3 Framework, and the NCSS National Curriculum Standards—not to mention the dozens of state standards and the new behemoth California Framework for History-Social Science—the field has spent adequate time on defining objectives and learning outcomes.

And, while the field may be contentious, I find there is important agreement across these documents concerning some general learning objectives that connect the disciplines. Do we not agree, for example, on the need for students to become critical consumers of information, to investigate questions, evaluate various forms of text, analyze evidence and develop claims; to learn analytical reading, writing, and speaking skills; and to develop and apply conceptual understanding? Is there not general consensus regarding such inquiry- and literacy-focused outcomes? If so, I would argue that this agreement warrants more "policy emphasis" on instruction to support such learning.

Whether there are discipline-specific core teaching practices is an interesting question that calls for further research across the field. The need for such work, however, should not preclude practice-focused teacher education. Here, again, I think it is important to consider instructional practice as more than discrete moves that result in student learning but rather as a central component of pedagogical content knowledge (PCK). Focusing on practice within the framework of PCK allows for different types of subject matter and a variety of learning outcomes. It provides a way to identify how more generic teaching practices (e.g., explicit strategy instruction, facilitating discussion, organizing group work, and formative assessment) might be "discipline specific." Here is another point that van Hover and I seem to agree upon: that the field would benefit from taking up, or at least considering, how core teaching practices in other subject areas might apply to teaching and learning history-social studies content, concepts, and skills.

Moreover, I also agree with van Hover that better assessments of learning across the field are needed. This is particularly the case at the state level, where low-level multiple choice tests have, in many instances, contributed to the construction of state standards that have reduced history and social studies to long lists of names, dates, and phenomena. But, I would argue again, this process does not necessarily need to focus largely on defining learning outcomes. Rather, we might be better served focusing on developing tools and strategies (practices) for formative assessment in relation to what are well-established history-social studies learning objectives. Part of this process involves identifying performance standards for students ("what student learning outcomes look like"), but also involves more research on how students learn, understand, and apply different types of history-social studies content, concepts, and skills, for which better assessments are needed in order to measure.

Finally, and perhaps most importantly for this exercise, I share Dr. van Hover's concern about "well-meaning policymakers" that "might try to enact (or impose) their own interpretations" of instructional practice that results in "unstable or unworkable policy." I think this would be a concern even if there were a critical mass of research regarding a specific set of history-social studies teaching practices, particularly at the "big-P policy" level. It does not take much to imagine state or district policy reducing the complexities of instructional practice to checklists of discrete moves. Based upon the field's track record with state standards and tests, we should be skeptical of such policy levers aimed at influencing classroom instruction.

So what does this mean concerning policy? Perhaps a stronger policy emphasis for high-leverage teaching practice might involve, in part, getting rid of existing history-social studies accountability policies that promote covering wide expanses of content in short periods of time and demonstrating learning through multiple choice tests focused on low-level recall on content. More constructively, I believe there should be a policy emphasis that supports the field in moving beyond defining content and skills to creating resources and tools to support teachers in building their subject matter knowledge across the history-social studies disciplines; developing understanding of how students learn in diverse history-social studies classrooms; and considering, practicing, and receiving feedback on instructional practice that intersects with subject matter and student learning. A renewed policy emphasis is necessary to make the time and resources available for such challenging work.

References

Evans, R. W. (2004). *The social studies wars: What should we teach the children?* New York: Teachers College Press.

Nash, G. B., Crabtree, C. A., & Dunn, R. E. (2000). *History on trial: Culture wars and the teaching of the past.* New York: Vintage Books.

van Hover's Response to Fogo's Commentary

As I read Brad Fogo's excellent piece "From Defining Content to Supporting Instruction: A Case for Core Practice Policy," I kept thinking about the role context plays in how we make sense of the complex interactions between education policy and history/social studies teaching and learning. I live and work in the Commonwealth of Virginia, a state that has proudly eschewed the Common Core Standards (CCS) and, by association, the College, Career, and Civic Life Standards (C3). So much so that about four years ago, when a group of faculty from the University of Virginia were asked to attend a state-level meeting about assessment with elected government officials, we were informed that we should avoid direct reference to the Common Core and instead, if absolutely necessary, could refer to the "movement under way in other states." The Virginia Department of Education website offers a side-by-side comparison of the Virginia Standards of Learning (SOLs) and the CCS, asserting that the SOLs are equally rigorous and identify learning outcomes that prepare all students for college and career readiness.

Yet in history and social science, despite the presence of historical (and social science) thinking skills in the SOLs, the multiple-choice high-stakes assessments measure factual content (van Hover, Hicks, Stoddard, & Lisanti, 2010). Yes, students have to analyze tables, graphs, and images to answer some of these questions but, for the most part, in order to pass these tests they have to know the facts (and be able to read and process information and to engage in test wiseness) (Reich, 2009). Recently, in response to a growing backlash against the sheer number of tests students take each year, the state has convened committees to envision education for the future and that are beginning to promote (in history-social studies) the removal of high-stakes multiple-choice tests in favor of district-developed performance assessments. In a new research project exploring student learning in standards-based settings, we are seeing the complications that ensue when new assessments (performance-based) are added on top of existing testing regimes (multiple-choice tests) (van Hover, Fitzpatrick, Cornett, & Hicks, 2017) and how well-resourced districts are making these changes more nimbly and appropriately than those with less support (both pedagogical and monetary).

So why this background about Virginia? Because I found myself agreeing with everything Fogo wrote *except* the call for a policy emphasis on core practices, perhaps due to my lived (and research) experience in Virginia. I agree with Fogo that education policy has for too long focused on defining what students should know and be able to do and that the transition to CCS and C3 offers an exciting opportunity for shifting the conversation (in participating states). I agree that the practice-based teacher education model has great potential to increase our attention to the interrelationships of teaching practices *and* student learning, which is absolutely vital. Yes, there are pitfalls everywhere in attempting to endorse or identify any "particular set of instructional practices for history-social studies" given the long, complicated history of the field. I concur that attention to pedagogical content knowledge (Shulman, 1987) serves as a useful framework to help think about core practices in history. I also think that Fogo is absolutely correct in suggesting that explicit strategy instruction, facilitating historical discussions, organizing and supporting group work, and formative assessment are core practices that have the potential to support student learning for the purposes of disciplinary literacy and inquiry.

Fogo's discussion of a policy emphasis, however, gave me pause. He argues that "the policy focus on reading and analyzing primary and secondary texts" lends itself to certain core practices and that "policy might help by supporting . . . research in history-social studies" and "go beyond simply identifying content for history-social studies classrooms to also focus resources and credentialing requirements on supporting the development of teachers' pedagogical content knowledge." I agree with the spirit of the statement, but am not optimistic that a policy emphasis could achieve the expected outcomes. Policies (both formal and informal) are constructed and implemented by people, and the unstable and highly contextual nature of policy and policy implementation (see Ball, 2008) means that well-intentioned ideas do not always yield the intended results. I wonder whether changing credentialing requirements would lead to meaningful and impactful change, or whether any policy could be enacted in ways that would actually support the development of teachers' pedagogical content knowledge or promote high-leverage core practices that contribute to student learning. Rather, I would argue that high-stakes assessments do more to drive changes in practice (for better or for worse), which points to the need for high-quality assessment in history-social studies that can create (if they exist) the "right" stakes and help us measure student learning in meaningful ways and build a case for core practices that contribute to student learning.

Thus, I return to the argument that before we initiate a policy emphasis on core practices, the field should engage in conversation to, as suggested by Seixas and Ercikan (2015: (1) "define models of cognition and learning" in history-social studies; (2) "design tasks and assessments" that measure those learning outcomes; and (3) "validate score meaning in those assessments" (p. 1). Some agreement needs to exist as to learning outcomes (CCS, C3, or otherwise) and how to meaningfully assess them to identify and provide empirical support for core practices that support student learning. Perhaps a Core Practices Consortium within our field would be an exciting place to initiate conversation that might lead to meaningful and lasting change in teacher preparation and teacher professional development, and most importantly, increase the focus on student learning in history-social studies.

References

Ball, S. J. (2008). *The education debate*. Bristol: The Policy Press.

Reich, G. A. (2009). Testing historical knowledge: Standards, multiple-choice questions and student reasoning. *Theory and Research in Social Education, 37*(3), 325–360.

Seixas, P., & Ercikan, K. (2015). Introduction: The new shape of history assessments. In K. Ercikan & P. Seixas (Eds.), *New directions in assessing historical thinking* (pp. 1–14). New York: Routledge.

Shulman, L. (1987). Knowledge and teaching: Foundations of the new reform. *Harvard Educational Review, 57*(1), 1–23.

van Hover, S., Fitzpatrick, C., & Hicks, D. (2017, April). Student learning in a standards-based setting: A case of the Byzantine Empire. Paper presented at the annual conference of the *American Educational Research Association*, San Antonio, TX.

van Hover, S., Hicks, D., Stoddard, J., & Lisanti, M. (2010). From a roar to a murmur: Virginia's History and Social Science Standards, 1995 to the present. *Theory and Research in Social Education, 38*(1), 80–113.

8

"WHAT KINDS OF ASSESSMENT POLICIES, PRACTICES, AND TOOLS DO SOCIAL STUDIES LEARNERS AND TEACHERS DESERVE, AND WHY?"

Reframing the Narrative: Research on How Students Learn as the Basis for Assessment Policy

Commentary by Bruce VanSledright,
University of North Carolina at Charlotte

In this chapter, my task is to address the question, What kinds of assessment policies, practices, and tools do social studies learners and teachers deserve, and why? Answering this question turns out to be more complex than at first it would seem, because adults—the ones who make many educational decisions, such as parents, politicians, psychometricians, and administrators—are wont to argue at length, and often vociferously, about what they think learners deserve by way of assessments. For example, many politicians crave accountability, test makers obsess over reliability, parents often focus on fairness, and most teachers fuss over learning (see Madaus, Russell, & Higgins, 2009). The issue of what *learners deserve* is rarely part of the discussion decision makers hold (teachers are typically an afterthought here also). Rather, adults typically argue about what sorts of assessments, policies, and tools *they, themselves, think they deserve.*

One additional adult group needs mentioning—educational researchers. They have posed an array of arguments as they attempt to bring evidence to bear on the assessment question. Recent scholarship has called attention to the importance of formative, diagnostic assessments conducted by teachers regularly in their classrooms (see e.g., Black & Wiliam, 1998; Ercikan & Seixas, 2015; Pellegrino, Chudowsky, & Glaser, 2001; VanSledright, 2014). This work often contrasts sharply with views held by politicians, for example.

What these observations make clear is that, as with so many things, how one answers the question posed depends very much on whom you ask. Who has the right or best policies and prescriptions remains open to debate. For my part in addressing the question, I am predisposed to pursue lines of argument that flow from educational research. My predisposition lies in that fact that I am an educational researcher who has studied the teaching and learning of history for many years. I also have been interested in the role curriculum and standards play in the teaching-learning process. That in turn led me to concerns about assessments, policies, and tools that aid in learning. My argument then is fueled by this research. It focuses especially on what that research says about what social studies teachers and learners deserve, because the research is rooted in the idea that assessment fundamentally needs to cultivate strong learners and promote deep learning. I believe that this argument is the most educationally defensible if we are to take learning seriously.

Understanding What Students Know in Order to Improve Learning

One of the pressing problems with using high-stakes standardized tests for accountability purposes is that they do very little to aid teachers in promoting student learning. When social studies teachers finally see the results of such tests, they are teaching entirely new groups of students (teacher looping practices aside) and can hardly use the results to assist learning difficulties of the students they no longer teach.[1] A second issue has to do with the test items themselves, whose scoring yields the results. They reveal that, say, Jessica scored 68 of 100, but they tell teachers very little about why. A third crucial limit is that, in the press for efficiencies and concerns about reliability and testing costs, they compress an otherwise rich and complex social studies curriculum into bite-size testable bits. Threats to construct validity are the result. In short, they do little to advance learning. More complex assessment practices and tools are available. But they are less efficient to administer and score, and therefore are more expensive. For teachers dedicated to improving learning, and for learners who are curious about their social worlds, the term *deserving* in this context seems deeply ill-suited.

To address these limitations and explore how assessment practice could be used to promote learning, the U.S. National Research Council empaneled an international group of educational assessment specialists and researchers, called the Committee on the Foundations of Assessment. Their lengthy report emerged in 2001 (Pellegrino et al., 2001).

The Committee argued that, for assessment practice to be most useful in promoting learning, it needed to occur frequently in classrooms, be undertaken by teachers, follow a formative (rather than summative) character, and be woven into the fabric of classroom learning practices. Such assessments were comprised of three pillars: cognition, observation, and interpretation. Cognition refers to a learning model that is drawn from the best research available on how students learn a subject (e.g., geography, history)—its pivotal concepts, substantive knowledge, and procedures. The Committee suggested that the model should specify progression in learning, that is, how some concepts and procedures must develop before more complex cognition and subsequent understanding can occur. The more data-based, precise, and detailed the learning model, the more powerful the assessments. The quality of assessments, and their deservedness for learners, rests on the quality of the research-based learning models.

Observation refers to the development and application of assessment tasks that allow teachers to observe ongoing student learning. Performance assessments are favored here because they ask learners to perform what they know, rather than simply state it. Interpretation is the process of making sense of the evidence of student learning (its fullness, partiality, or absence) derived from the tools used for observation. Interpretations of observational evidence can recursively inform the learning model, and therefore speak to students' growing or lagging subject matter cognition. That allows teachers to modify the model and their subsequent teaching practices to improve opportunities for learning from lesson to lesson, if such formative assessment practices are frequent.

Following this practice rigorously allows teachers to systematically diagnose students' learning difficulties, adjust their teaching efforts (e.g., revisiting a concept or procedure that students had not learned well, one on which future learning could depend), and thereby more successfully promote deeper understanding. The view of assessment here is rooted in concerns about validity: Do the assessments provide teachers *and students* with valid information about the development of key subject matter concepts, knowledge, and cognitive procedures? This is why the Committee stressed the importance of a cognitive model for guiding teaching practice, developing useful assessments, and making evidence-based interpretations.

Part of what so seriously limits the deservedness of contemporary high-stakes tests is the deeply impoverished or inchoate learning models that underpin them. A quick examination of tests that appear in released-item form on state education department websites reveals that the guiding learning model seems to be a belief that a learner must master the ability to recall a series of disconnected geographical or economic or historical facts (aka substantive knowledge) (e.g., Reich, 2009). Conceptual or procedural understandings are seldom if at all tested. The research work on learning in history makes repeatedly clear, for example, that conceptual and procedural (or strategic) understandings are crucial to making sense of a subject's substantive knowledge domain. The Committee's work was a concerted effort to redress this fundamental shortcoming.[2]

Cognitive Learning Models in Social Studies

Some arguably succinct learning models in social studies can be found in NCSS's *The College, Career, and Civic Life (C3) Framework for Social Studies State Standards* (National Council for the Social Studies [NCSS], 2013). Social studies teachers, curriculum developers, and specialists who are interested in developing classroom-based formative assessments can consult the C3 document for ideas on learning progressions in civics, economics, geography, and history.

The document lays out four key teaching-learning dimensions for each subject. It grade bands what teachers might expect students to know and be able to do cognitively in each dimension. It thereby implicates learning targets. Assessment tasks could be formulated from the learning progressions these dimensions imply. Elsewhere, I have attempted to articulate a research-based cognitive model specific to history education (VanSledright, 2011, Chapter 4). This model could also be consulted for teaching-learning guidance.

Tools: Observational Tasks and Interpretations of Learning

A number of scholars and organizations have developed observational tools useful for classroom-based assessments in social studies. From a longer list, here are several illustrative examples.

The state of New York endorsed the NCSS C3 Framework and then commissioned a resource toolkit that includes assessment tools that are targeted at classroom learning (see www.c3teachers.org/newyork/). This New York Social Studies Resource Toolkit was designed to build upon and cohere with New York's social studies standards. The approach focuses on asking questions, researching answers, and building evidence-based arguments in civics, economics, geography, and history, while also making classroom observations of those learning outcomes. Social studies teachers looking for assessment tools that they and their students deserve because they focus on learning and understanding social studies might find useable ideas within this toolkit.

The Common Core State Standards in English/Language Arts (CC-ELA) specified an array of learning goals for reading in history. Those goals share much in common with the inquiry approaches found in the C3 Framework. Since a number of states endorsed the CC-ELA, a market arose for organizations to create and sell assessment tools. One of these, the Partnership for Assessment of Readiness for College and Careers (PARCC) attempts to fill this market niche. They state on their website (www.parcconline.org/assessments) that "assessments should work as tools for enhancing teaching and learning. Assessments that are aligned with the new, more rigorous Common Core State Standards help to ensure that every child is on a path to college and career readiness." Because the focus in the history section of the CC-ELA appears linked to the learning models I referenced in the foregoing, the assessments PARCC creates are another potential source for ideas about the types of classroom-based observation tools at least history teachers and their students might find deserving.

The Stanford History Education Group (SHEG) has also entered this market with an array of classroom-based assessments in history, American history in particular (https://beyondthebubble.stanford.edu). Teachers are the principal target users of this work. The assessment tools are designed around research-based learning models in history, typically more explicit than what's found in the assessments of PARCC. The Stanford assessment work also features efforts to establish high levels of construct validity with concepts and procedures found in a history learning model (e.g., Smith & Breakstone, 2015). Related research-based and learning-model-driven assessments in history can also be found at the Centre for Historical Consciousness (CHC), housed at the University of British Columbia (www.cshc.ubc.ca/projects/#assessing_historical).

Using a history-specific learning model in evaluating Teaching American History grant projects over a 10-year period, colleagues and I developed a variety of observational tools applicable to classroom-based, diagnostic assessment. Examples of these tools can be found in two volumes (VanSledright, 2011, 2014). As with the work of SHEG and CHC, a crucial concern of these two volumes centers on how to use observational tools to yield strong evidence-based interpretations of learning. In line with the recommendations of the Committee on the Foundations of Assessment (Pellegrino et al., 2001), the volumes focus heavily on the development of a variety of interpretive scoring rubrics that would be useful to history teachers concerned with deepening their students' learning.

The foregoing illustrative examples are almost entirely history focused. This is intentional. Research-based, empirical learning models in civics, economics, and geography are relatively scarce and underdeveloped largely because *research on learning in these domains* are not on pace with the work in history (or in mathematics, science, or reading/literacy, for that matter). As a result, it remains more difficult to speak clearly about classroom-based assessment tools that are linked to robust learning models in these other social studies subjects. Therefore, to say or point to what assessment practices are more or less deserving for those subjects is, at present, a somewhat uncertain task. I say more about where this concern might lead in what follows.

Implications for Deserving Assessment Policy and Practice

If we accept the argument that the assessments teachers and students deserve are those that are anchored in learning and in guidelines drawn from assessment research (Pellegrino et al., 2001), then at least three implications follow. First, if the social studies community is to continue building research-defensible assessments and subsequently participate in assessment policy debates in meaningful ways, it needs more concerted research on how students learn civics, economics, and geography, and possibly history as well.

If, as the Committee on the Foundations of Assessment maintains, the cognitive/learning model is the pillar on which the other two pillars depend, then teachers and students are not likely to see many useful, deserving tools until the cognition pillar is more firmly developed in each subject. This implicates a significantly reconstituted research focus among those in the social studies research community. By this I mean, for example, that doing research on how prospective and practicing social studies teachers teach history or economics or geography nets us very little *without first extensively researching* how children learn those subjects. After all, what real guidance can social studies teacher educators or curriculum and professional developers offer practitioners about how to teach and assess if they operate from underdeveloped learning models?

Second, without robust learning models in all key social studies subjects and the assessment tools and practices that can flow from them, those in the community are ill-equipped to engage successfully in conversations about policy. To be blunt, with the possible exception of history, the community lacks vigorous *evidence- and learning-model-based* assessment examples to counter the widespread misuse of high-stakes tests as accountability tools. Standardized testing regimes are unlikely to fully disappear, even in a post-NCLB era. However, because such tests yield so little useful data for those who need it the most to improve learning, testing-as-accountability remains a practice vulnerable to deep criticism. Yet, we need much better alternatives if the social studies community has any hope of dislodging that practice's surface appeal.

This leads to a final implication. I want to believe that more deserving assessment tools and practices, those developed and deployed close to where learning occurs and that serve to improve it, could generate enough evidence of their power to create a compelling counter-narrative to the ostensible benefits argued in the accountability story so prized by non-educators. For example, if a social studies teacher gathers rich, diagnostic data about how her students learn and understand, say, geography and history, and she uses it to adjust her teaching practices to systematically improve on that understanding, she then possesses a powerful argument for showing how end-of-year, state-level tests are characteristically weak, suspect, and probably unnecessary by comparison, because they do nothing for all their expense to aid students. Her better approach, tools, and resulting data strike at the heart of the current testing-as-accountability policy delusions. However, in the end, we cannot anticipate such an outcome without more research work on student learning in social studies that can provide her with tools and practices she and her students need to build a compelling counter-narrative.

Notes

1 Efforts have been underway for a number of years to address this problem by having students take high-stakes state-level tests online. The hope is that then the results can be quickly scored and results sent back to schools much more rapidly. This solution, however, does nothing to address the second or third limitations I note next.

2 As a side note, a careful reading of the 2001 report of the Committee shows that all of the many examples they provide to illustrate their three-pillar argument are drawn from mathematics, science, and reading. I was unable to find a single assessment example in

social studies, presumably, in part, because the Committee could not locate learning models robust enough to generate them. I say more about this momentarily.

References

Black, P. J., & Wiliam, D. (1998). Assessment and classroom learning. *Assessment in Education: Principles Policy and Practice, 5*, 7–73.

Ercikan, K., & Seixas, P. (Eds.). (2015). *New directions in assessing historical thinking.* New York: Routledge.

Madaus, G., Russell, M., & Higgins, J. (2009). *The paradoxes of high-states testing: How they affect students, their parents, teachers, principals, schools, and society.* Charlotte, NC: Information Age.

National Council for the Social Studies. (2013). *The College, Career, and Civic Life (C3) framework for social studies state standards.* Silver Spring, MD: Author.

Pellegrino, J. W., Chudowsky, N., & Glaser, R. (Eds.). (2001). *Knowing what students know: The science and design of educational assessment.* Washington, DC: National Academies Press.

Reich, G. A. (2009). Testing historical knowledge: Standards, multiple-choice questions, and student reasoning. *Theory and Research in Social Education, 37*(3), 298–316.

Smith, M., & Breakstone, J. (2015). Historical assessments of thinking: An investigation of cognitive validity. In K. Ercikan & P. Seixas (Eds.), *New directions in assessing historical thinking* (pp. 233–245). New York: Routledge.

VanSledright, B. A. (2011). *The challenge of rethinking history education: On practices, theories, and policy.* New York: Routledge.

VanSledright, B. A. (2014). *Assessing historical thinking and understanding: Innovative designs for new standards.* New York: Routledge.

The Center Fails: Devolving Assessment Authority to Educators

Commentary by Gabriel A. Reich,
Virginia Commonwealth University

Problems

When I think of how to improve assessment policies, I think of the conditions under which educators and learners work and how those conditions could be alleviated so that their experiences together are more meaningful. In my history teaching and education-research experience, classrooms in which students and teachers are engaged in the challenging work of exploring questions that are of some interest to them are better places to be than classrooms in which these conditions are absent. Assessment plays an important role in creating these conditions. Unfortunately, over the past decade and a half, policies have made assessment one of the most unpleasant experiences teachers and students endure, falling short of their promised efficacy (Harman, Boden, Karpenski, & Muchowicz, 2016) and eroding the moral authority of teachers and schools (Nichols & Berliner, 2008).

Policy making and assessment construction are both design processes in which tradeoffs must be made, with each tradeoff representing a choice about which priorities are most important. Currently, assessment policies trade school and teacher power for state and district power, and standardized assessments trade greater reliability for lower validity. Below, I argue that teachers and learners deserve assessment policies in which those tradeoffs, and the values that inform them, are shifted towards greater teacher control and towards a focus on validity over reliability.

Shifting Tradeoffs: Professional Responsibility in Macro- and Micro-Institutional Contexts

Educational systems divide power between the macro- and micro-level institutional contexts. The macro level refers to districts, states, and the federal government. The micro level consists of teachers, students, and schools. Choices about the professional responsibility and decision-making power held at each level involve tradeoffs with profound implications for classroom practice. Current policies place more autonomy for making assessment decisions at the macro level. That facilitates some macro-level public responsibilities, such as ensuring that public education is delivered equitably in all local contexts. This is historically important, because local-level decisions have denied educational opportunities to marginalized students (see Ryan, 2010). By tying assessment to macro-level accountability schemes, however, teachers and learners are presented with one-size-fits-all assessment and accountability. In such a system, teachers have little say in how their students' learning is assessed, and those state-level assessments provide them with little information that can be used to improve the quality of their teaching. Thus, trading assessment over autonomy diminishes the power of teachers to make meaningful decisions that affect their own students' learning. Shifting these tradeoffs may allow stakeholders at the macro and micro levels to perform their duties more effectively.

Schools are publicly funded institutions that operate in the public interest. In regards to assessment and curricula, federal and state departments of education should continue to guide teachers' development of learning goals (e.g., the concepts, content, and skills students should master) and to collect data that allow comparisons of student achievement. The National Assessment of Educational Progress, or NAEP, is a low-stakes test that can measure, albeit crudely, student achievement at the school, district, and state level. A national test is preferable for these purposes because it allows easier comparisons between states, maximizes the efficiency of investment in test development, and is accountable to voters and education stakeholders in a way that private companies with state contracts are not. NAEP results provide policymakers with red flags when and where students are not being served adequately. A more robust national assessment system can provide information on the effects of inequality and the effects of interventions aimed at leveling outcomes at the local level, providing greater potential benefits to educators around the country. I am not suggesting, however, that measurement necessarily leads to improved achievement. Improved achievement occurs in schools where teachers, learners, administrators, and parents share a common purpose and trust that their fellow stakeholders are working towards that purpose.

Teachers and learners spend a lot of their lives in school, and the school atmosphere, be it sound or toxic, affects them deeply. Bryk and Schneider (2002) studied high-poverty schools in Chicago and found that the social well-being of a school had a more significant impact on student achievement than any other factor. Defining well-being as *reciprocal trust*, they found it more likely to exist in schools when stakeholders (teachers, administrators, parents, and students) listen to each other, go beyond their assigned duties, and perform their roles competently and with integrity by holding students' interests most highly. High-stakes accountability policies are predicated on the belief that such trust does not exist, and therefore behavior must be defined with clear goals measured by an authority that is remote from the school context. Thus, high-stakes accountability policies exacerbate the problems in low-trust schools and can erode trust in schools that have built it over time (Nichols & Berliner, 2008). In order to be effective, policymakers must consider how their proposals will impact schools as institutions. By trading some macro-level power for local autonomy, the proposal laid out below is designed to create the conditions in which relational trust can be built.

At the micro level, the classroom, teachers need some measure of autonomy in regards to setting learning goals and designing or selecting how those goals will be assessed and the power to review results and reconsider their practice. Current standardized assessments are not designed to provide teachers with that information (Reich, 2013, 2009; Rothstein, 2004). The reasons for this are technical. Every assessment choice involves a set of tradeoffs (Pellegrino, Chudowsky, & Glaser, 2001). Currently, policymakers have decided to trade accountability for relational trust, as was discussed above, and reliability for validity, an issue I will turn to now.

Shifting Tradeoffs: Reliability and Validity

Baked into current assessment policies is a burdensome concern for the reliability of test results, rather than their validity (Wineburg, 2004). Reliability refers to the extent to which a test will produce similar results when conditions are consistent. The primacy of reliability pushes test designers towards formats and items that discriminate between high and low performers amongst a representative sample of students. Although this is a perfectly legitimate function of a test, an over-reliance on reliability to vet the quality of an assessment leads designers to make choices that can compromise other important functions. For example, it is easier to get reliable results if one radically narrows the definition of the domain being measured and uses test formats that remove uncertainty from grading. In the U.S., this concern has led to an over-reliance on multiple-choice tests.

In the case of history, the value placed on reliability leads standardized-test developers to design exams that measure factual recall rather than other types of historical knowledge, concepts, and/or skills (Wineburg, 2004). It should not be assumed, however, that such measures of knowledge are accurate (Reich, 2009, 2013). Test developers generally do not collect evidence from test takers that would indicate whether or not content knowledge is evoked when answering questions, thus the extent to which scores represent factual recall is unknown (Reich, 2009, 2013). So then, why do we call such tests reliable? The key to understanding that is to consider the extent to which test results conform to social expectations. In other words, if students from wealthy districts outscore students from impoverished ones, social expectations have been met. It is only when *those* expectations are not met that the public outcry leads to a reconsideration of the qualities of the test itself.[1] Thus, the demand for high levels of reliability makes virtues out of sameness, narrowness, and consistently meeting preconceived expectations.

For teachers, however, the virtues of reliability are balanced with a number of other concerns. Amongst those concerns are the alignment of an assessment to learning goals (e.g., factual, conceptual, and skill-based), a level of challenge that is in students' *zone of proximal development* (Vygotsky, 1978), and results that yield information teachers can use to inform their instruction. The technical term for these concerns is *validity*. An assessment policy that prioritizes validity over reliability should place the power to design assessments in the hands of those whose job it is to translate content standards into learning goals that meet their students' needs.

A Possible Solution

Teachers and learners deserve assessment policies that, at the macro level, ensure that history is a key academic subject in all schools and, at the micro level, enhances trust between stakeholders and promotes their engagement with learning. Policies can support such work in several ways. First, a policy can require a certain number of credits for history/social studies, ensuring that all students get exposure. Second, states can require that districts and/or schools design or adopt assessments and hold them accountable through random, periodic audits in which schools must hand over copies of the assessments, reports on student success, and plans to improve instruction. Teachers in many districts are already required to discuss benchmark test scores and provide similar reports. The difference here is that there is more opportunity for teachers to play a role in designing the assessments and framing the results that they report. Capacity is uneven across and within districts, as are norms of practice. Some departments may opt to buy off-the-shelf multiple-choice tests and report on them, but a policy such as this would not require them to do so. Such a policy would give incentives to those educators who are more innovative and more concerned with student learning and the latitude to create assessments more authentically connected to their learning goals. In other words, teachers would have an incentive to engage in the cyclical process of assessment design, a process that has the potential to lead to deeper professional learning and growth towards teacher expertise.

The assessment-design process is an ongoing inquiry cycle into the meaning of curricular goals, the kinds of instruments that will elicit student performances that can be interpreted *vis à vis* those goals, and the interpretation of the results as evidence that students have or have not met the goals (Pellegrino et al., 2001). It is cyclical because the analysis of student work generated by assessments informs refinements to the goals, to the assessment instrument, and to the pedagogy that supports student success.

For example, a middle-school history department may decide that they want to focus on students' use of evidence to support a clear thesis statement. Over the course of several design meetings, they may create a set of assessments given at different points in all three years of middle school and a rubric that attempts to define success at increasing levels of sophistication over those years. It is highly likely that a number of problems will emerge when these assessments are administered. The instructions may be confusing, the assignments may be too difficult or too easy, and the rubric fields may not be clearly delineated from each other. The teacher team will have to review the results of the assessment, in particular strong and weak student performances evoked by it, and consider several possible changes. They can refine the assessment itself, redesign the rubric, and consider different instructional approaches that may be more helpful for students to reach this particular goal. Such conversations will also touch on other issues important to teacher development, such as considering the goals of instruction, what interests and motivates students, and how to make assessment taking a more interesting learning experience for students. Conversations such as the one just described constitute a more effective and fulfilling form of professional development than the models that currently dominate the field.

Conclusion

Currently, assessment policies include a set of tradeoffs that have not led to improved achievement. Assessment policies have reduced teacher control over key curricular and instructional decisions and invested more power with district and state administrators. These policies have also prioritized reliability of assessment devices over the extent to which such devices represent student performances that indicate whether real learning has occurred (i.e., validity). I argue that these tradeoffs should be reversed, that more power in regards to assessment be placed in the hands of districts, schools, and teachers, and that their efforts should be focused on choosing or designing assessments that measure student learning in relation to their priorities. The tradeoffs that I argue for will make it more difficult to compare performance across schools and districts, but this sacrifice may be worth the potential growth in teacher engagement and relational trust among stakeholders. The role of teachers will shift from executing the plans of others with "fidelity" to studying how to meet the needs of their students and designing assessments that provide them with information they can use to improve their practice. This approach can encourage the growth of relational trust within schools as administrators' work shifts from cajoling teachers for test results to ensuring that teachers have time to meet regularly, and that when they do so, they are focused on the work assigned. Web-based educational technology is already in use in many districts, including less-affluent ones, that allows teachers to share not just scores but the actual assessments and rubrics with parents. This transparency can help to build trust with families. Educators, learners, and the public at large deserve assessment policies focused more on learning than on assigning punishments and rewards. This proposal is a modest step in that direction.

Note

1 Examples of this phenomenon are somewhat anecdotal. There are times when marginalized students do well on tests, or when wealthy students do poorly in statistically anomalous ways and there is little public outcry. However, there are a number of cases when anomalous results lead to consequences that differ based on the relative status of the students affected. For example, when students in wealthy suburban towns outside New York City did poorly on new tests of physics and math (Math A Panel & Brosnan, 2003; Winerip, 2003), there was a public outcry and the test scores were thrown out with no negative consequence to the students. On the other hand, when Jaime Escalante's Latino immigrant students did well on the AP calculus exam, the results were questioned by the Educational Testing Service under suspicion that the students cheated. They had to retake the test to prove that they could pass it (Mathews, 1988). In the former case, the problem was understood to be with the test itself, in the latter with the students who took it. As a colleague of mine explained when I was worried how my marginalized and impoverished students would perform on a standardized history exam, "someone's gotta fail. Otherwise they'll say it was too easy."

References

Bryk, A. S., & Schneider, B. L. (2002). *Trust in schools: A core resource for improvement.* New York: Russell Sage Foundation.

Harman, W. G., Boden, C., Karpenski, J., & Muchowicz, N. (2016). No Child Left Behind: A postmortem for Illinois. *Education Policy Analysis Archives, 24*(48), 1–21.

Math A Panel, & Brosnan, W. (2003). *Interim report* (Independent Panel). Albany, NY: New York State Education Department.

Mathews, J. (1988). *Escalante: The best teacher in America.* New York: Henry Holt & Co.

Nichols, S. L., & Berliner, D. (2008). *Collateral damage: How high-stakes testing corrupts America's schools.* Cambridge, MA: Harvard Education Press.

Pellegrino, J. W., Chudowsky, N., & Glaser, R. (Eds.). (2001). *Knowing what students know: The science and design of educational assessment.* Washington, DC: National Academy Press.

Reich, G. A. (2009). Testing historical knowledge: Standards, multiple-choice questions and student reasoning. *Theory and Research in Social Education, 37*(3), 298–316.

Reich, G. A. (2013). Imperfect models, imperfect conclusions: An exploratory study of multiple-choice tests and historical knowledge. *The Journal of Social Studies Research, 37,* 3–16.

Rothstein, R. (2004). We are not ready to assess history performance. *Journal of American History, 90*(4), 1381–1391.

Ryan, J. E. (2010). *Five miles away, a world apart: One city, two schools, and the story of educational opportunity in modern America.* New York: Oxford University Press.

Vygotsky, L. S. (1978). *Mind in society: The development of higher psychological processes.* Cambridge, MA: Harvard University Press.

Wineburg, S. (2004). Crazy for history. *Journal of American History, 12*(29), 1401–1414.

Winerip, M. (2003, October 15). Trail of clues preceded. *The New York Times.*

VanSledright's Response to Reich's Commentary

Early in Gabriel Reich's essay, he introduces the concept of relational trust. He notes that research studies point out that successful schools with high achievement also demonstrate high relational trust among the many stakeholders that comprise the actors. By my lights, this concept and its relationship to testing and assessment policy could hardly be more apt. If relational trust is important for producing deserving assessments and their policies, as Reich and I suspect it is, we need to ask: Why is this relational trust currently in such short supply?

As the last several decades have shown, policymakers—and I am thinking especially of state and federal politicians who are most responsible for current educational policies—have become deeply enamored with school accountability. Standardized tests and the test results they produce have become the vehicle and the evidence. Accountability is simply another name for quality control. Quality control traces its origins to the business world and to management metaphors. How does a large business with many scattered production facilities insure that all its products meet the same exacting standards upon completion? It must have a robust quality control (aka accountability) structure in place that tests and certifies its products against the corporate standard. Quality product control enables advantages in business competitiveness and profits regardless of manufacturing facility, employees, different languages spoken, and local customs, norms, and work ethics.

The simplicity of this model and its built-in business metaphors, vocabulary, and logic possess immediate appeal. Many policymakers, who hail from business backgrounds and business law, appear to have it wired into their discursive circuitry. Therefore, accountability as testing and as product quality control in educational policy should probably not surprise us.

Couple this with an alarmist "educational crisis" literature and you have a recipe for doubling down on efforts to shore up the quality control apparatus.

The crisis literature also has the potent side effect of deepening suspicions among policymakers that educational workers at all levels (but especially teachers and the labor unions that defend and support them) cannot be trusted to produce adequate products (i.e., students) and generate sufficient value (i.e., profits). The deeper the perceived crisis, the more invasive and onerous the policy solutions become.

From this popular neoliberal, business *mentalitie*, we witness a vocabulary and language of teachers as laborers, students as products, schools as manufacturing facilities, school systems as businesses, and education as profit. Testing as quality control is designed to shore up production and subsequent profit by forcing teachers to do better work on the general suspicion shared among many business managers and politicians alike that all laborers are likely to slack off if they are not carefully supervised, disciplined, and incentivized by managers who act as powerful regulators of the process.

Teachers, for their part, seldom talk about their students as products, at least not wittingly. They also like to think of themselves as professionals, able to regulate their conduct and make independent judgments for the educational and socio-emotional benefit of their students. They often work alone among those students and are therefore compelled by classroom culture demands to act on their best interests. They operate *in loco parentis*.

Most teachers talk about their work in academic, supportive, and palliative terms. They liken what they do to caregiving, much the way doctors, social workers, and pastors describe their efforts. They think in terms of best outcomes for children and adolescents. How it turns out is shaped by a range of academic, socio-emotional, and spiritual possibilities. Teachers operate as embedded socio-cultural agents. As caregivers they sit between students and parents and must see to the needs of both, while simultaneously serving the larger communities in which they live. They do not typically speak of themselves as lone product assemblers working for a corporation that makes, say, cleaning products. They see themselves as public servants, willing to assist all who come through the door. They understand their work as a complex human endeavor intricately threaded through the fabric of society, an endeavor that defies simple market-based and business-management quality control solutions (Sandel, 2013). In short, their metaphors and discourse share very little in common with that of policymakers.

My point in this comparison is to show how these two different vocabularies and discourses cannot help but to lead to ongoing relational *distrust*. Teachers tend to believe that policymakers, with their ingrained business mentalities, simply do not get what education is about. Policymakers—trained on a long history of disdain for labor—consider teachers as recalcitrant slackers who need to be externally motivated to be better producers. If they were not, the educational crisis would have long ago disappeared.

Deep suspicion, unvarnished deficit thinking, and the power asymmetries that shape the policy landscape and reinforce distrust are not good ingredients in a recipe for relational trust. Nor are they useful to a process for developing sound assessment policies that teachers and students might deserve (see Cohen & Moffitt, 2009). In this sense, I must disagree with Reich that the assessment control tradeoffs he discusses have much hope of being reversed, even though I share the hope that they might be.

I am maintaining instead that for us to arrive at a place where we witness teachers and students getting the social studies assessments they deserve, they will need different tools and practices, not necessarily different policies per se. Because relational distrust has become so endemic, teachers, with help from those in higher education and in concert with local school systems, will need to work out these new tools and practices largely on their own. As I suggest in my essay, if this reconstituted classroom assessment work succeeds, teachers—those closest to and most knowledgeable about learners—will be equipped with far better quality control data than the paint-deep measures currently employed. Only then will they possess the necessary evidence and outcomes needed to undermine the shiny surface appeal of the simple-minded business solutions driving contemporary policies. And only then will there be real hope for the growth of relational trust and a reversal of tradeoffs.

References

Cohen, D. K., & Moffitt, S. L. (2009). *The ordeal of inequality: Did federal regulation fix the schools*. Cambridge, MA and London: Harvard University Press.

Sandel, M. L. (2013). *What money can't buy: The moral limits of markets*. New York: Farrar, Strauss, & Giroux.

Reich's Response
to VanSledright's Commentary

History/social studies assessment practices are dominated by a very narrow range of tools, such as multiple-choice tests and document-based questions. As the pendulum swings away from mandated end-of-year multiple-choice testing in many states, the question faced by history/social studies educators is how to design assessments that are superior to the ones being abandoned. The truth is that assessment practices have not kept up with other developments in the field, a failure that the Stanford History Education Group (SHEG) has ascribed to a "poverty of imagination" (SHEG, 2017) in history-assessment design.

Bruce VanSledright and I propose using policy to create the conditions under which this poverty of imagination might be challenged and overcome to the benefit of teachers and learners. We are both supportive of a shift in assessment practice towards the iterative design and research process put forth by the National Research Council (Pellegrino et al., 2001) and the value of newer models of assessment that have improved the state-of-the-art in history-assessment design. In particular, we both identify the need for assessments that simultaneously reflect a robust model of disciplinary achievement and meet the needs of teachers and students. A difference that I would like to highlight relates to the locus of control in the assessment-design process in regards to university-based history educators and K–12 teachers.

In framing issues of assessment design, it is important to first consider the nature of the K–12 educator and university educator/researcher divide. VanSledright and colleagues (2011) offer a clear contrast of institutional factors that affect the work-lives and perspectives of these two groups. That contrast has clear implications for how members of each group work with and think about assessment design and the data assessments yield. Researchers tend to be more concerned with educational theory, tend to see K–12 students more abstractly, and can spend a long time considering student-work samples. Teachers, on the other hand, tend to be more concerned with student development and are pressed to grade assessments quickly, but will see multiple examples of student work over the course of a year. These institutional differences lead to different perspective in regards to what assessments should accomplish, how they should be administered, and what they should focus on.

There seem to me to be three ways to approach this gap. One approach is to ignore the gulf and continue on doing basic research and building theory while leaving teachers to their own devices. A second is translational research, in which a model of cognitive development is translated for K–12 teachers and informs professional development and assessment models. A third approach is to work collaboratively with teachers to develop curricula and assessments. None of these approaches is "right" or "wrong" either intellectually or morally, and all provide benefits for the community, but each also has its weaknesses as well.

VanSledright's proposal is most closely related to the translational research approach. This method has been practiced and achieved notable successes, including the design of history assessments (Breakstone, 2014; Ercikan & Seixas, 2015; VanSledright, 2014). These approaches are crucial because they involve scholars with deep knowledge of the cognitive-developmental model of historical thinking/understanding. Their presence helps to temper the role of psychometricians, who tend to be more adept at constructing arguments from assessment data than at constructing assessments that tap into deep disciplinary concepts and skills.

There are two important limitations to the translational research approach, however. The first is that the disciplinary models that such assessments are designed to measure are themselves both limited and hotly contested amongst researchers and between researchers and the public (Ercikan & Seixas, 2015). The second limitation is the assumption that teachers understand, value, and seek to work towards such models of learning with their students. Thus, while they may be rigorous, assessments that emerge from translational research efforts can struggle to bridge the gap between the academy and K–12 education because the needs, goals, and desires of teachers and their students are less central to the design process.

There is much to be gained from a more collaborative approach to assessment design that includes expertise in the area of disciplinary thinking, as well as the expertise of classroom teachers. For the past two years, I have been engaged with local teachers in a project whose aim is to improve the quality of history and social studies assessment. We follow the assessment-design cycle laid out by the National Research Council (Pellegrino et al., 2001). At monthly meetings, teachers present existing and emerging assessment designs and the student work generated by those assessments. All the members of the group—the teachers, myself, and a graduate student—use structured meeting protocols (McDonald, Mohr, Dichter, & McDonald, 2013) to focus the conversation on the elements of the design and how designs might be improved. In that process, there are moments that call for an explanation of specific elements of assessment design or historical thinking. As the university expert in those areas on the team, I will provide such explanations and advocate for the elements that I care more about, such as alignment of assessments to goals that reflect growth in historical thinking. Likewise, there are moments when my ideas are challenged by the teachers for reasons such as class size, district mandates, or the intellectual challenges that their students face. This team approach has its own limitations as well. It is expensive, particularly in terms of the time and effort put in to it, and it impacts only a handful of teachers, albeit more deeply. Time will tell if assessment designs emerge from this process that can rival the innovations being developed by researchers.

The pendulum has swung. Our long experiment with high-stakes testing and accountability schemes is noticeably fraying at the edges. Terms such as "authentic," "rich," and "discipline-based" are now on the lips of policymakers, state and district leaders, and teachers. This is a time of experimentation, and I believe that to overcome our poverty of imagination we will need professionals who bring many different perspectives with them to work towards assessments that provide teachers with actionable information, information that will improve teaching and learning.

References

Breakstone, J. (2014). Try, try, try again: The process of designing new history assessments. *Theory and Research in Social Education, 42*(4), 453–485.

Ercikan, K., & Seixas, P. C. (2015). *New directions in assessing historical thinking.* New York: Routledge.

McDonald, J. P., Mohr, N., Dichter, A., & McDonald, E. C. (2013). *The power of protocols: An educator's guide to better practice* (3rd ed.). New York: Teachers College Press.

Pellegrino, J. W., Chudowsky, N., & Glaser, R. (Eds.). (2001). *Knowing what students know: The science and design of educational assessment.* Washington, DC: National Academies Press.

Stanford History Education Group. (2017). *Beyond the bubble: Our approach.* Retrieved from https://beyondthebubble.stanford.edu/our-approach

VanSledright, B. A. (2014). *Assessing historical thinking and understanding: Innovative designs for new standards.* New York: Routledge.

VanSledright, B., Maggioni, L., & Reddy, K. (2011). Preparing teachers to teach historical thinking? An interplay between professional development programs and school-systems' cultures. Paper presented at the annual meeting of the *College and University Faculty Association of the National Council for Social Studies,* New Orleans, LA.

9

"WHAT ROLES SHOULD FEDERAL AND/OR STATE DEPARTMENTS OF EDUCATION PLAY IN SOCIAL STUDIES LEARNING, TEACHING, AND CURRICULUM?"

Revising Federal Assessment Policy and Reprioritizing Social Studies Education Across States

Commentary by Bruce Lesh, Maryland State Department of Education

Social studies teaching, learning, curriculum, and assessment are, and have always been, contested. Controlling social studies content is associated with perpetuating or impeding beliefs about the nation's founding, the role of religion, the size and nature of government power, and the efficacy of capitalism. As we have seen recently in battles over standards and textbooks in Texas, in debates about American exceptionalism in the Advanced Placement United States History curriculum, and in the Joe Foss Institute's initiative to require all American students to take the United States Citizenship Naturalization Test, social studies remains a flashpoint of the culture wars. But while scholars, leaders, and practitioners have spent decades debating what should be taught and how it should be taught, the reality is that today's core policy problem simply is the survival of our discipline.

Since 2002 and the No Child Left Behind Act (NCLB) and continuing today with the current structure of the Every Student Succeeds Act (ESSA), state policymakers have had to work under the unfortunate reality that "if it isn't tested, it isn't taught." This is especially true in elementary and middle schools, where the federal government requires states and localities to test reading and mathematics once a year from grades 3 through 8, and to test science once in each grade band (i.e., elementary and middle). These specific accountability mandates in math, English, and science leave little room for policymakers to make substantive and impactful decisions regarding social studies. What latitude exists is narrow at best and nonexistent at worst; funding and instructional time flow toward what is measured, and social studies is not being measured. Essential to understanding the policy tools available to state social studies leaders is remembering that instructional time within school days, weeks, and years is finite and monetary resources are limited. When federal policy shifts its emphasis—and since 2002, the emphasis has been away from social studies and towards science, technology, engineering, and mathematics (STEM) and English—school systems must make decisions about how to allocate these two limited educational resources. The current decision to not place social studies within the federal accountability requirements has its origins in the detritus of previous federal policy.

Distortion and Decline at the National Level

It is important to consider the lessons of the last thirty years. The 1990s brought forth an intensification of national interest in social studies education, manifesting in the National Standards for History (NSH). The byproduct of intense, multi-year conversations among K–12 teachers, university historians, and curriculum specialists, the NSH provided clear frameworks for teaching and learning United States and world histories. But in 1995, the United States Senate voted 99–1 in a non-binding "sense of the Senate" resolution to condemn the National History Standards on ideological grounds (Nash, 2000). Although the National Standards for History still exist and are used widely by states and districts to develop curricula, discord over their creation and subsequent denunciation resulted in a lingering politicization of studying the past. History standards have become the third rail of social studies education: attempt to touch what is taught and how, and you will be shocked by the reaction.

Then came the exclusion of social studies from the federally mandated testing required by the reauthorization of the Elementary and Secondary Education Act, commonly referred to as No Child Left Behind (NCLB). Rather than resurface debates over what history should be taught, NCLB's testing requirements focused on English, math, and science. Left out of the federal accountability requirements, social studies was marginalized in the curriculum, leading to a dramatic decline in social studies instruction in schools, particularly at the elementary school level (David, 2011). Money, professional development resources, and new materials for curriculum, instruction, and assessment flowed to tested domains, while social studies educators were left wanting.

The rise and fall of the U.S. Department of Education–funded Teaching American History (TAH) grant program represents an example of how federal funding can elevate one facet of the social studies while simultaneously excluding others. Funded from 2001 through 2011, the TAH program provided three-quarters of a billion dollars to support the teaching of American history only, while other social studies disciplines—economics, geography, and government—lacked comparable resources. Although the overall merits of the TAH program are best addressed in another forum, what is relevant to this argument is that social studies leaders and practitioners have been walking through a proverbial professional desert for years, with little to slake their thirst for legitimacy and growth (Ragland & Woestman, 2010).

In sum, federal involvement in education policy has favored particular disciplines and perpetuated the politicized status of the social studies. In attempting to set national standards and testing requirements and selecting particular disciplines for funding support, the federal government distorts state priorities. The rise of the STEM movement—strengthened by federal investment and supported by the private sector as a workforce preparation generator—corresponds with the decline of the social studies, weakened by resource depletion. State social studies policymakers often are left without monetary resources that could support statewide assessments and professional development, placing them in a position of having to advocate for saving social studies curriculum and instruction. Yet because state departments of education are part of the executive branch of government, employees cannot lobby externally for legislation or work in concert with interest groups to promote the establishment or maintenance of state social studies assessments. The executive branch is in place to enforce existing law. Thus, the only options available to policymakers in state departments of education are to advocate for funding support within their institutions, wait for a legislative response, or hope for a state superintendent of education to use the bully pulpit to draw particular attention to the challenges facing social studies education.

In many states, leaders representing the social studies, the arts, physical education, world languages, and services for English language learners compete for a small pot of professional resources. But because of the visibility brought by the tested subjects, money oftentimes is diverted from the non-tested subjects to English, mathematics, and science. Districts desire professional development for the subjects that will be tested because these subjects will be part of public reporting, media attention, and accountability measures that are used to evaluate teachers, principals, schools, and districts. This exacerbates curriculum narrowing and pits disciplines against one another within a state department of education, in competition for limited funds. These factors explain why a state superintendent of education might be reluctant to advocate for social studies education directly, even if she or he was particularly dedicated to its purposes, practices, and effects.

Consequences of Social Studies Assessment at the State Level

With the absence of federally mandated testing for social studies, the difficulties of securing dedicated funds from state departments of education, and a lack of advocacy from state policymakers, many states simply have eliminated assessment in social studies. Since 2000, Oklahoma, Alabama, Illinois, Maine, New Hampshire, North Carolina, California, Indiana, New Jersey, Virginia, and Maryland have dropped all, or portions, of their social studies assessments (CS4, 2001; Woods,

2016). The worst-case scenario—faced by education leaders in California, Illinois, Alabama, New Hampshire, Indiana, and New Jersey—is to have all existing social studies assessments defunded and ended, while assessments in other domains are bolstered and updated in order to meet federal compliance mandates.

In Maryland, starting in 2001, the state department of education eliminated the Maryland State Performance Assessment Program (MSPAP) for grades 3 through 8. This led to a dramatic reduction of social studies instructional time at the elementary level, while math, English, and science teaching were maintained or increased, in accordance with their status as tested subjects by federal mandate (MSDOE, 2010). In 2008, as a cost-saving measure, Maryland dropped the High School Assessment (HSA) in American government—a test that previously had been required for graduation. Not part of federal accountability regulations, the exam was seen as low-hanging fruit at a time when resources for social studies education were in decline because of the economic recession. The impacts of this decision rippled through schools as class sizes in American government courses increased, staffing for district social studies offices decreased, and money for professional development migrated to the tested subjects. Absent a legal obligation to administer the exam to meet federal accountability requirements via NCLB or ESSA, state social studies professionals were left to advocate within their own agencies for the return of the exam or to wait for a legislative response. Through the efforts of interest groups such as the Maryland Council for the Social Studies and the Maryland Social Studies Advisory Committee, the HSA in American government was brought back in 2012. Seniors graduating in 2016 were the first cohort required to take and pass the test since the graduating class of 2008. This was accomplished by way of a state law that mandates assessment in American government for all high school students and requires the development of a middle school social studies assessment. In Maryland, social studies assessment, at least at the middle and high school levels, is returning to parity with English, mathematics, and science because of legislative actions that, in turn, are enforced by state-level policymakers and impact resource allocations for social studies education in schools.

Colorado's social studies assessment portfolio has fluctuated. In 2009, the state board of education approved a new set of social studies standards, developed by a committee of teachers, university professors, parents, and business leaders and co-chaired by former National Council for the Social Studies president Peggy Altoff and historian Fritz Fischer. Alongside development of the standards, some committee members and education activists pressed Colorado policymakers to commit monetary resources to ensure that history, geography, economics, and civics are taught with fidelity in all classrooms within the state. Simultaneously, the state social studies specialist traveled district to district in an effort to roll out and support adoption of the new standards. Unlike numerous states that left social studies to wither because it was not included in federal accountability mandates, Colorado's educational infrastructure attempted to ensure its survival. That survival has been tenuous, though, due to backlashes against standardized testing. In 2015, Colorado's legislature moved to sample testing in social studies in grades 4 and 7 and eliminated social studies testing at the high school level. The sample-testing data do not provide teachers with suitable evidence for instructional decision-making, and anecdotal reports from social studies educators in Colorado indicate that Colorado districts are deprioritizing social studies learning and teaching. So, despite a strong coalition of support for statewide social studies assessment several years ago, Colorado's current defenses for the discipline seem to be wavering.

Iowa, on the other hand, has never had statewide assessments in social studies. Exacerbated by the federal exclusion of social studies from accountability requirements, social studies at the elementary level in Iowa has atrophied. In a 2015 report, Iowa elementary teachers reported that on average, "social studies instruction only occurs during 5.7% of the instructional week." Only 42.1% of teachers reported in the same study that professional development in social studies had been made available to them in the past three years, and "less than one in five elementary school teachers (12.9%) reported that they had access to social studies professional development" (ISDOE, 2015). Although Iowa maintains, and in fact recently updated, their state social studies standards, the policy options available to Iowa social studies professionals are limited. Monetary resources have shifted to the tested areas, and social studies is left to hope for legislative mandates for assessment at the state or federal levels or to find financial support for professional resources from a pool of funds directed to tested areas.

What Could Be Done?

With the continued diminution of the social studies, particularly in the elementary context, American children may be receiving messages, explicitly or implicitly, that the knowledge and skills associated with our discipline are relatively unimportant. Because federal education policy intentionally privileges three of the traditional core subjects to the disadvantage of social studies, the most significant policy action that must take place is the revision of federal testing requirements. Either the federal mandate that states conduct yearly testing must be removed, or social studies must be placed on the same assessment schedule as science, mathematics, and English. This is an unfortunate compromise because it lends support to the worrisome argument that if it is not tested, it will not be taught; but as the aforementioned state-level cases demonstrate, this is the reality for the social studies.

Absent revised federal mandates for testing to include social studies or the elimination of assessment mandates altogether, my answer to this chapter's overarching central question is that the federal government should set a national expectation that social studies receive equal instructional time when compared to mathematics, science, and English. Although contests over what is taught and how it is taught will remain at state and district levels, the battle for equity among the disciplines could be negotiated by a federal mandate that social studies is taught to every student, every year, in every school. States could decide specific courses, content and learning standards, and assessment schedules, but they could not reduce the amount of time students have to learn social studies. States would be required to report yearly that their districts are teaching social studies in all grades as part of their ESSA plans. To require social studies education would provide state policy professionals with leverage for professional development monies to support social studies teachers, K through 12. States and districts would be free to craft policies that ensure a well-balanced social education, rather than one that is so heavily skewed towards STEM and English. This would remove the current distortions of disciplinary privilege that federal legislation generates as state social studies policymakers, leaders, and practitioners fight to keep social studies relevant.

References

Council of State Social Studies Specialists (CS4). (2001). *National survey of course offerings and testing in social studies, K–12.* Retrieved from https://higherlogicdownload. s3.amazonaws.com/SOCIALSTUDIES/9c660cd9-d474-45c6-86f2-ea70fd3258a7/ UploadedImages/survey2003.pdf

David, J. L. (2011). Research says . . . high stakes testing narrows the curriculum. *Educational Leadership, 68*(6), 78–80.

Iowa State Department of Education (ISDOE). (2015). *Social studies: A call to action: An analysis of survey results of teacher knowledge of social studies instructional practice, curricula, and associated needs.* Retrieved from www.educateiowa.gov/sites/files/ed/documents/ Social%20Studies%20report_11-16-15%20FINAL.pdf

Maryland State Department of Education (MSDOE). (2006). *Task force report on social studies education in Maryland: The challenge and the imperative.* Retrieved from http:// marylandpublicschools.org/about/Documents/DCAA/SocialStudies/SocialStudies TaskforceReport2010.pdf

Nash, G. B. (2000). *History on trial: Culture wars and the teaching of the past.* New York: Vintage Books.

Ragland, R. G., & Woestman, K. A. (Eds.). (2010). *The teaching American history project: Lessons for history educators and historians.* New York: Routledge.

Woods, J. R. (2016). *Education Commission of the States: State summative assessments: 2015–2016 school year.* Retrieved from www.ecs.org/state-summative-assessments- 2015–16-school-year/

When Good Ideas Make Bad Policies: Having the Courage to Change

Commentary by David Gerwin, Queens College/CUNY

It is important to acknowledge, at the outset, the minor, incremental impacts that federal and state education departments have on education, compared to other policy levers. A serious crackdown on poverty and racial segregation in communities and schools likely would produce huge gains in education. Ensuring that each child has preventative medical care, reducing incidences of domestic violence, and lowering incarceration rates all might contribute to sending children to school, ready to learn. That said, I want to make two points here about state education policy related to social studies education. First, good ideas, like strengthening teacher quality, can make bad policy, like laws and rules in New York State (NYS) that restrict prospective teachers' entry into the field. Second, many people in social studies education, including harried higher education faculty and K–12 educators, do not have much access to policymaking, and policymakers themselves face capacity challenges. Consequently, there is good reason for those seeking access to policymaking to collaborate with other stakeholders and press governments to gather data and study policies and their implications in situ, instead of making up their action plans on the fly.

Constraining Entry Into Teacher Education Programs

In April 2012, NYS Governor Andrew Cuomo empaneled a Race-to-the-Top-funded Education Reform Commission, which recommended that all graduate-level teacher education programs require a 3.0 GPA for admission and "use an entry assessment to verify that candidates are academically competitive with other graduate students" (New NY Education Commission, 2014, p. 8). The State University of New York (SUNY) adopted those standards for their teacher education programs. The City University of New York (CUNY)—separate from SUNY, though both receive public funding—committed to maintaining competitive admissions standards, but declined to require applicants to take the Graduate Record Examination (GRE), a commonly used standardized test for graduate-level admissions. Sometime in the overnight hours of March 31 and April 1, 2015, the NYS Legislature passed a package of budget bills that also contained several contentious education policies related to evaluating teachers' performance, awarding tenure, and addressing school "failure" (Harris, 2015). Among the mix of early-morning laws, legislators enacted the commission's recommendations, bypassing the NYS Regents and the legislative hearing process. On-time budgets have been a hallmark of Governor Cuomo's administration, a welcome change from budget bills that routinely were months overdue in New York, but the governor has taken to folding policy deals that might not hold up under normal scrutiny into the budget process, including the following:

> Each institution registered by the [NYS Education] Department with graduate-level teacher and leader education programs shall adopt rigorous selection criteria geared to predicting a candidate's academic success in its program, including but not limited to a minimum score on the Graduate Record Examination or a substantially equivalent admissions examination, as determined by the institution, and achievement of a cumulative grade point average of 3.0 or higher in the candidate's undergraduate program.

The GRE was not designed to measure anything about teaching, so it is hard to understand why it would predict such academic success. However, since teaching candidates have SAT or ACT scores that are below average for all college graduates (Ingersoll, Merrill, & Stuckey, 2014), perhaps this is an effort to strengthen teachers' general academic credentials—a mediocre idea stemming from a good impulse. In practice, the GRE costs $205 and adds nothing to teacher education program admissions decisions. It is simply a tax on prospective candidates and a boon for the GRE's developer, Educational Testing Service (ETS). There are no vouchers or waivers for this exam. The average CUNY student has a family income of $30,000 or less. The cost of teacher certification tests in New York— four of them required before initial certification—has climbed to over $1,000. Further, amidst these barriers to graduate-level teacher education, the legislature made no provision for systematically collecting and interpreting now-required GRE scores to glean any insights about the teacher workforce.

The 3.0 GPA admissions requirement, unlike the GRE, exemplifies a good idea that, when enacted as law, becomes bad policy. Of course, social studies teachers should be academically competent; but there are implications that the law fails to consider. First, it disadvantages prospective teachers who decide to change fields in the midst of their undergraduate programs. Some candidates in this situation score Cs in their first two years of classes, and As and Bs after discovering their callings in history or the social sciences; yet their overall GPAs remain below a 3.0 throughout their undergraduate studies. Second, for some CUNY students, undergraduate education involves a balancing act among academics, family obligations, and work, and one crisis in health care, immigration status, or family circumstance can push them off track. Other potentially successful social studies teachers arrived in the United States during middle or high school and gain English fluency with each passing semester, their grades over time reflecting that growing fluency. A strong academic performance in candidates' last two years provides more significant evidence of readiness for graduate education than an initial year or two of pursuing the wrong major or overcoming challenges in acclimating to college.

Equally troubling, the legislature assumes that students move directly from college into graduate education programs. The law makes no provision for applicants who have been out of school for years, whose undergraduate transcripts no longer represent their potential. My program arranged with our history department to allow such students to enroll in graduate history courses as non-matriculated students, providing them an opportunity to directly demonstrate their ability to succeed in graduate school. Rather than using an undergraduate degree and a GRE as proxies for that success, we constructed a program-relevant assessment of these potential applicants' academic abilities. The new state policy seems to shut the door on this accommodation.

Law schools, business schools, and other graduate programs are free to take into account extenuating circumstances, powerful recommendations, and singular accomplishments when admitting candidates that we are required, by law, to refuse. We have received applications from career-changing lawyers or businesspeople whose undergraduate GPAs, a decade or more old, were below 3.0, yet their graduate GPAs were exceptional and they had significant professional accomplishments. Bizarrely, we have argued with colleagues in the graduate admissions office not to read the word "undergraduate" literally.

The law allows up to 15% of any incoming class exemptions from these criteria—a provision that, I have been told, was won in a brief rearguard action by NYS Assembly Higher Education Committee members. This is an uncertain mechanism for dealing with exceptional cases because it relies on the random number of applications that makes up an "incoming class" in any given admissions period. It takes seven applicants with a GPA above 3.0 to admit one "exceptional" applicant. Rather than making reasoned decisions on a case-by-case basis, the random number and mix of applicants determines my admissions policy. I despise sitting on a deserving application while I await another few applications that might allow me to admit that candidate.

In *The Teacher Wars* (2014), Goldstein points out that, although policymakers may desire that teachers come from the same elite, selective undergraduate institutions that produce doctors and lawyers, the number of teachers needed nationwide dwarfs those in the medical and legal professions, particularly given high attrition rates in the field. A teacher workforce made up entirely of elite graduates is not possible in America's near-term future. Instead, Goldstein points to Shanghai's model of improving teaching: not changing the demographics of their teachers, but rather improving working conditions by ensuring that teachers spend less time alone in front of students and more time planning lessons, observing colleagues, and sharing practices that significantly increase student achievement. Goldstein's data and recommendations present an important corrective to the legislative grandstanding represented by requiring higher admissions standards for graduate teacher education. Further, they expose the drawbacks of legislators' typical efforts to improve teaching without spending money.

What this law and its resultant policies do, above all else, is to thwart entry into teacher education programs and irritate teacher education faculty in New York State, particularly those working with economically disadvantaged and educationally underserved candidates who might make exceptional teachers of similarly disadvantaged and underserved students. The deeply cynical act of stuffing the law into an overnight budget bill, without funding to study the outcomes of this legislation or support its policy implications, telegraphs a lack of interest in any complicated conversation about how admissions standards translate into admissions policies, or about what it takes to strengthen the success of early-career teachers and, in turn, their students. It is the clearest, and simplest, example I can provide of how not to make state policy, based on the alienating and self-defeating impact of taking a genuinely good idea and imposing it as an unfunded, poorly conceptualized, "one size fits all" legal mandate. This is a suitable paradigm for considering the enactment and impact of state education policy, in general.

Constraining Entry Into the Field of Social Studies Teaching

In 2013, in a manner analogous to the legislative process that changed admissions requirements for graduate-level teacher education programs, the NYS Education Department (NYSED) began to require edTPA completion for initial state teaching certification. As part of its 2009 Race to the Top application, NYSED committed to a series of reforms that included new certification examinations, one of which was to be a performance assessment of teaching. Until 2012, that performance assessment was to be developed uniquely for NYS; but then Commissioner John King Jr. (later President Obama's pick for a ten-month stint as US Secretary of Education) decided to adopt the edTPA, developed by Stanford's Center for Assessment, Learning, and Equity (SCALE) and administered by the Pearson Corporation. For NYS teacher educators, the best characterization of edTPA adoption and implementation is "last to the dance, first on the floor."

By contrast, Washington State spent four years piloting edTPA with its teacher education faculty, considering different scoring and consequentiality options and, crucially, collecting data. In 2013, when the National Council for the Social Studies' College and University Faculty Assembly (CUFA) sponsored a panel on edTPA, Terence Beck, a faculty member at the University of Puget Sound, presented discrepancies between scores that candidates' edTPA portfolios received from faculty and those determined by Pearson-monitored national scorers. No such stakeholder buy-in or data analysis efforts took place in NYS.

Instead, NYS piloted a few edTPA portfolios across the state in early 2013—scored entirely by Pearson contractors—and held brief training sessions for teacher education faculty at various state population hubs. The next academic year, candidates across the state were due to submit "consequential" edTPA materials and achieve the highest minimum cut score in the nation or be denied initial certification. In response to popular concerns about the edTPA implementation timeline, the NYS Assembly scheduled a hearing for April 2014. Days before the hearing, the NYS Regents approved a safety net policy that required candidates to submit a scoreable edTPA portfolio to the state for $300, but that allowed them to obtain certification if they failed the edTPA by taking a written certification test that preceded the edTPA, with a statewide pass rate of 99%. That safety net policy was renewed annually for four years, through June 2017.

Regardless of the affordances or constraints of edTPA and with gratitude for whatever role it played in securing $750 million in federal funding during an economic downturn, any policy that still operates under a safety net after four years would have benefitted from a phased introduction. I have served on two NYS edTPA taskforces since the test's initial implementation year, and I can report that we lack particular kinds of data that would enable stakeholders to consider the implications of current edTPA policies and envision future ones. We have pass rates on the exam and we know how many people have taken it, but we do not know how many people have student-taught without submitting an edTPA for certification. Based on program experience at Queens College (Gurl et al., 2016), the edTPA submission rate likely illustrates a greater threat to candidates' equity and access to the teaching field than their actual exam performance. In 2014, after the first year of consequential use, only two social studies candidates who submitted the exam failed it (generating a pass rate over 80%), but fully one third of the students who completed two semesters of student teaching that year had not submitted an edTPA by the following January. The state has not collected such data; nor, during the operation of the safety net, has the state gathered data on how students from the same program compare in their employability, effectiveness, and longevity in the field, holding the variable of edTPA outcomes equal.

There is an ironic correspondence between this disregard for the edTPA's impacts on teachers and the simultaneous ascension of NYSED Commissioner King to US Secretary of Education, which undoubtedly was spurred by the portfolio of reforms he haphazardly enacted in New York, including the edTPA. Statewide, educators and thoughtful members of NYSED have done their best to respond to and document the consequences of these reforms. State policymakers' impulses to mandate, rather than to provide educational agents with regulated options and supports for meeting policy goals and studying their efforts, highlights an aggravation with state and national policy initiatives. Policymakers pay constant lip service to "data-driven decision making," but edTPA policymaking in New York State has been devoid of extensive data collection and analysis. The state's certification management system contains information on what schools candidates attend, their certification areas, their races and ethnicities, and the tests they have taken. It could be an important source of data, though currently, it cannot be queried for research. Four years into the state's edTPA policy, that seems more like an excuse than an explanation.

Collaboration and Empirical Research as Policy Activities

Wilson (2009) envisions a world in which universities and K–12 schools that play roles in teacher education, alongside state departments of education, might "work with teachers to embed promising assessments in teacher preparation pathways and, over time, test the capacity of [these] assessments to predict a new teacher's success in the classroom" (p. 23). I would welcome such an effort. Collaborations that systematically include school partners, managed by larger, statewide (even citywide) bodies that prioritize data analysis and program improvement, would be a welcome departure from current circumstances. Within such a model, state mandates would involve data collection and interpretation rather than specific program requirements, and variations would be sources of empirical interest rather than anxiety.

We might pursue a similar approach to curriculum innovation. In 2014, NYSED allocated $3 million to the NYS Social Studies Toolkit, an ambitious set of curricular and instructional tools—written by NYS teachers and aligned with the C3 Framework's Inquiry Arc—designed to support inquiry-based social studies teaching in K–12 classrooms. (In the interest of full disclosure, I served that project as a paid curriculum reviewer). While resource download data are available, I know of no systemic efforts to study and evaluate Toolkit implementation efforts and outcomes, statewide. This, of course, would require funding, and there are good reasons to have invested all of the Toolkit money in the curriculum effort, as doing so resulted in well-designed, extensively piloted, copyright-cleared materials that are publicly available to any social studies teacher. It would be even better if the project were accompanied by some larger design to study its implementation and consequences for learners. Even still, its success was not grounded in a state mandate, but in collaboration among NYSED, teachers, local districts, and social studies education faculty.

I would like to see states commit resources to intensively study the impacts of policies that affect social studies teaching and teacher education. For example, at least one study of beginning teachers found that even such a basic distinction as "staying" or "quitting" does not effectively capture new teacher outcomes (Cochran-Smith et al., 2012). It seems reasonable, then, that studies might measure differences among teacher education program completion rates, certification exam results, student teaching evaluations, hiring data, and in-service evaluations as ways to interpret the effects of admissions testing, GPA, and certification testing standards. Right now, in NYS, there is no mechanism for following teachers through teacher education programs and into teaching; the legislature did not request such information. The studies that I proposed above would make discussing early-career outcomes with legislators an interesting project.

These kinds of initiatives, grounded in collaboration and serious inquiry, require some degree of stability. For instance, studying the early careers of social studies teachers from program enrollment through the edTPA and into the field means investing in and maintaining pathways to teaching over time, even if some new and exciting reform initiative comes along. Yet state governors and education commissioners serve for relatively short timeframes, and wreaking havoc and disruption within a state may well be rewarded with higher office. It takes restraint and a degree of humility to work with long-term civil servants in education departments, faculty in education programs, and leaders and educators in schools to take slower and smaller—but potentially better—steps.

References

Cochran-Smith, M., McQuillan, P., Mitchell, K., Terrell, D. G., Barnatt, J., D'Souza, L., . . . Gleeson, A. M. (2012). A longitudinal study of teaching practice and early career decisions: A cautionary tale. *American Educational Research Journal, 49*(5), 844–880. Goldstein, D. (2014). *The teacher wars.* New York: Doubleday.

Goldstein, D. (2014). *The teacher wars: A history of America's most embattled profession.* New York, NY: Doubleday.

Gurl, T. J., Caraballo, L., Grey, L., Gunn, J. H., Gerwin, D., & Bembenutty, H. (2016). *Policy, professionalization, privatization, and performance assessment: Affordances and constraints for teacher education programs.* New York: Springer.

Harris, E. (2015, March 31). Cuomo gets deal on tenure and evaluation of teachers. *The New York Times.* Retrieved December 12, 2016, from www.nytimes.com/2015/04/01/nyregion/cuomo-gets-deals-on-tenure-and-evaluations-of-teachers.html

Ingersoll, R., Merrill, L., & Stuckey, D. (2014). *Seven trends: The transformation of the teaching force (CPRE Report #RR-80).* Philadelphia, PA: Consortium for Policy Research in Education, University of Pennsylvania. Retrieved December 13, 2016, from http://repository.upenn.edu/cgi/viewcontent.cgi?article=1003&context=cpre_researchreports

New NY Education Reform Commission. (2014). *Putting students first: Final action plan.* Albany, NY: Author. Retrieved from http://www.governor.ny.gov/sites/governor.ny.gov/files/archive/assets/documents/NewNYEducationReformCommissionFinalActionPlan.pdf

Wilson, S. (2009). Measuring teacher quality for professional entry. In D. Gitomer (Ed.), *Measurement issues and assessment for teaching quality* (pp. 8–29). Thousand Oaks, CA: Sage.

Lesh's Response to Gerwin's Commentary

David Gerwin begins his response to this chapter's central question as follows: "It is important to acknowledge, at the outset, the minor, incremental impacts that federal and state education departments have on education, compared to other policy levers." Although Gerwin notes that this statement is a caveat to his larger arguments about changing policymaking, it represents a distinct difference between our two essays. I agree that other policy levers could have a significant impact on overall educational outcomes; equitable funding, stronger efforts to integrate schools, and greater access to challenging curricula for all kids could move the meter on broad educational outcomes. But the reality is that, with regard to social studies curriculum, instruction, and assessment, specifically—and thus, students' opportunities to learn social studies—federal policy has wrought major and deleterious changes.

As I argued, it is, in fact, policy generated by the U.S. Congress, and fleshed out by the U.S. Department of Education, that has placed social studies in its current fight for survival. Federal directives regarding what subjects are assessed force state departments of education to make difficult decisions regarding the distribution of the finite resources of money and instructional time. Failure to comply with federal directives on assessment places millions of dollars of federal education funding to states at risk. Fearing the loss of funding, states adhere to federal mandates to assess mathematics, science, and English. Because of these decisions—spawned by federal accountability requirements and manifesting in the form of curriculum constriction—social studies is on life support at the elementary level. Unfortunately, the Every Student Succeeds Act portends no great renaissance in social studies education, as it does not change the fundamental calculus of what is required by the federal government to be assessed.

Gerwin makes a strong argument that, too often in public education, solutions to issues become more problematic than the concerns they attempt to resolve. Federal assessment policies and their impacts on access to robust social studies education serve as case in point. The tendency for solutions to educational problems to miss their intended marks is partially due to the architecture of our political system and the presence of multiple entry points for policy construction. Whether it is the federal, state, or local level of government, or the legislative or bureaucratic apparatus within each level, potential solutions to a full range of educational issues come from multiple places, and thus, good ideas can metastasize into convoluted policies. Teachers and educational leaders represented by unions and associations, state legislators with varying degrees of education policy expertise, well-funded lobbying groups seeking to impact legislation, higher education faculty who draw from diverse bases of research, and state departments of education rarely work in unified, cohesive ways when attempting to affect policy, because of ideological differences and political network isolation.

Effective public policy at all levels requires consideration of the competing needs of constituent groups impacted by, and implementing, said policies. Gerwin's example of New York State's efforts to restrict entry into teacher education programs is an example of this. In principle, increasing the academic expectations for candidates entering the teaching profession, in an attempt to strengthen teacher efficacy and teaching quality, makes sense. But in practice, as Gerwin cogently suggests, such policy is loaded with debatable assumptions about how teaching can and should be improved. And a policy that restricts in "one size fits all" fashion, rather than differentiates to uphold a diverse teaching profession, can undermine its own intent to enhance teaching quality. By crafting policy in a way that acknowledges and attempts to meet the conditional needs of school community members, educators, teacher educators and researchers, and state actors, it seems likely that problematic assumptions may be surfaced and checked, and legislation and rules might be enacted in manners that attempt to reconcile the myriad complex problems that could result from their implementation.

Gerwin's argument that K–12 and college/university educators often lack access to policymakers is on point. Further, state education agencies are part of the executive branch of government and typically are not allowed to engage state legislative branches to influence policy. Instead, those agencies focus on implementing laws, usually under stringent conditions, without the ability to advocate for policy changes unless those changes are built into rule-making functions afforded to them. Despite these limitations, in Maryland, a modest attempt to encourage collaborative policy discussions has occurred. The state education department's office of social studies has facilitated meetings that brought together district supervisors, state specialists, social studies researchers, and teacher educators to discuss common issues and generate solutions to roadblocks associated with preparing social studies teachers.

Put differently, state departments of education can be nexuses for connecting a variety of stakeholders in the social studies world. The admittedly small step we have taken here in Maryland could serve as a model of policy action elsewhere, like Gerwin's home state of New York; but nothing will fully ameliorate the fact that state education officials serve "relatively short timeframes" and are limited in their ability to influence the legislature where most educational policy originates. Because of these factors, stakeholder networks looking to influence legislative and bureaucratic activity at state levels, in the interest of powerful social studies education, require persistence, stability, and longevity in their efforts, strategically and operationally.

In closing, I think it is essential that states challenge federal policy when its consequences are to restrict the resources available to states and schools for social studies learning, teaching, and curriculum development. Great opportunities exist to revive and strengthen social studies education at state levels, though as with many education policy issues, state-level efforts vary considerably from one to another. Places where social studies supporters have mobilized, legislators are interested in civic development, and state superintendents are secure advocates of social studies education find more parity with the other core subject areas than those where teachers' unions, among other groups, have rejected state social studies assessments on account of testing fatigue. That said, federal regulations leave many social studies educators in the conflicted and controversial position of advocating for their subject matter's inclusion in the assessment policy landscape while simultaneously wishing they did not have to do so.

Gerwin's Response to Lesh's Commentary

Austerity thinking accepts an underfunded public sphere as inevitable and seeks compromised strategies for making the best of a hostile environment (Fabricant & Brier, 2016). In social studies education, such thinking involves acknowledging minimal funding for professional development and resources and fighting with other disciplines for scarce dollars and time. Forging statewide coalitions to advocate for high-stakes social studies testing follows logically, as untested subjects cannot compete for resources on the same grounds as tested ones.

The 11,295 teachers who responded to the 2010 Survey of the Status of Social Studies affirmed this point (Passe & Fitchett, 2013). Elementary teachers in states without testing reported fewer hours of social studies instruction, and secondary teachers in high-stakes testing states reported more professional development hours. Unfortunately, teachers in testing states also reported having less control over curricular and instructional decisions. Ironically, in states where testing compels more spending on professional learning, the beneficiaries of that learning often are discouraged from pursuing ambitious new content and teaching practices (Patterson, Horner, Chandler, & Dahlgren, 2013).

Meanwhile, during the 2015–2016 school year, 81,389 students failed the New York State (NYS) Global History and Geography (GHG) Regents Examination. Disaggregating the 68% statewide pass rate, we find that pass rates were 50% for African Americans, 56% for Latino/as, 33% for English language learners, and 81% for Whites (NYSDOE, 2017a). The pass rate across New York City (NYC) was 57% (NYSDOE, 2017b). Currently, nearly all students who fail that assessment are denied high school diplomas until they can pass it.

In Bruce Lesh's home state of Maryland, only 75.7% of all high school seniors had passed the mandatory government assessment in 2015; yet, a set of safety net policies allowed 100% of those seniors to meet state graduation requirements (Maryland State Department of Education, 2015). In 2016 and 2017, Maryland

House members and Senators challenged these policies by filing two bills—HB0324 and SB0263, respectively—that would require Maryland students to "take and achieve a passing score on a civics test that consists of the 100 questions used for the civics portion of the naturalization test administered by the U.S. Citizenship and Immigration Services" in order to graduate from high school (Maryland General Assembly, 2016, 2017). These bills, if enacted as laws, would mandate replacement of the current state government assessment and end the use of safety nets for graduation. In its opposition to these bills, the Maryland PTA testified that such an assessment would reduce districts' capacities to set local, contextualized graduation requirements; conflate civic understanding with questions on a naturalization test; and potentially reduce the graduation rates of minority, immigrant, and poor children, similar to the effects of the GHG Regents Examination in New York (Maryland PTA, 2016).

The bottom lines are that (1) high-stakes, state-level graduation exams in civics and history are not going to bring back elementary social studies or direct more local resources toward powerful curriculum and instruction across the social studies disciplines; and (2) "to pass a lousy test in order to graduate from high school" is not a good answer to "why study human society?" Bruce Lesh knows this, as the author of a popular book that advocates in-depth historical inquiry (Lesh, 2011). That is why I am surprised by the position he took on federal and state policy in this chapter. He describes how the elimination of social studies testing led to increased class sizes in civics, reductions in district social studies staffing, and an outflow of professional development dollars to tested subjects—serious problems that he faces daily and that concern us all. He backs a test-centric solution out of desperation, in response to deteriorating conditions in public education, fundamentally accepting the premise of austerity thinking. This is a position I oppose.

Rather than focusing primarily on fighting for a larger slice of a vanishing pie, we need coalitions that situate social studies within a broader push to restore public funding for education, across all levels of government. As of this writing, the proposed executive federal budget for 2017–2018 eliminates the National Endowments for the Arts and Humanities; US Education Secretary Betsy DeVos seeks to shift federal resources toward charters and school privatization initiatives; the *Janus v. AFSCME* court case threatens to nationalize a "right to work" model for all public employee unions—including teachers' unions supportive of social studies education; and the State University of New York trustees recently voted to let charter chains issue their own teaching credentials after just thirty hours of supervised field work and a few courses—allowing those organizations to bypass state and national credentialing and accreditation rules. Austerity and privatization threaten material protections for educators and the communities they serve. They close spaces for public discourse and reduce people's collective capacities to advocate for public goods. They must be called out and confronted.

Despite these circumstances, student interest in social studies education surged this year in NYC, a hopeful development. President Trump issues daily statements and orders in ways that drive students to seek out their social studies teachers, providing a measure of vitality that teachers welcome, even as it becomes harder to prepare for state exams. Students scramble to understand how the 14th Amendment works, how federal judges can block an immigration ban without being fired, and what justifies impeachment proceedings. Undocumented immigrants and their children besiege social studies educators with questions about the effects of Trump's policies on their lives. Meanwhile, I hear anecdotally that social studies departments in affluent suburbs are shrinking as middle- and upper-middle-class students (and their parents) select math and science electives with their eyes on high-paying careers in a precarious economy. The contrast between vulnerable students seeking civic engagement while better-off students shun the humanities for "college and career readiness" further complicates the policy environment.

A stronger foundation for social studies would involve joining rather than competing with other subject areas. In the 1960s and 1970s, a considerable amount of social studies funding came from the National Science Foundation and was directed at projects in the social sciences. Currently, climate change is a scientific, cultural-psychological, and civic problem—and as past and present debates over global warming demonstrate, it is a problem best understood in historical context. Conversations about "big data" and its value to humanity are happening in mathematics, economics, and psychology. The arts have always been integral to understanding, discussing, and rethinking social problems. High-stakes tests will not advance the cross-disciplinary creativity and resources needed, at national and state levels, to address contemporary social problems through public education. They will not slow the campaigns of austerity and privatization. They will not "save" anything.

Bruce Lesh correctly anticipates a difficult time for social studies education in federal and state policy—budgetary policy, specifically—but that is a minor symptom of a major condition: public austerity in the interest of privatization. The entire sector of public education, including K–12 and higher education, is under assault, both materially and conceptually, and to narrowly advocate for state social studies testing is to concede that battle. Coalitions across disciplines, educational settings, and associations must organize to advance, in federal and state policy, a vision of education that emphasizes our common future, anticipates common problems, and preserves public scholarship and spaces for social, civic, and artistic activity. Our mobilization must be as compelling and inclusive as the assault is deadly.

References

Fabricant, M., & Brier, S. (2016). *Austerity blues: Fighting for the soul of public higher education.* Baltimore, MD: JHU Press.

Lesh, B. A. (2011). *Why won't you just tell us the answer? Teaching historical thinking in grades 7–12.* Portland, ME: Stenhouse.

Maryland General Assembly, Department of Legislative Services. (2016). *Fiscal and policy note HB 324 education—Maryland High School Diploma—civics test requirement*. Retrieved from http://mgaleg.maryland.gov/2016RS/fnotes/bil_0004/hb0324.pdf

Maryland General Assembly, Department of Legislative Services. (2017). *Fiscal and policy note SB 263 education—Maryland High School Diploma—civics test requirement*. Retrieved from http://mgaleg.maryland.gov/2017rs/fnotes/bil_0003/sb0263.pdf

Maryland PTA. (2016, February 11). *Testimony submitted for the record to the Maryland house ways and means committee for the hearing on education—Maryland High School Diploma— civics test requirement (HB 324)*. Retrieved from www.mdpta.org/bridge_legislation.html

Maryland State Department of Education. (2015). *2015 HSA test performance status*. Retrieved from http://mdk12.msde.maryland.gov/data/HSA/TestPerformanceStatus.aspx?Nav=1.5:5.1:10.99:15.12

New York State Department of Education. (2017a). *New York state report card 2015–16, global history and geography results*. Retrieved from https://data.nysed.gov/reportcard.php?instid=800000081568&year=2016&createreport=1&regents=1

New York State Department of Education. (2017b). *New York city report card 2015–16, global history and geography results*. Retrieved from https://data.nysed.gov/reportcard.php?instid=7889678368&year=2016&createreport=1&regents=1

Passe, J., & Fitchett, P. G. (2013). *The status of social studies: Views from the field*. Charlotte, NC: Information Age.

Patterson, N., Horner, S. L., Chandler, P., & Dhalgren, R. (2013). Who is at the gate? In J. Passe & P. G. Fitchett (Eds.), *The status of social studies: Views from the field* (pp. 289–300). Charlotte, NC: Information Age.

Advocacy

Policy Activity and Activism Among Teachers, Teacher Educators, and Researchers in the Social Studies

10

"WHAT POLICY PRIORITIES SHOULD SOCIAL STUDIES EDUCATION, AS A FIELD, ADVOCATE, AND WHY?"

Prioritizing Policy in the Social Studies: Orientation, Context, and Criteria

Commentary by Todd Dinkelman, University of Georgia

What policy priorities should social studies education advocate and why? Coming at this question as an interested observer, not a scholar, of educational policy left me struggling to even make sense of what the query entails. The realm of educational policy can seem a multi-level house of mirrors. Nearly everyone has ideas about what would make schools better, and nearly all of these ideas reflect and suggest policies. In the United States, education policy issues implicate federal, state, local, and classroom authorities, including, of course, individual teachers. Policies interact in complex ways in different contexts; they develop and change over time, serve some more than others, and support and shape systems of schooling. Some policies drive educational decision-making; others are ignored, unnoticed, and resisted. Few would argue that policy does not matter, this much is clear. Beyond that, the question is complicated.

Orientation: Creating Conditions for Meaningful, Democratic Learning and Teaching

Realizing that policymakers intend their policies to *do* something, I decided to approach this chapter's question by asking what I would like social studies policies to accomplish. The simple answer is that I would like to see policies move the social studies closer to fulfilling the democratic-educational promise that has long centered the field. For me, this means social studies would provide teachers and students with more and better opportunities to come together for meaningful learning around important content and social practices. Meaningful learning makes use of diverse knowledge, draws students into active engagement with powerful questions and problems, and develops critical thinking. Important social studies content not only resides in social science disciplines, but also looks to persistent social issues, matters of social justice and equity, and arguments about how power works and in whose interests. I want social studies to cultivate democratic ways of listening, talking, doing, and being among students. As policies require visions of enactment and consequence, this vision for social studies centers the policy orientation I employ in this chapter.

Another consideration grounds my approach to the policy question. I recently met a part-time graduate student and full-time social studies teacher in a research seminar I offered. Aubrey Jackson arranged to end her school day early so she could make the weekly three-hour drive to campus for the start of our class. I was impressed—no, more accurately, I was *moved*—by Aubrey's determination to spend twice as much time traveling to campus and back as she would spend in our seminar each week, where she was demonstrably eager to discuss social studies research. She reminded me of the great distances (in this case, literally) many social studies teachers will go to improve their practice.

Aubrey was a third-year social studies teacher. Her school is a large, Latina/o-majority, Title 1 high school in a small working-class city. There, she taught six U.S. history classes in a seven-period school day, leaving her little time for planning. With 30 or more students per class, her teaching load was over 180 students, slightly fewer than half of whom were designated English language learners. She also was head coach for three different sports teams. Aubrey was responsible for meeting these and other responsibilities in her school under internal and external policy pressures—what Cornbleth (2001) calls a climate of constraint and restraint—familiar to most social studies teachers. As an untenured teacher, Aubrey understood she could be denied next year's contract without "good cause."

Aubrey weighed heavily on my mind as I considered not just the proposed policy question, but also the aspirational view of social studies reform that centers my work as a researcher and teacher educator—one that looks more to what social studies might be than so often is. In colleges and universities, social studies faculty can find themselves separated from the working conditions many social studies teachers face; just as policymakers in state offices can find themselves similarly disconnected from what happens in schools. As a result, the interests of social studies researchers and policymakers risk diverging from those of social studies teachers. Learning about Aubrey's working conditions served as a powerful reality check in that regard.

The lived experiences of practicing social studies teachers are crucial to discussions of education policy, its enactments, and its consequences. For example, the math on how long it takes to give each of 180 students *a mere five minutes* of careful feedback on, say, an ambitious historical inquiry assignment is constant: it takes 15 hours in 2017—just shy of two full working days—the same as it would have two or three decades ago. Now, however, teachers like Aubrey find themselves working in climates of increasing centralization, standardization, test-based accountability, and resource austerity. They have witnessed waves of public assault on their profession, campaigns to denigrate public education, and ongoing efforts to link pay and job security to misappropriated value-added assessment schemes.

Social studies policy deliberation cannot stand apart from what the field asks of teachers and the very real challenges they face. In what follows, I discuss one prominent social studies policy initiative—the C3 Framework—as an example of an "inside the system" initiative. I cast C3 as a kind of policy work that may be necessary, but also is insufficient. That insufficiency points to a crucial challenge for those considering what policy priorities social studies educators should advocate: how to develop "inside-the-system" initiatives, within existing policymaking pathways, with an appreciation for the lived experiences of social studies teachers. I conclude by proposing several guiding questions to inform policy discussions— questions that might serve the interest of moving the field in some small measure toward more meaningful, ambitious, critical, and democratic ends.

A Caveat: Policy Priorities in the Political Past and Present

The history of modern U.S. schooling is one of competing purposes. Should schools serve the social order as is, or should they endeavor to generate something better? Is schooling about creating a compliant labor force to serve the capitalist state economy, preparing as many students as possible for college, or promoting greater equity and social justice? The persistent struggle over the meaning and means of U.S. schooling writ large reflects similar debates in social studies. Yet the democratic-citizenship rationale remains a common denominator across most arguments for social studies. Although all subject areas can profess that rationale, social studies stands apart for its unique relationship to the democratic ideal.

The history of social studies has not changed, but the present social and political context has. When the very idea of public institutions is under attack, the future of public schooling is an open question. Now more than ever, the social studies field needs to press forcefully against powerful educational reform currents that minimize the centrality of public goods, democratic practices, and the very idea of public schooling. In my view, members of our field should seek to permeate multiple levels of public activity—e.g., community councils and school boards, grassroots organizations, state departments of education, education groups that lobby on a federal level—to defend public education's democratic mission.

There is a rich tradition of such advocacy in social studies education; yet its present necessity as a counter-force to the ascendant conservative and neoliberal political and ideological climate seems especially significant. My argument herein is twofold—first, that the field should adopt a more avowed stance toward social studies as essential to the public project of democratic education; and second, that the field should follow through on this stance with direct action that addresses the institutional realities experienced by social studies teachers, most of whom labor under challenging working conditions.

Context: The C3 and Its Situation as an Inside-the-System Policy Initiative

The C3 Framework for Social Studies State Standards (herein, "C3") offers an interesting test case for the urgent stance I advocate here. C3 can be understood as a relatively high-profile, well-funded effort to latch the social studies car to what appeared to be a rapidly moving Common Core State Standards (CCSS) train, pulled by a powerful locomotive on a reform track laid by conservative and neoliberal critics of public education. The idea was, "The train has left the station; better to be on it than left behind."

Post NCLB, states rushed to rewrite social studies standards and develop elaborate and expensive (to the public, profitable to others) assessment systems (Au, 2009; Simon, 2015). Although this movement affected social studies teachers differently, the overall effect appears to have been that teachers hewed the same test-preparatory content-coverage line long normalized in many social studies classrooms, only now the approach was supported by state imprimatur. And whatever the intentions of those who wrote Race to the Top, it intensified the tying of teacher evaluation, retention, and pay to crudely drawn student and teacher performance assessments. These policy impacts not only pose a direct threat to social studies teachers who do not toe the line, but they are just as troubling for the manner in which they indirectly reshape ever-evolving discourses about what can be done in social studies teaching and learning. For a new generation of social studies educators, these policies work to delimit and institutionalize ways of seeing, understanding, and thinking about social studies.

In this context, C3 is a compromise document intended to serve multiple purposes and constituencies. The very title of the document foregrounds Common Core language and appends "civic life" in third place, behind "college" and "career," as a reminder of what social studies might add to the curriculum. The "Inquiry Arc," as a proper noun, speaks to both a generalized conception of inquiry *and* academic-disciplinary modes of inquiry. Civics is cast as an academic discipline and joins history, economics, and geography as the academic disciplines that matter most, with others relegated to "companion document" appendices.

Readers are assured the report is not just another in a long line of standards documents, but a *framework* that includes input from a broad array of professional organizations of different ideological positions (e.g., both Junior Achievement and Teaching for Change are acknowledged as "critical voices" stakeholders invited to review, prepublication) and allows states and teachers to address the question of what, specifically, is worth knowing. The result appears to have safely negotiated an interest group minefield in an attempt to secure social studies a seat at the reform table. For this and other reasons, the document is an impressive achievement in social studies literature, and perhaps a necessary strategic response at a key moment in a shifting policy climate.

Beyond this, the jury is still out on what C3 will *do*. Hitched as it was to the CCSS train, as that movement slows down or fades from view, C3 may very well follow. C3Teachers.org is an impressive effort to promote C3 via the web, professional learning opportunities, and shared resources. The framework may prove influential as states use the framework to update their standards documents and assessment policies. However, the field should remember the distance between state-level policy uptake and ground-level classroom practice. By the time C3 works through my state department of education and to teachers like Aubrey, will the new standards wash over them as yet another externally directed imposition, only this one more threatening because of its ties to value-added merit schemes?

Standards, and the frameworks upon which they are based, do not move teaching practice alone. They are one piece of a puzzle; others are teacher education and professional development, as well as persistent structures and grammars that give shape to life in schools—these latter pieces likely more significant than the former. Teachers generally do not shift fundamental assumptions about teaching social studies from encounters with framework documents, not even after the best professional development workshops. As I support C3's effort to center inquiry at the heart of social studies teaching and learning, from a policy perspective, I have concerns about the field putting too much of its energy and hope into this and similar inside-the-system documents, several degrees removed from teachers' lived experiences.

Criteria: Pursuing Policy Beyond Inside-the-System Initiatives

Even if C3 proves neutral with respect to life in social studies classrooms, it might be defended as a bulwark against the disappearance of social studies. Yet there is no neutrality in "getting in the game" of standards and testing as educational controls. The "something for everybody" nature of C3 is understandable, considering the compromises required by the political climate in which it was authored, and credit the document for foregrounding the importance of social studies to democracy. However, absent a more forceful, pointed, and critical statement about this relationship, I worry C3 ventures an unintended cost, perhaps in the form of opportunity lost to more urgently and forcefully press for redirection of educational reform currents toward a more robust vision of democracy. I also worry that a preoccupation with policy as standards and assessment regimes strengthens anti-democratic reform agendas that not only fail to take into account the lived realities of social studies classrooms, but actually make these realities more unsupportive of the kinds of meaningful, inquiry-driven education C3 seeks to promote.

I suggest that it is possible to defend democratic education by working within ever-evolving policy systems, and by actively resisting these same systems from without. We do not have to adopt one approach or another; and strategies should vary, as the playing field is vast and distributed, with myriad opportunities. In schools, social studies teachers might use parent-teacher meetings, committee and community meetings, and collaborative work with other teachers as spaces to garner support for more ambitious views of the field. State and national professional organizations already engaged in advocacy work must look for policy openings to assert the value of social studies in a time of assault on democratic traditions and institutions.

Social studies faculty in colleges and universities should continue to work "against the grain" in their programs and use the affordances of their positions toward more visible and public contributions to educational reform debates. Writing for a more public readership is an example. This consideration requires some rethinking of reward systems in higher education, currently built on research productivity that often circulates no further than a relatively small community of social studies scholars. Rather than perpetuate silo effects across potential advocacy groups, leaders in the field should push for conditions that would allow broader coalitions of social studies professionals to add clear, forceful voices to the growing movement of resistance toward attacks on public education. As well, social studies teacher educators should do more to promote the idea that advocacy work is a core professional responsibility of all social studies educators and to provide practical supports in helping new teachers learn how to do this work.

With these arguments as a backdrop, I propose several questions to frame the social studies field's thinking about future policy strategies and how to prioritize them:

- Does this policy clearly and forcefully assert a democratic vision for both public schooling and social studies education?
- Does this policy strategically resist anti-democratic forces that seek to undercut this vision?
- Does this policy facilitate school and classroom environments supportive of diversity, mutuality, inquiry, critical engagement with meaningful content, and shared deliberation?
- Is this policy likely to improve the on-the-ground working conditions for social studies teachers?
- Is this policy likely to encourage professional collaboration and strengthen decision-making among social studies teachers?
- Is this policy a promising way to contravene in systemic inequalities in K–12 education, higher education, and civil society?

If the answer to at least one of these questions is not "yes," I argue the policy under consideration should not be a priority for the social studies field. Conversely, if the answer to several of these questions is "yes," perhaps the policy should be considered high priority.

Of course, these questions invite disagreement; they offer no particular order of importance, and there are others we might add to this list. I acknowledge, once again, that educational policy is complicated. Still, Aubrey's case reminds me that prioritizing social studies policy initiatives hinges on their consequentiality to teachers' working conditions. It is hard to imagine that any efforts the field takes on in the coming years will move the field unless they better the demanding realities faced by the teachers most immediately charged with the democratic promise of social studies education.

References

Au, W. (2009). *Unequal by design: High-stakes testing and the standardization on inequality.* New York: Routledge.

Cornbleth, C. (2001). Climates of constraint/restraint of teachers and teaching. In W. B. Stanley (Ed.), *Critical issues in social studies research for the 21st century* (pp. 73–95). Greenwich, CT: Information Age Publishing.

Simon, S. (2015). *No profit left behind.* Retrieved from www.politico.com/story/2015/02/pearson-education-115026

Proposing a Seven-Step Social Studies Policy Advocacy Strategy

Commentary by Michelle M. Herczog, Past President, National Council for the Social Studies

The current political atmosphere in the United States represents a threat to the existence of our democratic way of life. Americans are becoming more distrustful of government institutions, politicians, and democracy in general (Pew Research Center, 2015). Frustration and cynicism have led to increased disengagement of citizens in civic arenas and low voter turnout, particularly among young people. Our nation is confronted with complex social and political issues never seen before (e.g., Peters, 2017); simultaneously, policymakers are making decisions that will impact the lives of all Americans for decades to come. Voting for candidates with an informed, critical lens is essential for the preservation of our democracy and our place in the world.

At the close of the Constitutional Convention in 1787, Maryland delegate James McHenry alleged that a woman approached the eldest delegate, Benjamin Franklin, and asked whether the framers had created a monarchy or a republic. So goes the story, Franklin told her that the new nation would be a republic, "if you can keep it." While this account likely is fictitious, according to the Library of Congress (n.d.), its message about the fragility of democracy resonates hundreds of years later. If something is not done soon to reverse current trends, we may be unable to "keep it." The dismal state of civic trust and engagement among adults is alarming. The future seems especially dire when we consider how the marginalization or elimination of social studies education might impact the civic potential of young people. Attention to high-quality social studies education is desperately needed to preserve and protect our democratic way of life.

Policy Intersections at State and Federal Levels

Social studies educators have long understood the importance of, and worked tirelessly to provide, high-quality instruction throughout students' K–12 educational experiences. Unfortunately, federal education policies that prioritized literacy and math skills in the "No Child Left Behind" era minimized the importance of social studies education, the effects of which trickled down to states and local school districts. At local, state, and federal levels, policy drives instructional priorities. Policy drives conceptions of what students need to know and be able to do in the form of standards, frameworks, textbooks, and instructional materials. Policy drives accountability systems that dictate what schools are required to accomplish. Policy drives what subject areas are assessed, when they are assessed, and how they are assessed. And finally, policy drives budgetary decisions regarding support for teachers in the form of instructional resources and professional development.

The social studies community has experienced the impacts of school policies that have marginalized or eliminated social studies education in elementary schools, middle schools, and high schools across the nation. It seems reasonable to imagine some relationship between the deprioritization of social studies education and a current electorate that is uninformed about and disengaged in our democratic institutions. And yet, we also know that there are places where policymakers have enacted initiatives that elevate the status of social studies education as part of a well-rounded education for all students. For example:

- In 2010, Florida passed the Sandra Day O'Connor Civics Education Act, which requires a middle-level civics course and high-stakes test, among other school-level accountability measures.
- In Hawaii, a required "Participation in Democracy" course, enacted by law in 2006, places a strong emphasis on experiential civic education. A subsequent effort to repeal the law was defeated.
- In Tennessee, legislation mandates project-based civics assessments at the middle and high school levels.
- A resolution passed by the Illinois Senate places the Illinois Civic Mission Coalition's "Democracy Schools" designation—an indicator of strong commitments to democratic education in specific school communities—on state school report cards.
- On August 21, 2015, Illinois Governor Bruce Rauner signed House Bill (HB) 4025 into law, requiring that future Illinois high school students complete a semester-long civics course. Course contents center on government institutions, current and controversial issues discussions, service learning, and simulations of democratic processes.
- Arkansas, Connecticut, the District of Columbia, Hawaii, Illinois, Kentucky, Maryland, New York, North Carolina, California, and other states have formally adopted and/or utilized the *College, Career, and Civic Life (C3) Framework for Social Studies State Standards*, which the National Council for the Social Studies (NCSS) published to strengthen the teaching of social studies and purposefully prepare students for civic participation at all grade levels.

At the federal level, policymakers, at the urging of social studies advocates like Ted McConnell, Catriona Macdonald, and Les Francis of the Campaign for the Civic Mission of Schools, introduced new provisions in the Elementary and Secondary Education Act—now known as the "Every Student Succeeds Act" (ESSA)—to strengthen social studies education. Further, in July 2016, the U.S. House of Representatives Appropriations Committee passed a 2017 appropriations bill that included, for the first time in several years, funding for civics and American history. The Committee *increased* these appropriations by close to $2 million beyond the level authorized in the ESSA in December 2015. Specific provisions, some of which were adopted and others of which were not, included competitive grants to support new curricular and instructional tools in civics, American history, and geography; partnership academies with museums, libraries, and research centers to improve the quality of civic and history education; and grants focused on the integration of technology, student wellness and enrichment initiatives, and instruction in civics and government, economics, geography, and environmental education (NEA, 2017; United States House of Representatives Committee on Appropriations, 2016).

These policy initiatives represent a relatively recent shift in tone related to the importance of social studies education for all students. Though public education primarily is funded through state coffers, states often take their cues on issues of resource allocation, assessment, and accountability from the federal government. This revitalized federal attention to "well-rounded education" hopefully will energize state and local policymakers to elevate the importance of social studies education in their schools. And yet, the past and present of education policy demonstrates a predicament for identifying what kinds of priorities the social studies should pursue as a field and how: policy forces flow in different directions at different levels—some strengthening and others weakening social studies education—all at the same time. The trick is determining what policy activities are most likely to influence a reversal of trends toward civic disengagement in a climate where social studies arguably is losing and gaining ground simultaneously.

Policy Activity at Local Levels, and Beyond

Does education policy matter? Absolutely. Can educators and community members impact education policy? Definitely. Most classroom teachers rightfully attend to the immediate and long-term educational needs of their students. They invest long hours in preparing lessons, gathering resources, delivering and facilitating instruction, utilizing formal and informal assessment to inform their work, and learning to improve their practice. They also know that if policies are not in place to support their abilities to operate as the professionals they were trained to be, their efforts will be underutilized, under-resourced, and sadly, unappreciated. Therefore it is important for all educators—teachers, administrators, and higher education faculty—to actively advocate for policies at local, state, and federal levels to support high-quality social studies instruction for all students across all grades. The challenge, of course, is finding the time and knowing what to do.

A number of social studies organizations have created advocacy toolkits for educators to use. These include NCSS (www.socialstudies.org/toolkit); the Campaign for the Civic Mission of Schools (http://civicmission.s3.amazonaws. com/118/64/1/190/AdvocacyToolkit.pdf); and the National Center for Learning and Engagement at the Education Commission of the States (www.ecs.org/ clearinghouse/01/16/12/11612.pdf). Since most educators are more comfortable in the hallways of schools than the hallways of government offices, these guides are extremely helpful. Whether leading an advocacy plan or helping others to implement one, social studies educators might consider drawing from several guidelines that I would recommend to organize efforts locally, statewide, and nationally.

A 7-STEP SOCIAL STUDIES POLICY ADVOCACY PLAN

1. **Identify specific advocacy challenges and opportunities:** What are the leading initiatives in the current educational policy arena? Whether it is Common Core, STEM education, or career and technical education, examine how social studies education can enhance schools' ability to meet new goals and objectives while strengthening students' equitable access to high-quality social studies learning experiences and their abilities to be prepared as informed, engaged citizens. Propose and press for win-win scenarios for including social studies education in comprehensive programming. Areas of direct influence include instructional time, funding for instructional materials and field trips for students, release time and funding for professional development, and assessment and/or accountability measures to ensure that social studies is valued to the same degree as other subject areas.

2. **Determine the key audiences:** This is *Civics 101*. For instance, determine if the policy you want to influence can be addressed at the local level. Local schools and districts tend to have a lot of control over the adoption of curricular and instructional resources and the allocation of professional learning and instructional time. In that context, your key audience will be local school board members, the surrounding community that elects them, and of course, stakeholders within the school. Identify and include local groups that could support your efforts, including community organizations, business leaders, families, and other constituencies. If the policy is directed by the state or federal government, target the policymakers who make the decisions you want to influence.

3. **Find out what audiences know and how they come to know it:** Do your homework. Conduct surveys, interview individuals and groups,

and collect information from media outlets to inform your work and strategies. Non-educators' knowledge of specific education initiatives can sometimes be minimal or misguided. That said, learn how your audiences prefer to be reached and interact with them via those means of communication. For example, are they influenced by public media, emails, surveys, face-to-face meetings, or recommendations from superiors?

4. **Define specific message points relevant to each audience:** This is critical. Know *what* and *how* to convey your message to school board members, families, business community members, state policymakers, and others in ways that are meaningful for them. For instance, when promoting social studies education, key areas of interest for school board members are funding implications and the need to align district policies and procedures with those at the state and federal levels. For families, it is about preparing their children to be responsible, engaged citizens. For the business community, it is about understanding historical trends, adapting to present circumstances, predicting future challenges, and considering the economic implications of these things.

5. **Establish measurable objectives and strategies for attaining them:** By measurable objectives, I mean intended outcomes of interacting with audiences and specific things you aim to accomplish as a result. Find the "sweet spot" for identifying objectives that are realistic and attainable, given current policies and the priorities of different actors. Be creative in pressing for these outcomes and accomplishments by meeting face-to-face with policymakers, making phone calls and sending letters or emails, inviting them to schools, asking them to speak at assemblies, or presenting them with an award or recognition.

6. **Plan your resources, timeline, and responsibilities for each activity accordingly:** Think about the resources you need to implement your advocacy plan and how to adapt those resources, as necessary, in the midst of your work. Map out activities, according to the objectives and strategies established previously, and invite others to help accomplish different tasks. Timelines with specific action steps will help keep everyone organized and moving forward.

7. **Evaluate the extent to which you have reached your objectives:** Take time to reflect on your accomplishments, whether large or small. Congratulate your team on their successes, no matter how trivial. Advocacy work can be taxing and often frustrating. It is important to recognize and celebrate the work that is accomplished and the relationships that are built. Simultaneously, identify which objectives you have met to what extents, and then return to earlier steps in the action plan to reflect on and revise your strategies if necessary, or to generate new objectives in light of accomplishments.

Our American democracy operates on the principle that the voice of the people should guide the policies and practices of our nation. When citizens disengage—not only those educated in America's schools, but also the educators, themselves—they can become victim to those policies and practices. If we believe social studies education is essential to the future of our communities, our nation, and our world, we must empower ourselves and others to influence educational policies that will prepare the next generation to be informed, actively engaged citizens of the 21st century.

References

National Education Association (NEA). (2017). *House Appropriations Committee action compared to ESSA authorization of appropriations.* Washington, DC: National Education Association. Retrieved from www.nea.org/assets/docs/FY2017-House-Appropriations-Committee-Bill-Compared-to-ESSA-Authorizations.pdf

Peters, M. (2017). Education in a post-truth world. *Educational Philosophy and Theory, 49*(6), 563–566.

Pew Research Center. (2015, November). *Beyond distrust: How Americans view their government.* Washington, DC: Pew Research Center. Retrieved from www.people-press.org/2015/11/23/beyond-distrust-how-americans-view-their-government/

United States House of Representatives Committee on Appropriations. (2016, July 22). *Departments of Labor, Health and Human Services, and Education, and related agencies appropriations bill, 2017.* Retrieved from www.congress.gov/114/crpt/hrpt699/CRPT-114 hrpt699.pdf

United States Library of Congress. (n.d.). *Creating the United States: Convention and ratification.* Retrieved from www.loc.gov/exhibits/creating-the-united-states/convention-and-ratification.html#obj8

Dinkelman's Response
to Herczog's Commentary

What a pleasure it was to read Michelle Herczog's thoughtful response to this chapter's social studies policy question. I am struck by how much we converge in our perspectives on policy priorities, without any communication or collaboration during initial response writing. Our points of agreement are considerable. We both share deep concern about the present social and political climate in the United States. We agree that policy matters, especially now, in an exceptional era when democracy is truly "at risk." With concern, we view the sometimes waxing, more often waning contemporary shifts in the importance of social studies as a mainstay of the modern school curriculum. Finally, we both believe that social studies offers unique potential to contribute to a more just and democratic society. For this reason, we both call on social educators to involve themselves in attempts to influence educational policy.

Herczog's response extends our mutual call for policy advocacy in important ways. Most noticeably, she draws on her rich experiences in the social studies policy realm to provide practical guidance, in the form of a seven-step advocacy plan. It is all too easy to invoke social studies educators' professional responsibility to be active in matters of policy that affect practice. But as Herczog observes, "the challenge, of course, is finding the time and knowing what to do." The plan she articulates is admirable for its concrete action steps, as well as the flexible way the steps apply to different sorts of policy work at local, state, and national levels.

For all the convergence, reading Herczog's response helped sharpen my thinking about what I hoped to convey in my first attempt, and what contributions I can bring to social studies policy conversations. Herczog casts the parameters of the policy playing field in recognizable, perhaps even conventional, terms. As a relative outsider to that playing field, the difficulty I faced in conceptualizing what counts as policies—a crucial consideration if the task at hand is to prioritize them—might signal a potential contribution in and of itself. Perhaps the field would do well to trouble conventional notions of policy.

The C3 Framework, NCLB, and Race to the Top are clear examples of policies, and they deserve the field's careful attention, for they definitely have consequences for students and teachers in social studies settings. However, less high-profile policies, maybe those not even considered policies in a conventional sense, are consequential as well. Returning to my initial response, myriad daily, on-the-ground policy activities shade the experiences of Aubrey and her students, sometimes with far more immediacy and force than educational legislation, standards frameworks, and state and district-level rules.

Previously, I used the language of "inside" and "outside the system" policies. Now I think there is more fitting language. Perhaps the distinction is more accurately captured by policies "in the conventional sense" and policies "in the unconventional sense," or maybe the discourse of "big" and "small" policies better captures the point. Whatever the labels, the distinction is more than semantics. My original discussion of the C3 Framework was not meant to draw attention to the compromises the document makes, nor was it intended to diminish the value of an initiative that brought together so many social studies stakeholders. Herczog provides an encouraging list of recent policy victories in our field, all of which can be read as policies in the conventional sense, and the accomplishment of C3 belongs on this list.

By drawing attention to the challenging realities faced by so many social studies teachers, my response was intended to broaden our sense of what counts as policy from big, conventional, inside-the-system initiatives to include smaller, ground-level policies and policy moves. We cannot overlook the local, sometimes unofficial activity that touches on a range of concerns that directly shape the prospects for ambitious visions of social studies education, as described, for example, in C3. Examples include policies that determine whether teachers in a particular school are scheduled one or two planning periods per day, and whether those planning periods are lost to administratively imposed "data team" meetings; whether innovative teaching practices are encouraged through merit schemes or opportunities for teachers to collaborate openly with each other; whether school or district-wide assessments encourage all history teachers to cover the same content at the same pace, regardless of class sizes and compositions; and whether teacher evaluations involve thoughtful feedback from teams of school leaders and colleagues or are conducted in drive-by fashion by overburdened administrators.

These sorts of policies likely merit high priority for Aubrey and countless other teachers working to deliver on the promise of social studies education in remarkably challenging, sometimes deeply unsupportive, environments. I am sure many of them find C3 helpful, and perhaps some even find the document, associated support materials, and workshops transformative. However, the idea of social studies as inquiry is not new. The history of social studies now marks generations of attempts to move teaching and learning in directions that better fit with a vision of an engaged, democratic citizenry, amidst a routinely criticized pattern of classroom practice that has proven remarkably persistent and seemingly untethered to reform efforts.

We would do well to read this history in ways that expand our views of the policy playing field. Social studies policy is developed and enacted not only in legislators', state agencies', and higher education institutions' meeting rooms, but also in the policy-laden spaces teachers and students inhabit every school day. Our policy priorities—and the kinds of steps to enacting those priorities that Herczog proposes—must reconcile with what happens in those spaces. It is worth asking how much of the field's energy should be devoted to bigger, conventional policy activity; smaller, unconventional policy activity; or some combination thereof.

Turning back to the chapter's central question, policy priorities for our field should be expansive. We welcome initiatives like C3 and the larger-scale policy accomplishments Herczog identifies in her response. We also should help educators and leaders generate and mediate smaller-scale policy instruments and activities that shape life in classrooms, schools, teacher education institutions, and communities. This expansive view of the policy playing field—and in turn, of what policy activity involves—may not make establishing priorities any easier, but it may help us direct our collective energies toward meaningful change in times of trouble for democracy and education.

Herczog's Response to Dinkelman's Commentary

Long discussions with my son, Brian, a philosophy scholar, remind me that life is complicated. This may sound like a simplistic orientation, but if we can accept and embrace the complexity of human issues, events, actions, and reactions, we can better position ourselves to realistically approach challenges and achieve meaningful, productive outcomes for ourselves and others. Reflecting on Todd Dinkelman's essay has reminded me that educational policy, like life, is complicated.

I think we agree that policy is important to social studies educators; it plays a significant role in what we teach; where, how, and when we teach it; and to whom. It has the potential to support high-quality instruction by providing teachers with the professional development, time, and resources needed to perfect their craft. Policy can codify outcomes we hope to achieve for all students. And it can potentially restore the dignity and integrity of social studies as a core subject area in the educational arena.

My professional experiences and the ideas shared by Dinkelman prompted me to reconsider three key themes related to policy priorities that social studies educators might address.

Marginalization of the Social Studies

I sincerely believe that policymakers are well intentioned and committed to providing a high-quality education for all students. No Child Left Behind was informed by a critical need to improve student literacy and math skills. It did not *require* schools to drop all instruction in social studies, science, visual and performing arts, physical education, and health education. And yet, we saw state after state, school after school, eliminate or marginalize these subjects to focus attention almost entirely on literacy and mathematics. So, was the problem in the policy or the interpretation and implementation of the policy, and at what levels? There are no simple answers to these questions. But we have learned that if policy does not explicitly call for the teaching of social studies as part of a well-rounded K–12 education, we run the risk of continued marginalization.

A current debate about re-centering social studies education hinges on its inclusion in state assessment and accountability systems. California, like many states, has adopted the Smarter Balanced assessment system, which measures competencies for literacy and mathematics. A recent legislative plan to adopt a state assessment for social studies has faced a great deal of scrutiny. What should it measure? What kind of test should it be? In terms of performance outcomes, how good is good enough? What should be the consequences of low scores for students, teachers, and schools? What effects will testing have on what gets emphasized within the social studies curriculum and what continues to be diminished, or is even further diminished? Is it a good idea to assess social studies alongside the other academic areas, if doing so creates additional strain on an already overburdened testing regimen for students? These are complicated questions, all of which have implications for the marginalization (or not) of social studies education.

Identifying Student Learning Outcomes

Dinkelman asks,

> Should schools serve the social order as is, or should they endeavor to generate something better? Is schooling about creating a compliant labor force to serve the capitalist state economy, preparing as many students as possible for college, or promoting greater equity and social justice? The persistent struggle over the meaning and means of U.S. schooling writ large reflects similar debates in social studies.

I think he is correct. What and why we educate students is an ongoing debate and one that continues to complicate the endeavors of well-intentioned policymakers.

By visiting schools and talking with social studies leaders across the nation, I have learned that there is great disparity among conceptions of *what* and *how* we should teach the social studies. For example, some state standards are characterized by broad, general social studies concepts, principles, and skills that all students should "know and be able to do." Other state standards are not just a mile wide but a mile deep as well, with long litanies of discrete knowledge that often are impossible to digest in an already limited timetable for instruction (assuming "digestion" is a worthy goal of social studies learning). Some states have no state social studies standards at all, leaving the identification of outcomes to the control of local school districts. And as I suggested above, layered on top of these discrepancies are different positions on how to measure learning outcomes and what to do with the evidence of those outcomes. Such positions are informed by both practical considerations (e.g., multiple-choice tests are efficient and cost-effective but do not measure analytical and deliberative skills well, while performance assessments could better assess these things but are expensive and time consuming to administer) and philosophical ones (see Dinkelman's question about what aims social studies education should promote).

Creating Conditions for High-Quality Social Studies Teaching and Learning

I wholeheartedly agree with Dinkelman that policy can and should support conditions for teachers to act, learn, and grow as professionals. Professional learning communities have proven to be powerful avenues for teachers to collaboratively analyze data, develop and revise instruction, and intentionally and strategically target students' learning needs. Innovative school leaders have reinvented school calendars and master schedules to make time for teachers to engage in these practices. But doing so is no easy task. As more demands, constraints, and unfunded policy mandates are placed on schools, it becomes harder to find the time to do the important work of planning, reflecting on, and revising instruction. And when teachers are not adequately compensated or recognized as professionals by their communities, morale dwindles, enthusiasm wanes, and talented educators leave the profession altogether.

Here again, we see educational policy operate as a double-edged sword. Providing teachers with resources to strengthen professional practice is profoundly important, yet over-prescribing how those resources must be used, and what results must come from them, is problematic. Similarly, while structured curricular guidelines may strengthen the instructional decisions of some teachers, they also can deteriorate trust in educators' professional knowledge and experiences. To conclude, once again, educational policy is complicated, but the problems and priorities addressed here, and in Dinkelman's and my original essays, are worthy of diligent attention at federal and state levels, and especially local levels. As Dinkelman eloquently concludes his essay, we will be unable to move our field forward unless we "better the demanding realities faced by the teachers most immediately charged with the democratic promise of social studies education."

11

"HOW MIGHT PUBLIC POLICY ENGAGEMENT AND POLITICAL ACTIVISM BE SITUATED WITHIN SOCIAL STUDIES TEACHER EDUCATION PROGRAMS?"

Teachers and Teacher Educators as Public Policy Actors in Today's Charged Classrooms

Commentary by Margaret Smith Crocco, Michigan State University

(with thanks to Stephen Vrla for his able assistance on this essay)

Without being flippant about the seriousness of this question, my rejoinder has to be, How not? Teachers and teacher educators are public policy actors; they enact the policies that (typically) other people have decided upon as means towards an end. Teachers and teacher educators can resist these policies, for example, trying to mitigate the damage that high-stakes testing has done to their students. Alternatively, they can support policies they believe to be unjust or deleterious, acquiescing enthusiastically or unenthusiastically to the overdetermined situation in which they find themselves as the objects rather than subjects of educational policy. But social studies teachers and teacher educators are always and everywhere agents of the state, whose work has consequences for the quality of citizenship and citizenship education in this country. It's a serious responsibility that must include engagement and activism if schools are to be the incubators of democracy that they should be in the United States.

In responding to the original prompt posed by the editors, I modified their question slightly to add teacher education to teaching. Given the highly charged political climate of the past year, it seems important to pair these two separate but related activities as we think about public policy engagement and political activism, especially in light of the many assaults on social justice that schools have confronted as a result of this climate.

No matter what a teacher or teacher educator does or doesn't do, he or she is engaged with public policy, and in a broader sense, with political action if not activism. By political action, I mean making and enacting choices with consequences for the distribution of and opportunities for exerting power in our society. By activism, I mean hands-on, direct, and sustained engagement with activities that are political in nature and aimed at influencing the way power is distributed or exerted in our society. Keep in mind here that teaching is a normative, indeed a moral, enterprise that unfolds at the nexus of values, choices, and decisions about what knowledge is of most worth, which students get access to what kind of knowledge, and what ends teachers should pursue in their classrooms. A teacher or teacher educator makes choices every day that affect all these issues. However, not all teachers or teacher educators protest, write letters, lobby, or go on strike (or not) over such issues. Encouraging future teachers to discuss and debate the role of political action and activism in their work as teachers is an important, and necessary, part of the work that we should be doing in social studies teacher education.

Over the last several decades, teachers and teacher educators have been subjected to a new policy regime in which their profession has become more highly regulated and the stakes in terms of compliance or non-compliance raised considerably. The policies shaping new regulations have come about as a result of political decisions. Years ago, for example, many states passed laws mandating teaching the Holocaust, Irish potato famine, or Seneca Falls, but little oversight was done to check whether these mandates were implemented at the local level. By contrast, when one state, New York, was awarded Race to the Top federal funds, school districts had little choice but to accommodate the new testing requirements. When states such as Michigan mandated that accreditation come only via the Council for the Accreditation of Educator Preparation rather than an alternative pathway, schools of education were required to comply or lose their accreditation. When edTPA was introduced into Wisconsin, schools and colleges of teacher education were given a grace period, but the accountability measure became consequential for students and colleges there within relatively short order.

Most social studies educators today share a commitment to citizenship education (i.e., educating for responsible participation in democracy and to social justice), that is, educating for equity, recognition, and inclusion (Adams & Bell, 2016). These concepts get defined differently. Moreover, the enactment of citizenship education varies from an emphasis on personal civic responsibility to more active and transformative approaches (Westheimer & Kahne, 2004). Pretending, however, that one can avoid politics and policy engagement as a teacher or teacher educator of any subject, but most particularly social studies, is an especially dangerous conceit. I would argue that pursuing a social justice-oriented form of citizenship education unavoidably situates the practitioner, whether teacher or teacher educator, in a space where political action is implicated. Do we teach our teachers that all students can learn? Do we teach future teachers that students bring cultural capital by way of language difference into the classroom? Do we broaden our understanding of diversity to include not only race and gender but also social class, sexual identity, or physical ability? How we answer these questions and bring their implications into action in college or school classrooms reflects a political orientation and moral choice about our students and the purposes of schooling.

Political activism goes further than political action, involving a range of steps that can run the gamut from activities contained within the context of one classroom to others that take an educator out into the streets, town halls, or state capitols. When we think of activism, we may imagine participating in the Badass Teachers Association or the New York Council of Radical Educators or the Women's March on Washington attended by many in the social studies community. We may think of blogging, protesting, writing letters to the editor of a local newspaper or representatives in Congress, or lobbying against state policies (Swalwell & Schweber, 2016). Doing citizenship education from a social justice orientation that is aimed at transforming rather than reproducing the social order may also lead a teacher to adopt perspectives on public policies such as tracking, testing, homeschooling, privatization, segregation, etc.

To be sure, public policy choices may be considered good or bad, both in terms of means and ends, especially along the lines of democratic values and goals related to equity and social justice. Greater engagement with policy by teachers, who have been called "street-level bureaucrats" (Hill, 2003; Lipsky, 2010) who implement policy enacted by others, may make it more likely that their perspectives will be considered in policy decisions about both ends and means. Likewise, teaching about climate change, animal rights, the dangers of smoking, the corrupting influence of big money and conflicts of interests in politics, LGBTQ student rights, and other controversial topics may, depending on the local context, be activist endeavors just as much as writing letters to state legislators or school boards about these topics.

For as fraught and polarized as the new educational policy era may be, history provides numerous examples of teachers and teacher educators called to enact "pedagogies of resistance" (Crocco, Munro, & Weiler, 1999, p. 1) against policies seen as unjust or inequitable. During the first half of the 20th century, teachers suffered a loss in their voice, stature, and power in the face of an educational reform movement calling for new, hierarchical approaches to school governance. Many women educator activists of this era organized themselves into teachers' associations (unions) that lobbied governments and initiated various community alliance efforts to support and sustain better outcomes for their students and themselves. Interestingly, teachers of this era were told that they could speak out about anything other than their own working conditions as they demanded equal pay for equal work, retirement pensions, and tenure. By contrast, many teachers and teacher educators today (at least those who continue to have tenure protections and are represented by unions) have earned the right to speak out about their working conditions but may not feel free to teach about local, state, and national elections for fear of losing their jobs.

Given these circumstances, debating public policy in classrooms seems perilous to some practitioners. Discussing and deliberating public policy is an important element of robust social studies, one advocated in the C3 Framework (National Council for the Social Studies (NCSS), 2013), where students are encouraged to "take action" after studying a topic, although in my experience, this step is the one that teachers have the greatest difficulty taking since they are so habituated not to engage. Some of the resistance to this teacher move may be conceptual in terms of adding this element to their lesson plans; some of it may be practical because teachers never have enough time to accomplish what they're supposed to accomplish. In a parallel vein, investigating whether the edTPA approach to accountability seems a prudent or punitive educational policy choice seems a professional duty for a teacher educator, just as understanding the implications of the No Child Left Behind Act was for classroom teachers. Both were public policy initiatives designed for certain ends—the improvement of the teacher education enterprise and closing the achievement gap, respectively. Nevertheless, many teachers and teacher educators have been understandably critical of the extent to which these measures have achieved these ends, as well as the means adopted to achieve them. Let's consider these two examples in a bit more detail.

First, edTPA is a policy prescription for teacher preparation programs designed as a portfolio assessment of a future teacher's knowledge and skills upon completing the teacher preparation program. This assessment has its supporters and detractors within the social studies teacher education community. Among the arguments used against it are its cost; its association with Pearson, a large educational corporation that represents the testing industry; the perceived unfairness of its evaluation process; the hurdle it represents for many students who want to become teachers but have difficulty with the assessment; etc. Among the arguments used for it are that it provides a national benchmark for teacher quality just as the tests for national board certification provide; its potential for improving quality within the teaching force; and its competency-based rather than multiple-choice approach to teacher evaluation. Individuals in both camps (pro- and anti-edTPA) believe in social justice and equity. Both groups acknowledge the pivotal role of the teacher in creating a high-quality classroom experience for learners. However, the two camps come to different answers on the question of whether the form of summative assessment represented by edTPA will advance, obstruct, or undermine the cause of social justice in education, and ask whether it will produce enough collateral damage in its execution as to make it untenable as a public policy initiative throughout teacher education. Activism against edTPA has taken the form of editorials in educational outlets, blogs, and research studies and professional presentations analyzing the effects of edTPA on different groups of teacher preparation students.

Second, the No Child Left Behind Act is notable for the degree of rancor ultimately generated within numerous constituencies by the law, especially its "highly qualified teacher" provision. State policymakers heard from district administrators, schoolteachers, and schoolboards about problems with this law, just as they heard from these and other constituencies about the Common Core, which also generated significant pushback, changes, and retrenchment at the state level. Right or wrong, such pushback and policy change would not have happened without policy engagement by teachers, parents, and the general public through the democratic process of using voice, standing, access, and activism to influence public policy and bring about change.

Teachers and teacher educators can disagree about whether policy choices are wise ones. However, *not* having an opinion about such matters seems unprofessional. Working to mitigate the negative effects of these policies, actively opposing them, or supporting certain policy mandates related to these policies are also responsible choices. At a more minimalist level, I've always found it surprising that anyone could debate the necessity of being conversant with current events as a social studies educator. Although this knowledge might or might not become a formal (accountable) part of social studies teacher preparation, lack of knowledge of contemporary national or global events and issues seems a serious dereliction of professional duty. Providing space within one's teaching, whether at the K–12 or the undergraduate/graduate level, to consider a national or state election, its candidates, and the issues at stake seems incumbent upon social studies teachers.

Similarly, professionalism as a teacher requires an understanding of current research so as to "do no harm," as medical doctors espouse. In other words, a teacher must avoid the educational malpractice that might result if he or she teaches in a fashion that undermines the notion that "all students can learn," or that enacts prejudicial ideas rooted in a "fixed mindset" rather than a "growth mindset" about all students' potential, especially if such frameworks are associated with class-based, racial, language, or gender identities. The "good and just teaching" (Cochran-Smith et al., 2009) at the heart of social justice practice includes knowledge of and commitment to the standards of professional excellence. This means keeping up with the public policy framework in which the educator operates, whether these are local school board elections, state politics, or federal policy initiatives. The same is true for teacher educators, who should model for their students forms of enactment of citizenship education that is aligned with social justice education.

Encouraging political activism as part of the work of social studies education needs to account for the risks teachers may face in pursuing activism in the face of injustice, whether it be picketing against the end of ethnic studies in Arizona, contesting the slashing of the state budget for education in Wisconsin (Swalwell & Schweber, 2016), or pushing back against the dehumanization of K–12 schooling under contemporary accountability regimes (Blevins & Talbert, 2016). History is replete with other examples of times when teachers were faced with difficult decisions about unjust political events. Did teachers and teacher educators speak out against the Nuremberg laws in the 1930s? Did they encourage their students in the 1950s to resist Jim Crow segregation, north and south? Did they speak out against Japanese internment in the US in the 1940s or McCarthyism in the 1950s?

And today, do social studies teachers and teacher educators believe they have an obligation to fight the silence found in "homophobic hallways" (Crocco, 2002) or address the "missing discourse" about gender and sexuality (Crocco, 2001) in the nation's schools? Do social studies teachers and teacher educators believe that speaking up and talking back to those in power about these issues is their professional responsibility as citizenship educators? I believe they should.

Sadly, we have too many examples in the history of our own professional organizations, including the National Council for the Social Studies and the American Educational Research Association, of not speaking out about social justice issues even if individual members did. In encouraging teacher educators to bring policy engagement and political action and activism into their programs, deliberating about the ways to do so should be encouraged at our professional meetings while also considering the risks attendant upon various courses of action related to these endeavors. Academic freedom, however embattled it may be, provides a great deal of space for taking up such topics within the college or university setting. For teachers, however, there may be a great deal less space. Still, consideration of the opportunities that do exist is an important conversation to have within teacher preparation programs as future teachers consider what it means to do citizenship education. Likewise, helping teachers figure out how to survive and yet subvert what they believe to be damaging to their students is a key obligation of teacher educators today.

Whatever way one defines political activism, public policy engagement, or social justice, these emphases are central to the work of citizenship education and the preparation of students and future teachers dedicated to democracy and a more equitable society. Recognizing that not all teachers or teacher educators will be in a position to take the same risks in how they enact their activism or exercise their rights to influence public policy, engagement is essential, not only as a matter of self-protection since so much educational policy today seems aimed at undermining the place of teachers and public schools in our democracy, but also because these activities are imperative for improving schooling for all students. Public schools, as Thurgood Marshall once said, is about more than just reading, writing, and arithmetic; schools are the places where we learn to live together. Nothing could be more important to the future of this country than this lesson, and teachers and teacher educators should not relinquish their responsibility in this regard nor underestimate their power to be positive influences in society and their students' lives. Whatever form their activism or engagement takes, it's not only a professional but a moral imperative to do so.

References

Adams, M., & Bell, L. A. (Eds.). (2016). *Teaching for diversity and social justice* (3rd ed.). New York: Routledge.

Blevins, B., & Talbert, T. L. (2016). Challenging neoliberal perspectives: A framework for humanizing social studies teacher education. In A. R. Crowe & A. Cuenca (Eds.), *Rethinking social studies teacher education in the twenty-first century* (pp. 23–39). New York: Springer. http://doi.org/10.1007/978-3-319-22939-3

Cochran-Smith, M., Shakman, K., Jong, C., Terrell, D. G., Barnatt, J., & McQuillan, P. (2009). Good and just teaching: The case for social justice in teacher education. *American Journal of Education, 115*(3), 347–377. doi:http://doi.org/10.1086/597493

Crocco, M. S. (2001). The missing discourse about gender and sexuality in the social studies. *Theory into Practice, 40*(1), 65–71.

Crocco, M. S. (2002). Homophobic hallways: Is anyone listening? *Theory and Research in Social Education, 30*(2), 217–232.

Crocco, M. S., Munro, P., & Weiler, K. (1999). *Pedagogies of resistance: Women educator activists 1880–1960*. New York: Teachers College Press.

Hill, H. C. (2003). Understanding implementation: Street-level bureaucrats' resources for reform. *Journal of Public Administration Research and Theory, 13*(3), 265–282. doi:http://doi.org/10.1093/jopart/mug024

Lipsky, M. (2010). *Street level bureaucracy: Dilemmas of the individual in public services. 30th anniversary expanded edition*. New York: Russell Sage Foundation.

National Council for the Social Studies (NCSS). (2013). *College, Career & Civic Life C3 framework for social studies state standards: Guidance for enhancing the rigor of K–12 civics, economics, geography and history*, Bulletin 110. Washington, DC: NCSS. http://doi.org/NA

Swalwell, K., & Schweber, S. (2016). Teaching through turmoil: Social studies teachers and local controversial current events. *Theory and Research in Social Education, 44*(3), 283–315. doi:http://doi.org/10.1080/00933104.2016.1201447

Westheimer, J., & Kahne, J. (2004). What kind of citizen? The politics of educating for democracy. *American Educational Research Journal, 41*(2), 237–269.

Critical Democratic Teacher Education as Policy Engagement and Political Activism

Commentary by Steven Camicia,
Utah State University

Teacher education programs have increasingly engaged with learning objectives related to social justice (Cochran-Smith et al., 2009). This stance requires that students, educators, and community members learn how to act in a way that engages with public policy through political activism. An underlying assumption of this activism is that educators must have a political stance, positions that occur within an increasingly polarized and animus society (Hess & McAvoy, 2015; Pew Research Center, June, 2016). The opportunities and constraints involved with taking a political stance are further influenced by pressures of standardization and accountability. Cochran-Smith (2010) describes dominant views that frame teacher education as something "which is regarded as a problem that can be solved by the 'right' public policies, based on evidence rather than values or ideals, and judged by outcomes rather than processes, resources, or curricula" (p. 445). This movement occurs within a countermovement that emphasizes social justice (Cochran-Smith et al., 2009). Although there is some overlap between these movements, the underlying stances are different. The former privileges a narrow range of dominant perspectives, while the latter focuses upon increasing the range of perspectives within teacher education and society. It is within these polarizing contexts, both epistemological and political, that teacher education programs must prepare students to engage with policies. What principles can teacher education programs promote that encourage policy engagement and political activism within the context of increasingly polarized communities?

In my response, I focus upon a framework for teacher education programs that draws upon my understanding of critical democratic education (Camicia, 2016) and social movement theory (Anyon, 2005; Snow, 2004). The term "critical" modifies the term "democratic" in order to focus examinations of education upon how inequitable power relations undermine democratic communities. An education for critical democracy places power relations as central to understanding how we can make democratic communities more inclusive and just. One of the strengths of this framework is that it places the relationship of power/knowledge as a central construct for understanding how the public policy and curriculum construct and deconstruct social inequalities in schools and beyond. Later, I illustrate this with examples from Utah and California that show the intersection of social studies curriculum standards, educational policy, and different societal contexts. Because political dynamics change within and between the communities in which teachers work, educators need a lens for understanding political landscapes and how they position public education and issues of equity. Four components are central to a lens of critical democratic teacher education: positionality, democratic dialogue, discourse analysis, and action. Along with this understanding of political and cultural landscapes, an understanding of social movement theory gives students, teachers, and community members tools for advancing social justice agendas.

Public education is situated within complex and dynamic webs of power relations with multiple stakeholders. Teacher education programs are charged with preparing teachers to collaborate with the communities they serve, as well as contexts of complexity and contingency. Unfortunately, larger societal and political pressures narrow curriculum and teacher education experiences. Programs that ignore complexity and embrace narrow perspectives perpetuate social inequalities by feigning neutrality. Stances of "neutrality" are used to justify apolitical stances on knowledge and society (Apple, 2004). In contrast, social studies teacher education programs can examine how power functions inside and outside of schools in order to identify ways to increase social justice. This examination focuses upon how inequality works at the level of epistemology, language, and resources.

Critical democratic teacher education provides a framework for providing political stances in teacher education that challenge all forms of oppression. An analysis of the way power functions provides a tool for policy engagement and political activism. One of the key components of this framework is positionality. Students in social studies teacher education programs can examine how students, educators, and community members are located within networks of power that are relational. Maher and Tetreault (1993) write:

> Gender, race, class, and other aspects of our identities are markers of relational positions rather than essential qualities. Knowledge is valid when it includes an acknowledgment of the knower's specific position in any context, because changing contextual and relational factors are crucial for defining identities and our knowledge in any given situation.
>
> *(p. 118)*

Positionality creates a reflexive point for teachers to understand themselves as embedded in schools and communities that treat people differently depending upon their positionalities. My students and I have used autoethnography in my social studies and foundations courses as a way to increase critical consciousness. In critical ethnography, individuals examine experiences as they are embedded in cultural and political contexts. Arellano, Cintrón, Flores, & Berta-Ávila (2016) write that this awareness "allows individuals to recognize that their experiences of social and economic inequalities are not the result of their individual actions, but rather are derived from larger sociopolitical conditions" (p. 46). An awareness of positionality connects individual experiences with an understanding of larger social structures that construct and maintain social inequality. This is in contrast to dominant narrow perspectives of evidence and knowledge that exclude multiple and critical perspectives from expression in schools. Carlson (1998) writes, "To refuse to see or recognize the identity of those who have been oppressed or discriminated against because of that identity is to deny that oppression and discrimination exist" (p. 95). Positionality provides a lens for understanding how power functions through schools, society, and policies to construct and maintain social inequalities. Positionality grounds and increases the power of social sciences such as economics, geography, history, and civics by tying them to lived experiences of students, educators, and community members. Social studies disciplines can become transformative by engaging knowledge at an embodied level. These examinations can help students and educators better answer questions such as: How do educational policies impact people inequitably in relation to their positionalities? How are the social sciences organized in curriculum to privilege some positionalities while marginalizing others? The answers to questions like these help situate education and knowledge within the contexts of embodied power relations.

The second component of a framework for critical democratic teacher education involves a focus upon the relation of positionality with democracy and inclusion. Harding (1993) writes, "An effective pursuit of democracy requires that those who bear the consequences of decisions have a proportionate share in making them" (p. 3). The legitimacy of democracy depends upon inclusion. Positionality provides the material to examine knowledge and perspectives that are often marginalized and excluded in schools and society. It is a place where narratives and counter-narratives challenge and deconstruct "neutral" perspectives that marginalize people and their perspectives. This expression of positionality can form the basis for dialogue around social issues. Through dialogue and deliberation, teachers can better understand how to implement critical democratic education in their classrooms, as well as use the same principles to engage with policy deliberation and political engagement. Without an understanding of positionality, it is difficult to see how democratic dialogue can be authentically inclusive (Boler, 2004). This understanding can form the basis for asking a question such as: How can we increase democratic inclusion in policies and through political engagement? Positionality and inclusion frame deliberation around policies and actions.

The third component of my proposed framework involves discourse analysis. Discourse analysis focuses upon opportunities and constraints surrounding what can and can't be expressed, and as a result, what can and can't be understood. Interpreting Foucault's meaning of discourse, Hall (2001) writes that discourse:

> Defines and produces the objects of our knowledge. It governs the way that a topic can be meaningfully talked about and reasoned about. It also influences how ideas are put into practice and used to regulate the conduct of others. Just as a discourse 'rules in' certain ways of talking about a topic, defining an acceptable and intelligible way to talk, write, or conduct oneself, so also, by definition, it 'rules out', limits and restricts other ways of talking, of conducting ourselves in relation to the topic or constructing knowledge about it.
>
> *(p. 72)*

A focus upon meaning at this level is often missing but influential in our understanding of knowledge construction and society. Discourse analysis provides a key for understanding how social issues can be discussed and understood on an authentic level that is inclusive and aware of how power helps or hinders inclusion. Social studies teacher education programs can examine the ways that inequitable power relations within society are maintained by the ways that discourses delimit the norms and rules that govern communication. I recently examined the ways that educational policies influence discourses surrounding LGBTQ individuals and issues in public schools (Camicia, 2016). After examining social studies standards and other texts from California and Utah, I identified discourses that govern what can and can't be said related to LGBTQ inclusion and exclusion. This inclusion and exclusion touched the lives of students, educators, guardians, and community members. For most intents and purposes, Utah schools ban LGBTQ perspectives from curriculum while California has rewritten the K–12 Social Science Framework to include LGBTQ individuals. Educators in both states pointed to the standards as a way to guide inclusivity while gaining protection from stakeholders in communities that do not want inclusive schools. In addition, educators in both states emphasized the need to use the intersectionalities of identities and positionality as a central component of the social studies curriculum. In Utah, we are currently challenging policies that prohibit LGBTQ individuals and issues from inclusion in curriculum (Dobner, 2016).

By examining the discourses that prohibit inclusion, teacher education programs can better focus upon how to engage with policy and political action. Students in social studies methods courses can examine the discourses that serve to marginalize members of their community and beyond. In my methods courses, we examine the ways that discourses of racism, sexism, ableism, patriarchy, classism, cisgenderism, heteronormativity, and nationalism influence the political and cultural landscapes of our schools and communities. We do this through the examination of instructional materials and pedagogies as they relate to our positionalities in classrooms and society. We ask questions such as: What perspectives and positionalities are and are not reflected in these materials and our classrooms? What discourses function to privilege some perspectives over others in society? A critical democratic education uncovers the ways that these meanings and representations are influenced by discourses of inequality.

In consideration of positionalities, democratic dialogue, and discourse analysis, teacher education can strengthen discourses that increase social justice in policy and political engagement. A critical democratic education framework challenges the idea of a public sphere and deliberation that are composed by apolitical knowledge where the best reasons should prevail. This view was undermined by the results of the 2016 United States presidential campaign where reason gave way to the discursive terrain. Because discourses shape the intelligibility of reason, an apolitical view of knowledge often covers the very inequalities that such a system of reason might claim to ameliorate. By connecting reason within political and cultural landscapes, teacher education can take a social justice stance on policy and political engagement. Lenses of critical race theory, feminist theory, postcolonial theory, critical disability theory, and queer theory provide means for identifying discourses that can provide more inclusion within education and democratic communities.

The fourth component of my proposed framework involves action. With an understanding of the ways to increase perspectives in teacher education and society, we can frame our message of inclusion in ways that resonate with a variety of stakeholders and decision makers. Collaborations with the communities in which schools are embedded are key. Some social movement theorists conceptualize the framing of an issue as a powerful tool within a social movement's repertoire (Snow, 2004). Social movements increase their likelihood of success when they are able to align the frames of the movement with frames of stakeholders. Teacher education programs should identify the frames of various stakeholders and decision makers in order to understand how to influence positive changes toward social justice. The frames that increasingly dominate education and teacher education can provide the locations for these strategic changes. There is no shortage of dissatisfaction with frames of standardization and accountability. Social studies teacher education programs can engage with these frames by focusing upon the underlying logic of these frames and attaching a new kind of logic that will increase the quality of teacher education. For example, the frame of standards can be aligned with a framing of positionality and discourse as a more authentic form of standards, inclusion, and problem solving. This is critical thinking in both senses of the word critical.

I'm well aware that in proposing critical democratic teacher education for social studies programs, I'm placing myself toward a pole in our polarized society. However, I believe that the model that I propose is the only one that will lead to authentic democratic dialogue and justice. It is a position that also challenges dominant assumptions of polarization. Because power and discourse operate in tandem with reason, it is necessary to include an analysis of power and discourse in democratic dialogue in education. This level of inclusivity can increase the legitimacy of democratic dialogue because it excavates places of knowledge, language, and meaning. Social studies teacher education programs can increase inclusionary discourses in policy by intensifying a critical democratic framework through the way that social sciences are experienced in schools and communities. The biggest challenge that teacher education programs face is the dominant perspective in policies that position students, educators, and education as apolitical. Education is political, and the only way to work toward equity is to engage with critical democratic education authentically. This can provide the grounds for equitable and inclusive social movements that engage with policy and activism.

References

Anyon, J. (2005). *Radical possibilities: Public policy, urban education, and a new social movement.* New York: Routledge.

Apple, M. W. (2004). *Ideology and curriculum* (3rd ed.). New York: RoutledgeFalmer.

Arellano, A., Cintrón, J., Flores, B., & Berta-Ávila, M. (2016). Teaching for critical consciousness topics, themes, frameworks, and instructional activities. In A. Valenzuela (Ed.), *Growing critically conscious teachers: A social justice curriculum for educators of Latino/a youth.* New York: Teachers College Press.

Boler, M. (2004). All speech is not free: The ethics of "affirmative action pedagogy". In M. Boler (Ed.), *Democratic dialogue in education: Troubling speech, disturbing silence* (pp. 3–13). New York: Peter Lang.

Camicia, S. P. (2016). *Critical democratic education and LGBTQ-inclusive curriculum: Opportunities and constraints.* New York: Routledge.

Carlson, D. (1998). Who am I? Gay identitiy and a democratic politics of the self. In W. F. Pinar (Ed.), *Queer theory in education* (pp. 92–101). Mahwah, NJ: Lawrence Erlbaum Associates, Publishers.

Cochran-Smith, M. (2010). Toward a theory of teacher education for social justice. In A. Hargreaves, A. Lieberman, M. Fullan, & D. Hopkins (Eds.), *Second international handbook of educational change* (Vol. 23, pp. 445–467). New York: Springer.

Cochran-Smith, M., Shakman, K., Jong, C., Terrell, D. G., Barnatt, J., & McQuillan, P. (2009). Good and just teaching: The case for social justice in teacher education. *American Journal of Education, 115*, 347–377.

Dobner, J. (2016, October 21). In a national first, LGBT advocates sue Utah schools over 'anti-gay' laws. *The Salt Lake Tribune.* Retrieved from www.sltrib.com/home/4494330-155/lgbt-advocates-sue-utah-schools-over

Hall, S. (2001). Foucualt: Power, knowlege, and discourse. In M. Wetherell, S. Taylor, & S. J. Yates (Eds.), *Discourse theory and practice: A reader* (pp. 72–81). London: Sage Publications.

Harding, S. (Ed.). (1993). *The "racial" economy of science: Toward a democratic future.* Bloomington, IN: Indiana University Press.

Hess, D. E., & McAvoy, P. (2015). *The political classroom: Evidence and ethics in democratic education.* New York: Routledge.

Maher, F. A., & Tetreault, M. K. (1993). Frames of positionality: Constructing meaningful dialogues about gender and race. *Anthropological Quarterly, 66*(3), 118–126.

Pew Resarch Center. (2016, June). *Partisanship and political animosity in 2016: Highly negative views of the opposing party—and its members*. Retrieved from www.people-press. org/2016/06/22/partisanship-and-political-animosity-in-2016/

Snow, D. A. (2004). Framing processes, ideology, and discursive fields. In D. A. Snow, S. A. Soule, & H. Kriesi (Eds.), *The Blackwell companion to social movements* (pp. 380–412). Malden, MA: Blackwell.

Crocco's Response
to Camicia's Commentary

Steven Camicia's response to the question: *How might public policy engagement and political activism be situated within social studies teacher education programs?* suggests that we share commitments to social justice in contemporary teacher education. I agree with Cochran-Smith's assessment that such concerns have grown more commonplace in teacher education. In the face of neoliberalism's growing influence within education, this development may surprise those who feel that this ideology has only created academic cowards who put their heads in the sand in the face of threats to tenure and academic freedom. That said, although many scholars and practitioners of teacher education share a commitment to social justice, they may differ about how this commitment ought to be enacted in public policy and politics.

I agree with Camicia that critical democratic education is necessary in the face of assaults on democracy, both as a political system and form of "associated living" (Dewey, 1916, p. 101). Such assaults include, for example, the US Supreme Court's decision in the *Citizens United* case; the role of "dark money" in distorting political processes; the unprecedented level of gerrymandering in many states; voter suppression; the prison-industrial complex; and the spread of sexist, racist, and xenophobic online media, to name a few. Likewise, neoliberalism has brought widespread privatization of education at the K–12 level, with for-profit charter schools, online "virtual" schools, and demands for parental "choice" in the form of vouchers. These have been matched in higher education by the rise of for-profit institutions offering little value to students who, if they are lucky, graduate saddled with high-interest loans and low-value degrees. These "innovations" represent just a few of the global initiatives reflecting the role of venture capital, technological disruption, and decline in faith in the public sector over the last several decades.

Thus, I agree with the four-point plan for infusing social justice concerns into teacher education that Camicia advocates: an emphasis on positionality, democratic dialogue, discourse analysis, and action. These components will promote social justice–oriented teacher education programs that support future teachers in making judgments and considering responses to local policymaking and political issues. Nevertheless, I am not convinced that these elements will necessarily lead everyone to similar conclusions about which options are best in dealing with the complex issues in educational policymaking today. I don't mean to suggest that this is what Camicia assumes. However, in the polarized political climate in which we operate these days, it's important to reaffirm the right of our students to come to their own conclusions about what social justice demands. By briefly focusing on two examples, first, school choice and charter schools, and second, inclusion of LGBTQ topics in curriculum, I hope to promote further dialogue on these issues.

Many advocates of parental choice, charter schools, and vouchers see themselves as working "for the kids," as they like to say, with the implied contrast being educational policies that protect adults, aka teachers and teachers' unions. I am not a proponent of charters, choice, or vouchers, but I do believe that some individuals who support them are sincerely interested in improving educational outcomes for all students, especially those who have been poorly served by their schools' culture of acceptance of dismal outcomes for certain categories of students. My point here is simply that individuals who believe in social justice may differ in their views of how best to achieve the goal of addressing opportunity and achievement gaps in American education.

In teacher education, I suspect that proponents of greater regulation of teacher preparation programs through strengthening accreditation policies or mandating edTPA believe that these proposals will improve teacher quality. For example, the "Deans for Impact" group seems to believe that teacher preparation programs have been unwilling to consider how their graduates might be implicated in achievement and opportunity gaps. Other policymakers endorse Teach for America or the New York City Teaching Fellows since they see these programs as serving populations in difficult-to-staff settings. As policy responses, I disagree with these approaches but can accept that they stem from concerns for equity and social justice.

In terms of infusing LGBTQ topics into curriculum, I assume that the different responses in California and Utah emerged from democratic processes of decision-making in two contrasting state contexts. The outcome in Utah might reflect the judgment of citizens in a state where one religion dominates politics and policymaking. In California, the policymaking dynamics reflect the state's more diverse composition. My own commitments would be with California's choice. However, if Utah's choice was decided democratically, my response, like Camicia's, would be to encourage students to reflect on their own positionality in relation to this issue, engage in deliberation and discourse analysis, and consider actions aligned with their views of social justice. If I were teaching in Utah,

I would not be surprised if my students' reflection and analysis led them to judgments and responses different from mine.

Those of us who advocate critical democratic education need to accept that deliberative processes may not lead in the direction of our own policy choices. Good people can differ about the ways to achieve shared aims of equity, inclusion, and social justice. I hope that all social studies teacher educators affirm the importance of having students engage in considering and responding to public policy issues as they prepare to become teachers of social studies.

Reference

Dewey, J. (1916). *Democracy and education*. New York: Macmillan.

Camicia's Response
to Crocco's Commentary

The democratic mission of public schools is central to Crocco's response, and the power to control what is known and valued must be inclusive and socially just for schools to serve that mission. This requires democratic engagement and activism. For these reasons, I particularly appreciate the range of perspectives represented in Crocco's response. The question of engagement and activism is located within various contexts where teachers function as mediators between spaces of policy, pedagogy, students, and communities. The between spaces point to teaching as a political act, regardless of approach or perspective. As Crocco emphasizes, a lens of engagement is central to interpreting these contexts because public schools have a responsibility to be inclusive of diverse students, educators, and communities. This democratic view of inclusiveness can guide how social studies teacher education programs promote engagement and activism toward social justice.

The engagement that educators experience is also placed within contexts where multiple policy structures function to discourage a range of engagement. Teacher educators, teachers, and their students are increasingly surveilled by policies and accountability systems, while their protections of free speech and engagement are increasingly under assault. This encompasses a violence where knowledge, values, objectives, and successes are prepackaged and defined. Engagement under these circumstances is often defined by those who enthusiastically and competently follow a narrow range of guidelines imposed from the top. While these policies are ways to indicate a certain type professional standard, it is important to keep in mind that this is one type among a range of standards and perspectives. The effect of narrowly defining objectives and measures through policy is to produce a discourse of engagement where only narrowly defined objectives are allowed. Under this discursive regime, engagement and activism outside of these parameters is framed by policy and accountability systems as misinformed, unrealistic, or deficient. This is a policy context in which schools serve antidemocratic ends because the perspectives of students, educators, and community members are shut out of schools. I say antidemocratic because the perspectives of those who are impacted by curriculum and instruction are shut out of the decision-making process surrounding policy, curriculum, and instruction. This is counter to social studies education and democracy.

I appreciate Crocco's focus upon the expansive roles of policies such as edTPA and the No Child Left Behind Act as examples. While educators committed to social justice represent multiple perspectives on these policies, the narrowing of curriculum and instruction that results from these policies and accountability measures is difficult to deny. This narrowing can be viewed as increasing quality, but an overreliance on these policies can have opposite effect. This is particularly salient when it relates to the relative absence of social studies education in elementary schools. As is to be expected with public issues, people approach policy from multiple vantage points. As the ends of standardization and efficiency have permeated almost every space of our education system, our challenge is to find ways for our social studies teacher education programs to work within a system while challenging it to be more socially just. This involves thinking of the ways that discourses of standardization and efficiency assume an end at the expense of other possible ends. Engagement and activism in this context means questioning these ends and means in order to envision more possibilities for social justice.

Social studies education is uniquely positioned to foster positive engagement with various types and scales of communities. Within our historic, geographic, and economic realities, inequitable hierarchies force exclusion and injustice. Social studies teacher education programs can focus upon understanding these systems and developing student, teacher, and community opinions that lead to action and social justice. Crocco's focus upon deliberation and opinion formation are key steps toward social action. These social actions can also be informed by others who have examined social change. As social movement theorists (e.g., Tarrow, 1998; Tilly, 2004) tell us, movements have tools that are transferable to other movements, and these tools can be powerful forces of change. Movements can also frame their meanings to align with dominant discourses in order for positive change to occur (e.g., Benford & Snow, 2000; Binder, 2002). When applied to social studies teacher education programs, this implies transformative strands in curriculum and instruction that are both communicative and strategic. The framing of social justice gains traction toward change when it appeals to a new form of standardization that ironically increases perspectives rather than decreases them. This is communicative in that multiple perspectives and deliberation are valued. This is strategic because movement and action occur within dominant policy contexts that are antidemocratic. The reading of these antidemocratic contexts in strategic ways opens possibilities for citizenship education, democracy, and social justice.

I end my response by referencing Crocco's question, "How not?" We, social studies teacher educators and teachers, are embedded in contexts that require opinion formation, stances, engagement, and action. As we know, to not take a stance is a stance. To not act is action. Crocco applies this to multiple areas of our profession ranging from our classrooms to different scales of communities to our professional organizations such as NCSS and AERA (American Educational Research Association). Work toward democratic and socially just communities relies upon inclusion in the spaces within and between these various contexts.

References

Benford, R. D., & Snow, D. A. (2000). Framing processes and social movements: An overview and assessment. *Annual Review of Sociology*, *26*, 611–639.

Binder, A. J. (2002). *Contentious curricula: Afrocentrism and creationism in American public schools.* Princeton, NJ: Princeton University Press.

Tarrow, S. G. (1998). *Power in movement: Social movements and contentious politics* (2nd ed.). New York: Cambridge University Press.

Tilly, C. (2004). *Social movements, 1768–2004.* Boulder, CO: Paradigm Publishers.

12

"WHAT CAN THE FIELD OF SOCIAL STUDIES EDUCATION LEARN FROM POLICY RESEARCH AND REFORM IN OTHER DOMAINS?"

Policy Parables: Lessons of Education Policy From Outside the Social Studies

Commentary by Paul G. Fitchett, University of North Carolina at Charlotte

In December 2015, in a rare moment of bipartisanship, President Obama signed into law the reauthorization of the Elementary and Secondary Education Act of 1965 under a new moniker, the Every Student Succeeds Act (ESSA). Perhaps telling of its prioritization at the federal level, social studies rarely is mentioned in this new law, alluded to only once on page 219, Section 4104. Implicitly, the law tasks the states with resourcing school districts in support of social studies learning and teaching. This ambiguity can be perceived as either a boon or a disadvantage for social studies education policy. The lack of clear accountability mandates potentially grants states the freedom to design standards and curriculum, offer resources, and test students on social studies–related content and concepts as they see fit. Some social educators might view this lack of clarity as propitious, freeing teachers and students from the constraining environments experienced in mathematics, English/language arts, and now science classrooms. Others recognize that, in practice, if social studies is not included in policy talk, it is subject to being placed on the proverbial back burner.

Regardless of where one stands on this continuum, ESSA offers potentially new directions for social studies researchers, educators, and related scholars advocating for the field. Historically, however, success in advocating for social studies has been mixed, perhaps suggesting that it is time to look outside the narrow confines of social studies research. In the following conversation, I highlight two lessons that social studies educators can learn from policy research and reform outside of the field.

Focusing on the Aims and Capabilities of Education Policy: Lessons From Mathematics

Examining the historical landscape of educational policy, Cohen and Moffitt (2009) note that successful implementation of policy relies upon the alignment between the *aims* of the educational policy and *capabilities* of those set to execute it. When the aims of policy are too ambitious, those expected to administer said policies are left under-resourced, impeding the progress of enactment. Conversely, when the capabilities of those administering policies outpace the given aims, resources are wasted and the full potential of policy actors (namely teachers and students) is left unrealized. Finding the balance between aims and resources is ostensibly the goal of good education policy. Without it, the best educative intentions may fall flat. Even worse, poor initiatives may do more harm than good. For inspiration on how aims and capabilities shape policy for good and bad, social studies educators can, without irony, look toward the past.

The California mathematics reform movement of the late 1980s and early 1990s illustrates a cautionary tale of what can happen when academics work in conjunction with state bureaucrats and highlights the importance of aligning policy goals to teacher professional development to impact instructional practice. Highly touted and inspired by the mathematics practices emphasized by Ball and Lampert (e.g., Ball & Cohen, 1999; Lampert, 2009) and the curriculum advocacy of the National Council of Teachers of Mathematics (1989), the 1985 California Mathematics Framework included a set of reformed standards encouraging higher-order mathematical reasoning and inquiry-based instruction, which differed from the pedagogical experiences and training of many teachers in the state. Program developers recognized that effective policy required the communication of standards, sufficient professional development, and assessment that aligns with the new learning and teaching objectives (Cohen & Hill, 1998). Proponents of the reform noted that new assessments, which would measure learning differently from previous tests, probably also would contribute to lackluster scores as teachers and students adjusted to the curriculum. With a carrot-stick mentality, they posited that poor scores in year one would incentivize teachers to adjust their instruction to the curriculum. Predictably, scores dropped; but rather than weather the storm of scrutiny, the assessment and eventually other reform elements were dropped among partisan battles over the quality of the test and ideological differences on the purpose of mathematics education (Schoenfield & Pearson, 2009).

Closer scrutiny of the policy's history reveals substantial flaws in its implementation. Importantly, California employed only three individuals to train and support thousands of teachers in the state. Lacking sufficient support (i.e., capability), teachers failed to adjust instructional practices according to the demands (i.e., aims) of the new standards. Many teachers simply amalgamated reform-based pedagogy within existing practice, producing inconsistency in how teachers used the standards to inform their instruction (Cohen & Ball, 1990). Additional studies found that teachers who were exposed to targeted, reform-oriented professional development taught in ways that were more consistent with the mathematics framework (Cohen & Hill, 1998), suggesting that the policy's impact on instructional practice (i.e., capabilities) correlated with the level of resources provided to teachers. Because California failed to substantially support the policy at the teacher-support level, the fidelity of its implementation suffered. Consequently, the ambitious aims of the California Mathematics Framework outmatched the capabilities of the street-level bureaucrats (i.e., teachers) needed for the policy to flourish.

The California mathematics reform movement offers an important policy parable for social studies educators. As a field, we should first recognize that national endeavors to move policy forward require state-level support. Ambitious national initiatives like the *College, Career, and Civic Life (C3) Framework for Social Studies State Standards* are only as successful as their ability to coordinate with front-line policy brokers in states. From the National History Standards movement of the 1990s to the banning of ethnic studies in Arizona, to more recent boycotts of revised Advanced Placement standards in U.S. history, partisan forces often challenge more progressive social studies education policy aims and stymie policy enactment in the process. As a result, the curriculum in many cases remains inert and the full capabilities of teachers and students to engage in more substantive learning and teaching fall short. Given society's tendency to polarize around social studies curriculum issues, it is perhaps incumbent upon advocates of particular reforms to recognize limitations. Working within the culture and confines of existing bureaucracy is more likely to win over support among policymakers and policy actors than radically partisan proposals.

It is also important to remember that policy is only as successful as those who practice it. Teachers are the ground-level implementers for much of education policy. Without their support, the majority of education policy is dead on arrival. Aspiring policy requires the support and know-how of teachers. The New Social Studies movement of the 1960s, notably the *Man: A Course of Study (MACOS)* curriculum reform, included laudable goals for young learners, asking them to take on the disciplinary work of social scientists to better understand humans, culture, and society. However, *MACOS*'s enactment was partially stymied, like the California math reforms, by its incongruence with how social studies teachers were prepared to teach at that time (Fitchett & Russell, 2012)—a prime example of mismatched aims and capabilities within curricular policy. What the California mathematics reform and *MACOS* suggest is that states and districts have to invest in the policy-to-practice bridge, which requires both financial and human resource support. Moreover, transforming teacher pedagogy is a difficult endeavor. While recent curriculum reforms and accepted practices in teacher education suggest that practitioners are moving away from the folksy sit-and-get orientation of social studies learning and teaching, there is still hesitation on the part of some classroom educators to move away from the privileging of content transmission.

Having teachers buy into pedagogical reform takes time and convincing. Professional development efforts require coordination with any substantial policy reform that impacts social studies teaching and learning. Otherwise, classroom teachers will, at best, simply absorb new practices and shelve curricular materials. At worst, they will remain (willfully?) ignorant of policy, thus undermining ambitious initiatives.

Finding Space for Compromise: Lessons From Balanced Literacy

As noted above, social studies, perhaps more than any other subject area, is highly politicized, partially due to the aims and purpose of social studies instruction. One of the central tenets of social studies education and its associated disciplines generally is agreed to be the nurturing of democratic citizens. How that development should look pedagogically differs across ideological camps. For the sake of brevity, as noted by Evans (2006), one can bifurcate the aims-pedagogies relationship in social studies into traditional and inquiry/experiential categories. Traditionalists hold fast to heritage history and personally responsible citizenship approaches, believing that democratic practices are established by teaching foundational content and concepts. Knowledge is something to be gained, not scrutinized or challenged. Conversely, inquiry/experiential educators privilege the process of investigation, tools of the disciplines, and the variability of student perspectives. These teachers tend to take a more critical stance on democratic citizenship by challenging social, political, and economic institutions and canonical representations of historical understanding. The social studies wars, as they are referred to, suggest a substantial divide in what constitutes the purposes and practices of social studies. These schisms can (and do) inhibit policy implementation, as policymakers themselves are political agents that tilt toward either of these poles. Rather than taking polarizing positions, perhaps it is time for social studies to consider a third alternative—compromise. To find a salient example of such compromise, social studies can look toward another disciplinary war: the readings wars.

Few would contest reading's foundational place in education. It permeates all other subject areas and remains a cornerstone of educational attainment. However, the process of teaching reading emerged as a source of substantial controversy over the last several decades. Two camps, entrenched in their own epistemic traditions, marked the battlefield (Schoenfield & Pearson, 2009). One side, the phonics approach, emphasized the sounding out of letters to form words, following the rules of Standard English vernacular, and privileging direct instruction approaches. The alternative, whole language, focused on building and using diverse reading strategies, including social and linguistic cues, and cooperative reading and meaning-making. For years, the two sides amassed groundswells of support in defense of their respective traditions and ire toward their counterparts. Phonics supporters suggested that foundational reading skills were necessary for literacy, and that whole language falsely assumed that students would eventually develop these skills. Whole language advocates suggested that emphases on children's interests, strategies, and collective meaning-making cultivated literacy more powerfully than the lockstep, procedural phonics approach. However, twenty years ago, a curious thing happened; a compromise position arose, known as balanced literacy. Combining teacher-directed instruction and phonic rules with the use of sight words, cooperative reading groups, and student text choice, balanced reading has developed into one of the most widely accepted approaches toward literacy instruction in U.S. K–12 schools (Spiegel, 1998). This truce does not suggest that compromise options are always widely heralded. Criticisms of (off)balanced literacy abide, from objections to scripted, teacher-centered instruction on one side of the debate to accusations of deficient skills training on the other (Frey, Lee, Tollefson, Pass, & Massengill, 2005; Ravitch, 2010). Controversy surrounding its enactment aside, the concept of balanced literacy has created a unique opportunity for the development of policymaking and policy tools in reading education.

Because social studies learning and teaching remain firmly ensconced in politics and partisanship, policy compromise within the field is a hard sell. However, while framing social studies as apolitical is perhaps unrealistic and unwise, it is perhaps possible to mitigate some of the more polarizing aspects of social studies instructional purposes and cultivate a broader appeal among policymakers. Does the C3 open the door for compromise in social studies? Rather than presenting a specific set of content standards, which led to the castigation of the National History Standards from the political right, the C3 Framework emphasizes an inquiry arc, toward the ends of higher-order thinking and reasoning. It avoids propping up of one set of content standards over another as a source of political contention, leaving the selection of content relatively open, and instead promotes an inquiry model as a tool for practice. C3 definitely is not without its critics who question its lack of content specificity as an epistemological "cop-out" and hold skeptical the lack of disciplinary research undergirding the inquiry arc in social studies, outside of history (Au, 2013).

Given that it is still relatively new at the time of this writing, the C3's potential to inspire or inform compromise among various camps is yet to be seen. Yet, I would argue that consensus and compromise is needed to move policymaking forward in social studies. As noted previously, ESSA buries social studies fairly deep, garnering significantly less attention than do mathematics, science, or reading/language arts. Perhaps more telling is the former Teaching American History grant program, which intentionally funded projects that promoted history, but "not as a component of social studies." Such policy language suggests aversion toward the field and further marginalizes the subject area. It also reinforces antipathy by policy pundits who have previously referred to social studies as "tot sociology" and a social science quagmire (Ravitch, 1987). Members of the various camps represented, and not represented, in this commentary do not have to abandon principles wholesale. Rather, I suggest an armistice built on the idea that developing democratic citizens is the shared end goal of all social studies instruction. Finding compromise, one that is solidified by major stakeholders of social studies education and communicated across policy actors, is one potential way forward.

Concluding Thoughts

Taken together, these two lessons perhaps oversimplify recommendations for social studies education policy moving forward. However, I would argue that big ideas require a touch of pragmatism when they move from the academic sphere to the classroom. A healthy balance of aims and capabilities drives policy forward. Meeting lofty educational goals requires taking stock of the instructional resources available and providing support to policy implementers (i.e., teachers). Achieving policy aims vis-à-vis capabilities necessitates avoiding a rigid top-down or bottom-up mindset at development and implementation stages. Social studies should implement a blend of both (Fullan, 1994), in which central office bureaucrats (curriculum supervisors and state officials) provide resources and craft policy based upon on the resources and capabilities of implementers (teachers). Yet, the complexities of policy development and execution are not only contingent upon the power dynamics of a given bureaucracy. Within these open systems, varied ideologies hold sway over which policies emerge and take root. The politicization of social studies content and educational purposes further complicates policy in the field. Rather than remaining entrenched in camps, social educators seeking to move the field forward and improve its curricular relevance should leave their foxholes and begin the messy work of compromise. The examples provided above do not offer a clear path for social studies policy in the twenty-first century. However, they offer cautionary tales of education policy development and implementation worthy of taking note.

References

Au, W. (2013). Coring social studies within education reform. *Critical Education, 5*(4), 1–15.

Ball, D. L., & Cohen, D. K. (1999). Developing practice, developing practitioners: Toward a practice-based theory of professional education. In L. Darling-Hammond & G. Sykes (Eds.), *Teaching as the learning profession: Handbook of policy and practice* (pp. 3–32). San Francisco, CA: Jossey-Bass.

Cohen, D. K., & Ball, D. L. (1990). Relations between policy and practice: A commentary. *Educational Evaluation and Policy Analysis, 12*(3), 331–388.

Cohen, D. K., & Hill, H. C. (1998). *Instructional policy and classroom performance: The mathematics reform in California.* Philadelphia, PA: Consortium for Policy Research in Education, University of Pennsylvania.

Cohen, D. K., & Moffitt, S. L. (2009). *The ordeal of equality: Did federal regulation fix the schools?* Cambridge, MA: Harvard University Press.

Evans, R. (2006). The social studies wars: Now and then. *Social Education, 70*(5), 317–321.

Fitchett, P. G., & Russell, W. B. (2012). Reflecting on MACOS: Why it failed and what we can learn from its demise. *Paedagogica Historica*, *48*(3), 469–484. doi:10.1080/00309230. 2011.554423

Frey, B. B., Lee, S. W., Tollefson, N., Pass, L., & Massengill, D. (2005). Balanced literacy in an urban school district. *The Journal of Educational Research*, *98*(5), 272–280. doi:10.3200/ JOER.98.5.272–280

Fullan, M. G. (1994). Coordinating top-down and bottom-up strategies for educational reform. In R. J. Anson (Ed.), *Systemic reform: Perspectives on personalizing education* (pp. 7–24). Washington, DC: U.S. Department of Education.

Lampert, M. (2009). Learning teaching in, from, and for practice: What do we mean? *Journal of Teacher Education*, *61*(1-2), 21–34.

National Council of Teachers of Mathematics. (1989). *Curriculum and evaluation standards for school mathematics*. Reston, VA: NCTM.

Ravitch, D. (1987). Tot sociology: Or what happened to history in grade schools. *American Scholar*, *53*(3), 343–354.

Ravitch, D. (2010). *The death and life of the the great American school system: How testing and choic are undermining education*. New York: Basic Books.

Schoenfield, A. H., & Pearson, P. D. (2009). The reading and math wars. In G. Skyes, B. Schneider, & D. N. Plank (Eds.), *Handbook of education policy research* (pp. 560–580). New York: Routledge.

Spiegel, D. (1998). Silver bullets, babies, and bathwater: Literature response groups in a balanced literacy program. *The Reading Teacher*, *52*(2), 114–124.

Divergence and Values in Education Policy: Lessons From Other Academic Domains

Commentary by Kevin W. Meuwissen,
University of Rochester

"Policy activity," as a unit of analysis, is inordinately large and complex, from the passage of state laws and adoption of administrative regulations to the evolution of schools' social networks around perceived threats to educators' practical choices. In light of this chapter's potentially unwieldy central question, I framed what follows by focusing on policy instruments and activities that aim to impact teaching and learning more than, say, school leadership or financial operations. I also drew from the academic domains of science, mathematics, and literacy because they have commanded the lion's share of policy efforts to affect curriculum, instruction, and assessment. In doing so, I relied heavily on the expertise of other scholars[1] who explore and seek to understand the relationships between policy and practice, both generally and domain-specifically. In the end, two themes related to this chapter's question endured:

1. No matter what policymakers purport to do and how policies are built to accomplish their intents, many agents across multiple levels of implementation— from state and district leaders to classroom teachers—interpret and act upon those policies variously, and often divergently; and
2. Those interpretations and enactments are contingent upon agents' shared (or unshared) social and political commitments and the extents to which they see policy as a stabilizing or undermining force.

We must recognize, too, that policy initiatives are situated within aims-context relationships, and that contexts are multifarious. For example, attention to math and literacy education as matters of international competitiveness and national security intensified with the Soviet Union's launch of Sputnik in 1957, and then again with the National Commission on Excellence in Education's 1983 report, *A*

Nation at Risk. Concurrently, alongside Cold War fear-fueled efforts to systematize and sequence math and reading curricula and instruction, the 1965 Elementary and Secondary Education Act's situation of public education within a national civil rights framework generated new programs that aimed explicitly to close opportunity and achievement gaps between economically disadvantaged children and their wealthier, and whiter, counterparts. These two potentially incongruous contexts—education for economic competition and social justice—and the increasing political fetishization of private-sector accountability and efficiency priorities have generated considerable challenges in mathematics and literacy, from policy inconsistencies to relatively quick abandonment of programs and other instruments that failed to produce immediate student achievement gains.

Theme 1: Many Agents Interpret and Enact Policies Variously, and Often Divergently

Intersections of policy and practice represent decisional crossroads—places at which policy agents choose how to proceed, hopefully (but not always) on the grounds of improving learning and teaching. The crossroads metaphor emphasizes the many variables that play into policy enactments and underscores how particular pathways lead to commitments of human and material resources toward some ends and away from others. These pathways are multilayered, not unidimensional, on account of the following conditions (Cohen & Moffitt, 2010):

* Scale: does policy embody something broad and comprehensive, like "teacher assessment and evaluation policy in New York State," or small and specific, like "classroom policy on cell phone use?"
* Systematicity: is policy an enmeshed, coordinated structure of rules and mechanisms or a particular tool and procedure for using that tool?
* Ambiguity: to what extent is policy language and its prescriptions open to enactors' interpretations?
* Consequentiality: is policy intended to codify or alter particular practices, or both, with more or less severe repercussions for those affected?

For example, the creators of the Next Generation Science Standards (NGSS)—a large-scale, national project in which writers and policy actors negotiated content priorities, conceptions of science learning, and coherence with the Common Core State Standards (CCSS)—intended for the NGSS to be adopted by states without modification. State representatives then had to decide whether to accept the standards writers' recommendations (e.g., California), hybridize the NGSS with state-level priorities (e.g., Oklahoma), or reject the standards outright (e.g., Wyoming). Colston and Ivey (2015) explored the implications of those decisions in Oklahoma, where political resistance to the NGSS's emphasis on climate change amidst a national movement toward NGSS adoption resulted in a state standards revision that used the NGSS's disciplinary language and practices as models but remained ambiguous about human-environment interactions.

Of course, adopting standards and supporting their implementation in schools involve different decisional crossroads altogether. Colston and Ivey reported that, "in response to the political resistance and prescriptive power enacted" through the Oklahoma science standards, district-level science coordinators "organized to mobilize the full NGSS, including evolution and climate change standards" (p. 782). The coordinators' activism juxtaposed with several state policy decisions that repudiated robust, NGSS-aligned science teaching and learning, including (1) cutting budgets for statewide science education leadership, district-level coordinators, and professional development for teachers; and (2) increasing the power of state testing mandates, while concurrently omitting physical and environmental science content related to climate change from those tests. Meanwhile, in Oklahoma classrooms, about half of all science teachers expressed doubts about the consensus around anthropogenic climate change, prompting decisions to either teach climate science as fundamentally unsettled or avoid the topic altogether. The other half found their pedagogical efforts stymied by dwindling time, a lack of professional learning opportunities, and misrepresented content in school-sanctioned material resources, despite the work of district-level coordinators.

This example illustrates how numerous agents can interpret and enact education policies divergently, and that those enactments are contingent upon the scales, intended consequences, and social contexts of policy. There is another factor to consider: fidelity to disciplinary rationales for improving learning and teaching, which are intricate and can expose ambiguities—and thus, divisions—among actors' educational stances and degrees of expertise. The 1990s saw marked changes in mathematics curricula in the United States, spurred by the National Council of Teachers of Mathematics (NCTM) standards and states' and districts' attempts to implement them in classrooms. In a personal communication, math education researcher Jeffrey Choppin identified several decisional crossroads related to scale, the systematicity of policy uptake, and ongoing support for new practices:

> The NCTM standards really were the first time that anyone looked at research on math thinking and learning to write guidelines for teaching. This was followed by a huge investment—$100 million by the [National Science Foundation]—to systematically develop curricula based on those standards, on a large scale. . . . The problem—well, problems—were that there was only about 10% penetration of the new curricula across K–12 [schools]; commercial publishers began competing with the curricula, saying that their products were updated to align with the standards, even though the changes were often superficial and not aligned with the standards at all, so that corrupted the process; and then, after a few years, there was some political backlash from politicians, mathematicians, back-to-basics

types, who were opposed to the standards by orthodoxy and claimed that they weren't improving math achievement. It was hard to argue with them because measurements were low-level so they didn't pick up any complex effects, and implementation was dodgy; fidelity was an issue. . . . In one district, you might have a group of respected math teachers and leaders; they have social capital in their school, they're active in other professional networks, they study their own teaching, they look for PD related to math learning. And in another district, you might have teachers opposed to change, under an administration that doesn't really understand math learning and teaching, and they're just throwing new rules and expectations at the teachers. . . . You can have ambitious standards and good curricula, but if teachers can't pull it off, if they don't have the will and the networks and resources to help them pull it off, we're not going to see effects.

(November 18, 2016)

Relatedly, in a study of schools' responses to NCTM- and state-supported curricular reforms in Michigan, Spillane (2000) found that district-level coordinators who supported new modes of math teaching (e.g., new kinds of math problems, uses of manipulatives, and cooperative learning strategies) often misunderstood or overlooked the epistemological rationales for those reforms—in other words, the fundamental disciplinary conceptions of how mathematical practices generate knowledge, and what math knowledge and practices are good for, cognitively and socially. Spillane discussed this dilemma as follows:

[Reforms with recognizable themes and strategies] act as Trojan horses of sorts, packaging functional goals in a set of familiar instructional forms that can serve as cognitive hooks or handles for local enactors. As a result, they may find their way more easily into local school districts because they capture the attention of district leaders. The intents of reforms, however, frequently are never unpacked by district leaders: they never find their way out of the Trojan horses. Therefore, although policies that come in familiar forms with easily understood remedies make their way into local school systems, their functional intent often is never appreciated.

(Spillane, 2000, p. 171)

One lesson that we can draw, here, is that decisions in larger-scale domains—e.g., adopting standards or using fiscal and regulatory instruments to force particular educational priorities across a state—inevitably delimit decisional possibilities among agents in smaller-scale domains. Another is that policies and related instruments probably are necessary but insufficient mechanisms for change. Just as important, if not more so according to Sykes and Wilson (2016), are persistent opportunities for enactors to rationalize and develop expertise in new practices, to build social relationships around those practices, and to observe their demonstrable effects. And yet, given Colston and Ivey's, Choppin's, and Spillane's arguments above, failures within complex, large-scale, somewhat ambiguous policy systems seem inevitable. This predicament represents a decisional crossroads as well: agents at all levels could choose to acknowledge the risks of policy failure, particularly at points where failure is common (e.g., measuring outcomes and revising implementation goals at state levels; understanding policy aims and achieving curriculum fidelity at district and classroom levels), and to generate resources and take actions that promote resilience in light of those risks.

Theme 2: Policy Enactments Are Contingent Upon Actors' Social and Political Commitments and Their Conceptions of Policies as Stabilizing or Undermining Forces

Above, Choppin used the term "by orthodoxy" to characterize the "political backlash" toward the NCTM standards, suggesting that actors' conceptions of education policies can be just as ideological as they are practical or empirical. Certainly Colston and Ivey's (2015) research on the fate of the NGSS in Oklahoma demonstrates as much, explicating links between political circumstances and the aforementioned functional barriers to science education. During the state standards revision process, for example, (1) the state superintendent of education publicly critiqued the "liberal" principles of national science standards, suggesting that state-level standards should better represent Oklahomans' core values; (2) gag orders were imposed by the Oklahoma State Department of Education (OKSDE) on members of the standards drafting committee to prevent public discussion of what would be included and excluded; and (3) the OKSDE removed language related to environmental and evolutionary science from the state standards between committee approval and legislative adoption.

An artifact of how political commitments play into education policy and its enactments is the "wars" metaphor, which science (e.g., Osborne, Collins, Ratcliffe, Millar, & Duschl, 2003), math (e.g., Schoenfeld, 2004), and literacy (e.g., Pearson, 2004) scholars have used to represent educational-ideological differences. The values on which these differences pivot include beliefs about whether education is fundamentally a public or private good, and relatedly, whose interests ought to be served by it; what the social and intellectual benefits of education are, and how human and material resources should be organized to realize those benefits; and what kinds of grounds or warrants are valid for justifying education policies, their instruments, and their intended consequences. On the last point, literacy researcher Caitlin McMunn Dooley, currently a deputy superintendent at the Georgia Department of Education, noted in a personal exchange that the growth of empirical research on literacy learning, with evidentiary implications for teaching practice, corresponds with an emerging consensus among literacy experts that the so-called reading wars is an outmoded metaphor. And yet, while numerous professional organizations "have been helpful in pushing high-quality information out through policy statements, publications, and research journals, these things are routinely ignored by legislators. . . . We educators and scholars haven't really figured out the practices of policy advocacy and lobbying." In other words, as much as we might like to imagine empirical evidence to be a primary warrant for policy, frequently it is not.

Across domains, a key factor in advocating for or against policy seems to be the extent to which agents see it as a force of stability or sabotage, particularly with regard to resource allocation and decisional capacity. For instance, several authors in this volume present arguments for and against state-level standardized testing in the social studies, on the grounds of (1) its potential to leverage parity with other disciplines and command stronger curricular and professional development resources for teachers (i.e., a stabilizing force); or (2) its inhibitive, potentially deleterious effects on the kinds of social studies education that might otherwise incorporate more diverse subject matter, inquiry and investigation, and divergent thinking among students (i.e., an undermining force). Relatedly, Dooley explained how the inextricability of the CCSS and high-stakes testing simultaneously stabilizes and undermines literacy education:

> The CCSS set high standards and are written clearly, but they don't take into consideration the digital revolution we're experiencing currently; and they promote a narrow view of literacy with old and non-diverse texts. So they may prevent us from innovating and relating more with the kinds of multimodal texts that are ubiquitous in society. . . . I hear colleagues in social studies bemoan that the subject isn't tested as much as ELA, and therefore, it's considered less important; and I keep saying be careful what you wish for. Testing has not improved ELA outcomes. Testing narrows curricular focus. . . . Social studies has an opportunity to maximize the flexibility that comes from being untested to innovate and build coherence in areas like digital citizenship and critically evaluating online sources.
>
> *(December 23, 2016)*

To conclude, it would seem that parallels across domains, in terms of their political volatility and the challenges of pressing for policies that align with disciplinary principles and empirical research, could be fruitful common grounds for collaborative policy work. Specifically, both science and social studies share a kind of susceptibility to political-contextual circumstance; discord over the nature and purposes of science and contentious scientific knowledge bears some resemblance to contests over what history is and what kinds of history should appear in school curricula. Where might this collaborative policy work take place, and what could it involve? At national and state levels, professional organizations should prioritize two key aims and share resources to support those aims: (1) influencing legislative and administrative activity more persistently and effectively; and (2) helping teachers and leaders differentiate powerful, well-warranted educational approaches from poorly designed alternatives that hucksters allege are policy-aligned. These are especially important goals in the so-called digital age, when professional organizations' roles as coherent voices for their fields and preeminent sources of curricular and instructional guidance seem to be diminishing in light of other readily available associations and resources.

Locally, the trajectory from principles to policies to procedures and practices often is scattershot and, thus, subject to inconsistency. In light of this dilemma, Dooley's suggestion that "having school leaders who understand literacy development probably is more important than the policies themselves" triangulates well with one of Choppin's claims: "without administrators who understand how to support math learning, teacher leaders who are in daily contact with other math teachers, and regional support networks that can translate policy to practice, the chances of sustainable change are pretty low." In other words, local and regional networks serve two key functions: (1) adapting curriculum and instruction to inconsistencies among policies, district procedures, and their underlying principles; and (2) promoting coherent practices over time.

Reflecting upon the challenges Colston and Ivey (2015) discovered in their work, another role of regional support networks—alongside gatekeeping state policies and local practices—might be to elucidate and reinforce the social values served by instruments like the NGSS or the National Council for the Social Studies' College, Career, and Civic Life (C3) Framework, in ways that carry acceptable meanings and implications for agents with different priorities and commitments. On the relationship of values to public policy, Kahan and Braman (2006) note, "it is only when they perceive that a policy bears meaning congenial to their cultural values that citizens become receptive to sound empirical evidence about what consequences the policy will have" (p. 169). This argument may be just as germane to teachers' and school leaders' conceptions of what education policy consists of, is meant to do, and actually does as it is to citizens' interpretations of public policy, more broadly.

Note

1 Several math, English language arts (ELA), and science education scholars offered considerable time and thought in support of this chapter, though the author is solely responsible for its final content. They include Jeffrey Choppin (University of Rochester), Caitlin McMunn Dooley (Georgia State University), Joseph Henderson (Paul Smith's College), and David Long (Morehead State University).

References

Cohen, D. K., & Moffitt, S. L. (2010). *The ordeal of equality: Did federal regulation fix the schools?* Cambridge, MA: Harvard University Press.

Colston, N. M., & Ivey, T. A. (2015). (Un)doing the next generation science standards: Climate change education-actor networks in Oklahoma. *Journal of Education Policy, 30*(6), 773–795.

Kahan, D. M., & Braman, D. (2006). Cultural cognition and public policy. *Yale Law & Policy Review*, *24*(1), 149–172.

Osborne, J., Collins, S., Ratcliffe, M., Millar, R., & Duschl, R. (2003). What "ideas-about-science" should be taught in school science? A Delphi study of the expert community. *Journal of Research in Science Teaching*, *40*(7), 692–720.

Pearson, P. D. (2004). The reading wars. *Educational Policy*, *18*(1), 216–252.

Schoenfeld, A. H. (2004). The math wars. *Educational Policy*, *18*(1), 253–286.

Spillane, J. P. (2000). Cognition and policy implementation: District policymakers and the reform of mathematics education. *Cognition and Instruction*, *18*(2), 141–179.

Sykes, G., & Wilson, S. (2016). Can policy (re)form instruction? In D. H. Gitomer & C. A. Bell (Eds.), *Handbook of research on teaching* (pp. 851–916). Washington, DC: American Educational Research Association.

Fitchett's Response
to Meuwissen's Commentary

In his response to the question of what social studies can learn from outside the field, my colleague, Kevin Meuwissen, adeptly lays out two cogent and interrelated themes. First, he argues that education policy implementation varies across multiple organizational levels. Second, he notes that context plays a key role in how various policy actors interpret and enact policy.

Supporting his first theme, Meuwissen offers a useful exemplar in the Next Generation Science Standards (NGSS) and the varying degrees that states adopted them. Specifically, he draws attention to Oklahoma, which partially adopted the NGSS and undermined science education with cuts to instructional resources and an open hostility toward climate change education. In reading Meuwissen's interpretation of events, I wonder if part of the tension traces back to what education policy purports to accomplish and the realistic extent that national standards movements can influence state-level policy decision-making. The purpose of public policy, and Meuwissen and I agree on this point, is to solve a dilemma or problem. State policymakers, whose decisions reach into schools and classrooms, debate, deliberate, and attempt to address "problems" in education. National standards movements receive pushback; particularly when politicians or their constituency perceive encroachment from outside organizations and interests—groups that do not share the ideology of the policymakers. Thus, the national standards themselves constituted the "problem" abandoned or only implemented piecemeal. Instead, as Meuwissen points out, ambitious teachers work against efforts to sabotage standards. I argue that it is unrealistic for national standards movements, like the NGSS or the Common Core Standards Initiative, to expect wholesale adoption among the states. National standards movements utilize the same top-down perspective that drives other education policy initiatives. Instead of the policymakers at the state level being the progenitors of large-scale policy, the ideas of outside organizations drive decision-making, setting the stage for inevitable role conflict.

Linking context to the enactment of policy, Meuwissen states the "orthodoxy" (i.e., ideological rigidity) can undermine policy implementation. He notes that policy constrains teacher decision-making agency. However, policy without boundaries and stipulations is not policy at all. I contend that effective policy should bind organizational actors within a set of parameters for the purposes of fidelity, efficiency, and efficacy. Maverick, ambitious teachers might undermine oppressive, poorly conceived policies (i.e., initiatives to downplay climate change), but the structure of policymaking implementation often mutes their voices and obscures their actions.

So then, how to address these persistent themes of ideological conflict and lack of communication across policy actors? The examples provided by both Meuwissen and myself illustrate a lack of coordination at both the bottom and the top. An important step involves shifting the policymaking process, from top-down hierarchy to a more inclusive model. Datnow and Park (2009) classified three implementation and policy analysis perspectives: technical-rational, mutual adaptation, and sense-making/co-construction. Technical-rational perspectives, which dominate policy development, focus on a top-down and one-direction process in which policymakers craft policy that is enacted by lower-level bureaucrats. This perspective, exemplified in Meuwissen's anecdote of Oklahoma's half-hearted adoption of the NGSS, fails to consider the context in which policy is implemented. Proponents of this approach are relatively disinterested in policy implementation's local context. Rather, they fixate on programmatic fidelity and a macro-level view of policy effectiveness. The top-down structure of the technical-rational perspective does not adequately consider the work of teachers, whom Lipsky (2010) refers to as the street-level bureaucrats. As the classroom brokers of policy, teachers make daily decisions on the implementation of various programs and initiatives. The mutual adaptation perspective, a pushback to the normative structures of policymaking, promotes policymaking through a bottom-up process, privileging unique education contexts and the work of teachers (Fullan, 1994). While seemingly emancipatory for educators, the mutual adaptation perspective also focuses on implementation fidelity (or lack thereof), instead of the construction of policy. A third and more desirable option, the sense-making/co-construction perspective, recognizes education policy construction as a complex, co-dependent process (Datnow & Park, 2009). It emphasizes the importance of bringing the various actors—including legislators and teacher-implementers—to the policymaking table. Lawmakers and other upper-echelon bureaucrats have the authority to resource a given policy and dictate initiatives to subordinates. However, schools, ground-zero for many education policies, are loosely coupled systems in which classroom teachers have substantial control over their day-to-day decision-making once the door closes and the bell rings (Ingersoll, 2009; Weick, 1976). Teachers and other street-level bureaucrats remain uniquely situated to shape the enactment of policies—or, as Thornton (2005) contends, serve as curricular-instructional gatekeepers. The sense-making/co-construction approach embraces this symbiosis.

In a similar vein, Meuwissen argues for "influencing legislative and administrative activity more persistently and effectively" and "helping teachers and leaders differentiate powerful, well-warranted educational approaches from poorly designed alternatives that hucksters allege are policy-aligned." These are aspirational goals. Yet, what does it look like? Fortunately, the field can draw from an example of teachers engaging policymakers in a co-dependent, pragmatic policy approach. Recently, Illinois school teachers worked with state legislators to require a high school civics class (Healy, 2016). Using components of the NCSS C3 Framework, teachers negotiated with state lawmakers to craft and endorse standards that emphasize an inquiry-based curriculum. The initiative's success is grounded in the co-dependent relationship among the many policy actors. Teachers and social studies advocates received funding from the civic-minded philanthropic Robert R. McCormick Foundation to develop, pilot, and train teachers around these standards. Encountering a groundswell of interest among teachers across Illinois, state legislators in both major parties were compelled to support their constituency. This example typifies the collective work of teachers, policymakers, and others in the community committed to social studies education policy. The policy addressed a problem unique to the state context: a lack of inquiry-based civic education at the high school level. Proponents of the initiative adopted a framework established by a national organization (i.e., NCSS), but developed standards specific to the needs of policy context. The process of constructing and implementing policy in Illinois brought together multiple groups from within and outside education bureaucracy.

Social studies education can establish itself as a vital component of the broader policy agenda only to the extent that it addresses problems distinct to the education context. Regrettably, I doubt that many state legislators are particularly sensitive to social studies needs or concerns. If we continue to submit to a technical-rational approach to social studies education, realization of the field's more ambitious ideas remains unattainable. However, as the Illinois example suggests, social studies stakeholders educating and working with other actors has the potential to move policy in new and innovative directions.

References

Datnow, A., & Park, V. (2009). Conceptualizing policy implementation: Large-scale reform in an era of complexity. In G. Sykes, B. Schneider, & D. N. Plank (Eds.), *Handbook of education policy research* (pp. 348–361). New York: Routledge.

Fullan, M. G. (1994). Coordinating top-down and bottom-up strategies for educational reform. In R. J. Anson (Ed.), *Systemic reform: Perspectives on personalizing education* (pp. 7–24). Washington, DC: U.S. Department of Education.

Healy, S. P. (2016). Teachers at the center: Recent efforts to strengthen the civic mission of schools in Illinois. *Social Education, 80*(6), 375–377.

Ingersoll, R. M. (2009). *Who controls teachers' work: Power and accountability in America's schools.* Cambridge, MA: Harvard University Press.

Lipsky, M. (2010). *Street-level bureaucracy: Dilemmas of the individual in public services* (30th year ed.). New York: Russell Sage.

Thornton, S. J. (2005). *Teaching social studies that matters*. New York: Teachers College Press.

Weick, K. E. (1976). Educational organizations as loosely coupled systems. *Administrative Science Quarterly, 21*(1), 1–19.

Meuwissen's Response to Fitchett's Commentary

In *Democratic Education*, Amy Gutmann evokes Kant's claim that the "two human inventions which may be considered more difficult than any others" are "the art of government and the art of education" (1999, p. 3). Then, she fuses the two, explaining that "we do not collectively know good education policy when we see it; we cannot make good education policy by avoiding political controversy; nor can we make principled education policy without exposing our principles and investigating their implications" (p. 6). These contentions are the bases of my response to Paul Fitchett's commentary, in which he drew from policy arenas in mathematics and literacy education to make two primary points: (1) that the most significant impacts of policy are found in its implementation, and thus, we must acknowledge the limitations of large-scale policy proposals and the consequentiality of ground-level actors' knowledge, commitments, and modes of enactment; and (2) that compromise and consensus are pathways to envisioning and creating policy that stakeholders on different sides of an issue might not have imagined without them.

We Do Not Collectively Know Good Education Policy When We See it

Pressman and Wildavsky (1984) argued the following about economic development policy, not education policy, yet its relevance to the latter in undeniable: by the time policy implementation reaches the people whose lives it is meant to improve, it might scarcely resemble its original design. Consequently, it is hard to determine—though we must try—what goods education policy serves, for whom, and to what ends in the midst of enactment, given its evolution through a perpetual churn of contextualized negotiations among stakeholders. Fitchett's and my commentaries on mathematics reforms in California and Michigan demonstrate our agreement about this; and his "balanced literacy" discussion led me to consider what lessons social studies education might draw from that phenomenon, comparatively. Synthesizing scholarship in these two domains (e.g., Cohen & Hill, 2008; Stein & D'Amico, 2002), I suggest that collectively knowing good education policy, despite persistent flux, involves maintaining inextricable relationships among all four elements of the model below, through persistent funding and interaction:

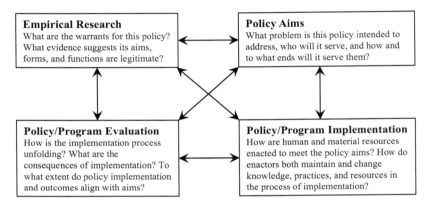

FIGURE 12.1 A network of education policy elements

Implicated in this model's questions are different conceptions of what makes policy "good." For instance, empirical researchers can inform those who make policies and run programs by helping to address the question, "on what grounds are this policy and its approaches justified?" while program evaluators speak to scholars and policy actors on questions like, "how, how well, and to what ends is this policy working?" This network of roles and connections seems just as important to the viability and vitality of social studies policy—from grant-funded curriculum and professional development programs to national, statewide, or local efforts to grow communities of practice around the C3 Framework—as it does to other domains. Without any one of these elements, the process of learning from policy—and thus, of imagining and enacting better policies in the future—faces considerable obstacles.

We Cannot Make Good Education Policy by Avoiding Political Controversy

Fitchett notes, "successful implementation of policy relies upon the alignment between the aims of the . . . policy and capabilities of those set to execute it."

He posits a sort of Goldilocks dilemma of enactment: ambitious policy aims and insufficient resources frustrate stakeholders and stymie progress, while dismal policy leaves capable implementers uninspired and their wealth of resources underutilized. While I agree with these points, I also would argue that Fitchett's dilemma has no "just right" solution in cases where policy implementation is a matter of ideological competition, not pragmatic compromise. Consider my example of reducing resources for science education in Oklahoma, or the State University of New York (SUNY) Board of Trustees' proposal allowing charter school networks with high achievement test scores to circumvent state teacher certification requirements by creating their own alternative credentialing programs (NYS Register, 2017).[1] In these cases, policymaking and implementation are not merely matters of finding sweet spots among different degrees of ambition and resource allocation, but matters of agonistic pluralism among values systems—like the extent to which broad scientific expertise or narrow local interests should play into educational decisions, or the contest between prioritizing charter schools' "freedom to innovate" and protecting students' rights to learn from experienced, professionally educated teachers.

We Cannot Make Principled Education Policy Without Exposing Our Principles and Investigating Their Implications

One problem with holding up compromise and consensus as gold standards for stakeholders is their potential to generate rather tepid ideas, practices, and educational consequences. This is a lesson learned from our science education colleagues, who find their subject matter and disciplinary practices at the center of acute ideological conflicts and watered-down campaigns, now more than ever (Hursh, Henderson, & Greenwood, 2015).[2] In social studies education, the language of "developing democratic citizens," often used in policy documents to justify the domain's existence, is a kind of consensus language that could just as easily reinforce a conservative reverence toward political institutions that maintain social and economic hierarchies as it could a progressive effort to identify pressing social problems and build political capacities to address them—a point made years ago by Westheimer and Kahne (2004) that remains germane to the C3 Framework's principle-neutral and practically vague "Taking Informed Action" dimension today.

In the end, Fitchett's commentary and others in this book enliven Gutmann's contentions in several ways. First, complexities and volatilities within discrete policy problems lend themselves variably to agonistic competition (e.g., uses of standardized test scores to evaluate teachers) and compromise and consensus building (e.g., development of the C3 Framework, the balanced literacy movement). Second, to acknowledge controversy, expose principles, and investigate their limitations as expectations for policy work inevitably means engaging with ideas that may be normatively unpalatable but worthy of serious consideration—for example, the idea that teacher unionization might hinder some measures of productivity, despite its importance to teacher activism, or that support for small class sizes does not correspond well with quasi-experimental research on the matter. On the flip side, we must persist in advocating for empirical evidence that gets ignored or corrupted through policy—for instance, that replacing whole staffs of teachers in underperforming schools, creative as their replacements may be, demoralizes and destabilizes school communities and reduces professional capital. Finally, we must recognize and adapt to changes in educational policy and practice landscapes, with an eye toward improving conditions for ground-level enactors and the people they serve. For example, given commercial interests in establishing footholds in the educational marketplace through policy, I wonder about the consequences of splintered, redistributed expertise and activism through social media—combined with declining participation in national educational organizations—for developing and delivering coherent policy messages about social studies curriculum and instruction, assessment, and funding. Returning to this book's introduction, these and myriad issues left undiscussed in this volume are why Fitchett and I think the field of social studies education ought to pay more attention to policy, in scholarship and practice.

Notes

1 New York charter schools have notoriously high teacher turnover rates and must maintain staffs of at least 70% state certified teachers, by rule. This proposal would grant charters flexibility to address the second challenge in light of the first by creating alternative credentialing programs out of fast-track field experiences and 30 contact hours of instruction, conducted by other charter school teachers or online. Language in the NYS Register justifies this policy move on the grounds of enabling charter schools to find high-quality teachers without being bogged down by onerous and irrelevant state certification rules, and freeing teachers from having to balance teacher education programming alongside the regular demands of planning and instruction, working with students and families, and attending school meetings.
2 I would argue that "environmental education" is just as much political or social studies education as it is science education.

References

Cohen, D. K., & Hill, H. C. (2008). *Learning policy: When state education reform works*. New Haven, CT: Yale University Press.
Gutmann, A. (1999). *Democratic education*. Princeton, NJ: Princeton University Press.
Hursh, D., Henderson, J., & Greenwood, D. (2015). Environmental education in a neoliberal climate. *Environmental Education Research, 21*(3), 299–318.
New York State (NYS) Register. (2017, July 26). *Rulemaking activities: Governance, structure and operations of SUNY authorized charter schools pertaining to teacher compliance*, Vol. XXXIX, iss. 30, pp. 23–25. Retrieved from https://docs.dos.ny.gov/info/register/2017/july26/Rule%20Making.pdf

Pressman, J. L., & Wildavsky, A. B. (1984). *Implementation: How great expectations in Washington are dashed in Oakland: Or, why it's amazing that federal programs work at all, this being a saga of the economic development administration as told by two sympathetic observers who seek to build morals on a foundation of ruined hopes.* Berkeley, CA: University of California Press.

Stein, M. K., & D'Amico, L. (2002). Inquiry at the crossroads of policy and learning: A study of a district-wide literacy initiative. *Teachers College Record, 104*(7), 1313–1344.

Westheimer, J., & Kahne, J. (2004). What kind of citizen? The politics of educating for democracy. *American Educational Research Journal, 41*(2), 237–269.

INDEX